Eber & Wein Publishing's

Who's Who
in American Poetry

John T. Eber Sr.

MANAGING EDITOR

A publication of

Eber & Wein Publishing

Pennsylvania

Who's Who in American Poetry: Vol. 1

Library of Congress
Cataloging in Publication Data

ISBN 978-1-60880-399-6

Proudly manufactured in the United States of America by

Eber & Wein Publishing
Pennsylvania

Who's Who
in American Poetry

The Captain

I sailed the seas,
upon the sea I saw
a gail on the horizon,
the fear inside us all.
Courage cried the captain,
courage he did call.
For as the storm waged war around us,
the ship looked mighty small.
The vessel did take water,
we fell down on our knees.
Faith cried the captain,
faith is what you need.
Faith can scale the mountains,
it can also bridge the seas.
We found strength in the captain's words
and rose up off our knees.
We did battle with the tempest,
the ship came through the squall.
We grew up just a little bit, the captain did
applaud.
I told you, you can do it,
to believe is all you need.
You'll find the strength to face each day.
If you keep your faith in me.

Greg Werkmeister
Williston, ND

[Hometown] Sac City, IA; [DOB] March 21, 1961; [Ed] graduated Central High, Minneapolis, MN; [Occ] self-employed; [Hobbies] hunting, fishing, writing poetry; [GA] marrying my wife

I was born in Iowa and moved to Williston, ND in 1981. I met and married my wife Lola in 1985. We had three kids: two boys, Grant and Jese, and one daughter, Mandy. We also have eight grandkids. My favorite is my granddaughter Brooke. I love hunting, fishing and poetry.

Pain Killers

The pill in the bottle
suppressed the pain but not all
it came back the next day
had to take more for the memory to go away

The pill in the needle
gleeful relief so lethal
was it worth the cost
it felt like I was lost

The pill on the line
a snow white cloud nine
but clouds don't last forever
and down I came from my fruitless endeavor

So many pills
all said to cure the ill
needles, bottles, lines and capsules
just need one to heal my soul

Each affects me in another way
so I think I'll take them all today

Anastasia Luetkens
De Pere, WI

[Hometown] DePere, WI; [DOB] June 1999; [Ed] homeschool; [Occ] author; [Hobbies] art, animation, writing

My name is Anastasia and I am a self-taught artist. I love the fall when the leaves are all different colors. I love all animals and stand-up comedy. I like to make people stop and think through my writings. I think people rely on too many medications. This poem is about how pills just mask the problems most of the time. The world we live in creates a lot of unnecessary stress, we get judged on how we look, clothes, religion, even hair color, causing people depression and anxiety. I like to use my writing as a way to bring these issues out and hopefully bring a positive message to people.

Tides That Flow

What is the essence found today?
What wanders through the mind?
What's lost into forgetfulness
From passageways behind?

And have past years with ample dress
Rewarded what you've done?
Or is there nothing there to charm
When time-space life's been spun?

Should what awaits you cause alarm?
What happens when bell's rung?
Is there some journey left to take
From seeded actions flung?

Or is there nothing in life's wake
No echo bounce at play
From actions good and bad you make
In time spent on the way?

Perhaps all life's a shadow show
With essence strewn on tides that flow!

John Gilbert Fuller
Warrenville, IL

[Hometown] Indianapolis, IN; [DOB] March 9, 1929; [Ed] BA's, JD; [Occ] writer, poet; [Hobbies] photography; [GA] The Forest Holds a Secret Place

I attended Shortridge High School in Indianapolis, IN and the The Taft School in Watertown, CT. I received my bachelor's degree in American and English literature from Brown University and my Juris Doctorate from Northwestern University Law School. During the '60s, where I wrote the novel Portrait of a Boy, *I lived with my wife and children in Vienna and then Barcelona. My poetry has been published here and abroad in various publications since the 1970s. A volume of my poetry,* The Forest Holds a Secret Place, *was published in 2004 by Woodbridge Publishing Company of Haworth, NJ.*

My Sister, My Sister, My Friend

When the world is against you and there's no one there
Better think again because someone cares.

But who is that someone who gives a hand?
Why it's someone who's your biggest fan.

It comes from a sister who knows you inside out
Someone who believes in you and never has a doubt.

Someone whose courage you can depend upon
Someone who will always talk to you on the phone.

Someone who loves you when things get rough.
Someone who will stick up for you and be mighty tough.

Yes it's your sister who fills the bill
Who will love you always and always will.

Kathryn Gardner
Greenbrier, AR

[Hometown] Greenbrier, AR; [DOB] July 1946; [Ed] BA in fine art; [Occ] artist; [Hobbies] yard work, flowers; [GA] four grandchildren

My sister was ill so I wrote the poem to tell her how much she meant to me. I hadn't written anything for some time and this got me interested in writing again.

Two Realms of Life

We live in a world with two separate compartments
    That can be categorized as self-contained departments
The first is intellectual, which deals with reason
    And is totally unaffected by feelings or season

The intellectual realm permits problems to be solved
    Through serious thought and with learning involved
Intellectual accomplishments determine success
    They foster achievement and eliminate mess

Stay in this realm for issues intellectual
    And avoid concerns emotional or sexual
Logic and planning lead to successful conclusions
    And steer you away from erroneous illusions

The other realm is the emotional life
    It's filled with hazards and potential strife
Included are feelings of fear and love
    With anger and aggression added to the above

It's essential to realize in which realm you are dealing
    Whether rational thought or emotional feeling
So you can find solutions in an appropriate manner
    And live your life in a way that is banner

Maurice Levy
Hilton Head Island, SC

I am an Emeritus Professor of Pediatrics and past Associate Dean for Faculty Development at The Medical College of Georgia. I have published over one hundred professional articles, two books and numerous poems, which relate to important issues in my life. Hopefully, anyone reading my poetry can feel my passion for the subject. My first wife of fifty years, Loris, passed away in 2005, and I am now married to Michele Kamet Levy. I have three children, Arden L. Levy, MD, Andrea H. Levy, MD and James M. Levy, JD. In 2008, I was diagnosed with pancreatic cancer and have been declared disease free after surgery and treatment. I totally cherish my life and continue to encourage and support medical education.

Restless in Paradise

Said Adam to Eve,
In the Garden of Eden,
"Get out of my way, dear,
I'm going to Sweden.
I'm tired of animals,
Heavenly flowers and fountains.
I want to feel snow,
And ski down the mountains.
You could come too, Eve,
If the effort you'll make,
But get rid of the fig-leaf,
And shoot that damned snake!"

Delores Habiby
Marion, IN

[Hometown] Marion, IN; [DOB] October 23, 1932; [Ed] two and a half years of college; [Occ] retired teaching assistant in special education, nineteen years; [Hobbies] playing the piano, painting, reading, TV; [GA] raising four children successfully

Over the years, I found my poetry changing from rather serious and introspective to a more lighthearted and sometimes humorous style. Upon arising one morning recently, I found myself wondering if our first parents were like most of us. Did they get tired doing the same things every day? Did they ever think about leaving the Garden and long for a change of scenery? My mind took flight. Hence, "Restless in Paradise" came tumbling out.

Times

There are times
    when the world explodes
    when it pans out
    into oceans and countries
    into people
And the world is massive
    and complex
    and harsh
There are times when the world
    consumes me
    burns through my bones
    cracks open my veins
    screams in my bleeding palms
Larger, and larger
    growing and dying and growing again
    scything down faces I don't know
    slamming me with emotions I don't want
Then I stop
    and turn away
    close my eyes, clench my fists
And I clamp down on the edges of the universe
    I fold it
    I break off minute pieces of flesh
Then I press it down
    mold it like clay into a manageable size
    compress it
    and confine it in the cramped margins of my skull
Smaller, and smaller
    far away, detached
    calmer, and sad

Bailey S. Collins
Great Falls, MT

[Hometown] Great Falls, MT: [DOB] April 25, 1998; [Ed] up to high school junior and one college class; [Occ] author and student; [Hobbies] writing, reading, acting, swimming, horseback riding; [GA] meeting Brandon Mull and Christopher Paolini

This poem is the product of long forty-five minute periods spent in a dimly lit Honors English classroom, listening to different people talking about how to write poetry. So these words emerged amid boredom and pretension— those two greatest sources of inspiration. I've always been an advocate for creativity over structure, and I just really wanted my own personal way to talk about poetry. To join it in its own dimension, if I could. It was really a challenge, trying to find the right, fitting words to describe something that's dominating purpose for existing is to describe everything.

Wandering

In fields of ash and embers,
A wall with no end.
Of years and wasted waiting.
These fires set and blown out,
A minefield of my making,
I've traveled without end.

In the wind there is no promise
No breath, nor yearning, no you
Nothing is nothing is nothing is nothing…
Is me.
Wanting to be heard,
And you in your armor resplendent as the sun.
You wear it like a talisman with the cracks showing.
My arrows fly not to maim but to show truth,
Truth…the very thing hidden from you.

When your sun finally sets in the realm that hides you,
When the silence becomes your friend,
When your mind is clear and your heart is still,
And alone no longer feels like strength,
Maybe then you will find me reaching through your wall.

Michelle F. Long
North Carolina

[Hometown] San Francisco, CA; [DOB] December 19, 1965; [Ed] BA in design from San Francisco State; [Occ] student; [Hobbies] painting and animal rehabilitation

This poem is about loving a person who has built an emotional wall around themselves that is so high nothing you do can break through. It's also about hope in healing yourself and them. This was inspired by my finding someone who opened doors in my world and allowed me to show my heart fully in a way I had never been allowed to do my whole life. He remains in my heart to this day, and I still hope.

Do Your Part

God calls us to be channels of His love and grace,
For a wounded humanity, take action, make haste.
Violence around the world is what we see,
In the newspapers, in homes and on TV.
Our country's foundation, values are shaken,
A lifetime of dignity, respect taken.
Brutal murders, lack of civil rights, justice for years,
Take a stand. There's been enough sorrow, tears.
Just take a little time to evaluate *you*.
Stop hurting others, as people so often do.
Prayer, love, humility, kindness and hope,
Are lasting tools which help us cope.

Jean Turpeau White
Silver Spring, MD

[Hometown] Washington, DC; [DOB] August 30, 1934; [Ed] Boston University, BS; Temple University, MEd; Temple University, EdD; [Occ] professor; [Hobbies] painting, gardening, writing poetry, needlework; [GA] married fifty-one years to Dr. Donald L. White, four wonderful children, four wonderful grandchildren

The Clown

The carousel was silent
The Ferris wheel is dark
No more sounds of happy laughter
In the now-deserted park.

A sudden cloak of sadness
Has descended on the place
A melancholy image upon the
Sad clown's face.

Gone all anticipation of the
Happy shouting crowd,
The world was feeling dreary
Like the darkness of a cloud.

Reminders of the good times
A prize dropped in the grass,
A partly eaten sandwich
A half-filled soda glass.

They all knew why the sadness
The softly weeping clown,
Because they were a circus
Just a circus leaving town.

Jo Ann Blunkall
Paonia, CO

[Hometown] Paonia, CO; [DOB] July 23, 1941; [Ed] high school; [Occ] retired housewife; [Hobbies] writing; [GA] mother of five children

I am a seventy-three-year-old grandmother.

Pain

A day without pain
  Is a day of splendor and joy.

A day without a tear
  Is a day the mind doesn't register pain.

A day without sleep
  Is a day without strength and energy.

A day without understanding
  Is a day in anguish.

A day where kindness is received
  Is a day of sublime joy.

John Andra
Pittsburgh, PA

[Hometown] Pittsburgh, PA; [Ed] two engineering degrees and business graduate courses; [Occ] project engineer, nuclear rocket scientist, worked in high energy physics; [Hobbies] model railroad, restoring classic cars; [GA] being granted two patents, numerous patent disclosures, meeting in my lab one of the four men that made the hydrogen bomb a reality with Oppenheimer.

In my last position before retirement, I traveled three weeks out of four in a month. I started writing poems related to my experiences in meeting people across the United States. After a few writings, I found that once I focused on a topic, the words just seemed to flow, like someone above was holding my pen.

If Only...

Ah, if only the world were more serene
and mankind were less prone to deprive,
a more delightful life would be routine.

Some people are antisocial and mean.
Their goal is to mislead and connive.
Ah, if only the world were more serene.

All long for a chance to live and be seen,
more just want the opportunity to thrive.
A more delightful life would be routine.

They only want a life that doesn't demean,
and a friendly climate in which to strive.
Ah, if only the world were more serene.

Most humans want a life that is clean,
and not one of altercation and strife.
A more delightful life would be routine.

Most people are of an unassuming mien,
and not piqued by those who contrive.
Ah, if only the world were more serene,
a more delightful life would be routine.

Gordon Bangert
Vail, AZ

[Hometown] Weirton, WV; [DOB] June 26, 1930; [Ed] BS in business; [Occ] accountant; [Hobbies] photography, games of skill; [GA] publishing my poems

The urge to write poetry emerged when I was seventy-one years young. Finding the precise word to convey my thoughts is a challenge I enjoy. My home now is near Tucson, AZ, where I live with my wife, Yolande. Choosing a subject that inspires others can be difficult, but I continue the search.

The Tree at Rockefeller Center

One hundred years I stood
in forest field and wood
Sheltering squirrels, harboring birds,
holding their nests in my arms.

I weathered all storms and smiled at the sky;
my roots drank the rain and I flourished.

Now I am chosen the fairest of trees
to delight eyes of all the beholders;
Torn from my home and all I have loved
and brought to the mighty arena—

Raised and bedecked with shimmering lights
in stone canyons of midtown Manhattan.

You gaze, entranced as my sight grows dim,
my limbs grow weak, my sap runs dry.
And I die slowly, feeling you watch
with smiles of joy and wonder at

How gloriously I die for your pleasure.

Cheryl Cardran
New York, NY

[Hometown] Haverhill, MA; [DOB] June 19, 1949; [Ed] BA in English literature, MA in drama, JD in law; [Occ] dog walker; [Hobbies] reading, writing, walking in nature; [GA] maintaining my integrity

Although I have taken a number of turns as I make my way through this life, writing has always been with me. This poem was inspired by my years in New York City where, every Christmas season, a magnificent tree is worshiped and sacrificed for the short-term enjoyment of thousands.

Christmas with the South Hills Chorale

We gather in September for the Christmas concert
I greet old friends and my uncut diamonds
I seek the first gem and my voice cracks
Fun and work and anticipation is back

The mix of sacred and fun have been chosen with skill
The compositions are intricate and require precision
The leader teaches and teases to bring out the best
Each week for months so I can sing them with zest

There is an appreciation of the dedication and talent of others
In the emerging beauty of the song
In the transformational moments that you know will come
In the desire to share and linger with the throng

It's the gift of listening to music from rock to symphonies
Joy of making it on the saxophone and guitar
The memory of nights that came before
When we sang about a star

Now onstage before 400 music lovers
All 80 are prepared and revel in the moment
When the audience joins in spirit with the singers
And the sounds of the season ring out with joy

Charles F. Mateya
South Park, PA

*[Hometown] Pittsburgh, PA; [DOB] February 25, 1958; [Ed] MS in public health; [Occ] full-time caregiver;
[Hobbies] listening to music, singing; [GA] master's thesis*

*I enjoy reading science and novels. I wrote my first poem in tenth grade as an assignment. My English teacher
liked it and encouraged me to keep writing. This poem is about a hobby I've been doing for three years, singing
with a group of eighty men and women. We perform large spring and Christmas concerts. I began singing in
a barbershop quartet in The Music Man in high school. In the South Hills Chorale, we work hard and the
resultant music is beautiful and fulfilling.*

Summer Outing

Hurry home from work—don't fool around
'Cause we're heading to Hocking Hills in a-bound!
We'll drop Preshihs off at Camper—making sure all's okay
Then check out the yummy Amish buffet
Antiquing at Rempel's Grove Mall
If we're lucky—not finding anything at all
So tell everyone at work, you'll see them later
'Cause you're not missing any more of this nice sunny weather
Cruising 33 as clock strikes one.
Packed goodies in basket for a nice picnic brunch
Dodging Lancaster patrol with their lights all aglow
You'd think it was the 4th of July fireworks show!
Stopping at Jolly Pirates for coffee and fritters
With all this traffic, we're getting the jitters!
Arriving at Lost Hollow and checking out the campers
We headed to Bush's for a home-cooked dinner
Prowsing through Logan's Antique Mall
Buying more junk—just having a ball!
Really enjoyable day—now driving home
Soon seeing trooper on-our-tail with bubble lights on
Pulling me over for no reason at all
I wasn't about to take this lunatic's fall
Telling him I was not speeding over and over again
He replied, "You was the leader of the pack, Madam!"
Handing me a warning for supposedly going 72
I was mad as a hornet but what could I do?
Well, I have a notice for something—nary a clue
Should he stop me again, "I'll call 911, wouldn't you?"

Patricia Burchett Wilson
Marysville, OH

[Hometown] Marysville, OH; [DOB] July 28, 1943; [Ed] high school, IBM keypunch school; [Occ] retired owner of Marysville Doverette Dance and Baton Drill Team; [Hobbies] writing, traveling, listening to music; [GA] completing genealogy book: Warpathawk Clan Legacy

At an early age, I realized a definite difference between my four Buckeye siblings and myself, West-Virginia-born. Instead of playing with dolls, I had a pencil in hand jotting down rhymes, songs, drawing sketches or just enjoying the sounds of nature—listening to birds and other animals tending to daily chores nearby. In recent years, I've finished two books: Our Family Genealogy Book *was a tremendous endeavor and* A Coal Miner's Daughter: Childhood Memories *about my journey living in Lynco, West Virginia coal country.*

Anniversary of My Birthday

I am thankful to God for completing another year;
I feel healthy and I am happy to be here.
I know God's lavish love because He told me so;
He sent His word so that I would know.
God is extremely old—The Ancient of Days;
He works in mysterious ways.
God's ways are past finding out;
Study of the King James Version Holy Bible removes doubt.
The wage of sin is eternal death;
But the gift of God is Eternal Life through Jesus Christ's last breath.
Jesus shed his precious blood to pay for all sin;
By faith in God's grace we may safely enter in.
Only Almighty God can forgive sin;
His grace and mercy wins.
Come boldly to the throne of grace;
The Son of God died and lives again for the entire human race.
Jesus has gone to prepare Heaven for us and will soon return;
For those who love him and His love is not spurned.
God says, "If you love Me, keep My commandments."
Sin is transgression of the Law; His grace gives us obedient power.
The door to the Kingdom of Heaven is opened wide;
Now whosoever will may come inside.

Bernice Hooks
Los Angeles, CA

[Hometown] Los Angeles, CA; [DOB] September 27; [Ed] art school graduate, LACC; [Occ] writing, art, leisure; [Hobbies] piano, singing and playing hymns; [GA] Cambridge Who's Who and author of a book

I am the author of one book, Reflections Before Dawn Volume I. *I have been a member of Cambridge Who's Who 15th Edition for years and received many entrepreneurial offers. I am in the Hall of Fame and Who's Who in International Poetry. I have received many certificates and awards from many poetry organizations. It is a privilege to communicate with such a wide-reading audience. I study bible prophecy in Daniel and Revelation and realize bible prophecy is being fulfilled. We live in a grand and awful time. As the world grows more wicked, true remnant Christians will be persecuted and not allowed to buy nor sell. Revelation chapter 13, verse 17. Go to Reg6.com to learn more about the mark of the beast and how to avoid getting it. Those who get the mark of the beast will get the seven last plagues and lose their souls.*

I Miss You

I miss you like dark the light
I miss you like day the night
I miss you like silence the noise
I miss you like quiet the voice

Without you there is no sun in the sky
Without you there are no stars in the sky
Without you the birds are not singing
Without you the children are not playing

The world without you lost its meaning
The world without you just stopped being
The world without you became a sad place
The world without you put on its sad face

I want to hear the birds are singing again
I want to see the children are playing again
I want to see the sun up high in the sky again
I want to see the stars in the night sky again

I want you by my side again
And I don't want to lose you ever again

Zsigmond Torok
Dana Point, CA

Immortality

You tell me that is getting old, I tell you that's not so!
The house I live in is worn out and that, of course, I know,
it's been in use a long, long while, it's weathered many a gale
I'm really not surprised you think it's getting somewhat frail
The color's changing on my roof, the windows are getting dim,
The walls a bit transparent and looking rather thin
The foundation's not so steady as at once it used to be
My house is getting shaky but my house isn't me.
My few short years can make me old; I feel I'm in my youth
Eternity lies just ahead, a life of joy and truth
I'm going to live forever there; life will go on—it's grand!
You tell me I am getting old? You just don't understand
The dweller in my little house is young,
just starting on a life to last throughout eternal day.
You only see the outside, which is all most folks see.
You tell me I am getting old? You mixed up my house with me.

Janet L. Emery
Sun City, AZ

[Hometown] Martinsburg, WV; [DOB] June 8, 1937; [Ed] eight years of grade school, four years of high school, four years college; [Occ] retired RN; [Hobbies] write, work puzzles, listen to CDs; [GA] decide to write a poem

I am a regular churchgoer. I was born and raised on a farm in West Virginia. During break times at work, I would recite something. My fellow co-workers said you should write a poem. Because I live in an elderly community and I respect my elders, that is what I write about.

My Perennial Valentine

My love for you is like the sky,
There is no end in sight.

Each day that we must be apart
Ends with a lonely night.

The only consolation found
Is in lovely thoughts of you,

The only person in my life
To change gray skies to blue.

The day I took you for my wife
Shall always be a treasure.

For the solace you have bought me
Defies a man-made measure.

As long as fate shall deem it,
I shall have you by my side.

And as long as we are together,
You shall always be my bride!

Paul W. Brumley
Fayetteville, GA

[Hometown] Flushing, NY; [DOB] February 27, 1931; [Ed] high school diploma and military studies; [Occ] cable splicer, foreman, Yellow Page salesman, owner of air freight delivery service; [Hobbies] boating, golf; [GA] marriage and parenting

"My Perennial Valentine" was written for the love of my life at the time I realized just how fortunate I was to have been joined to such a special partner!

Don't Let It Be True

You are a mountain that shields from the wind
A character that could never blend
A force that could make me smile
And make all the pain worthwhile
I don't think I can let you go
You are my guard against any foe
Don't let it be true!
You were among the brave, the few
So I can't contemplate you not being here
It was always my biggest fear
And now it has come true
I wish I could tell you how much I will miss you

Raven Kohrs
Hubert, NC

[Hometown] Killeen, TX; [DOB] March 17, 1994

My mother is Christine Palmer and my father is Theodore Kohrs. This poem is in loving memory of Raymond Cooper—a father, grandfather, husband and friend. We miss you.

Potter's Field Equipoise

Beneath the turf of Potter's Field,
Lie those of ignoble means.
Shadows once their ambiance,
Mocked presence cruelly deemed.
Ignored upon life's passing, petrified as stone.
Evaporated memories, lost tales of life now prone.
Trifling and pathetic caste, to all except to God,
Reduced to tags and numbers rotting casket's cryptic sod.
Fleeced of pride and dignity, discarded pauper waste,
Incarcerated relics, left for darkness to embrace.
Bequest of thee thou holy grail, it's legacy they reap.
No longer restless slumber, but blest delightful sleep.
Sentiments thus recognized, in accordance too thy will.
Futile casements open wide, no longer visions still.
It is now their time for glory, repressive energy now past.
Divinity engulfed by grace—justice theirs at last!
For who's not to say, the humblest ones, the poorest souls on earth.
In heaven reign as richest, dire poverty their mirth.
As for those endowed who feel that wealth is all that life should yield?
Come meditate upon the turf of hallowed Potter's Field.

Edward A. Nicholson
Locust Valley, NY

[Hometown] Locust Valley, NY; [DOB] October 14, 1936; [Ed] high school; [Occ] VP of Marketing, writer; [Hobbies] baseball, Detroit Tigers; [GA] book, Boxer George, the Pet Santa

I wrote "Potter's Field Equipoise" in tribute to those who have passed through this life as poverty shadows without fanfare. And even though forgotten in this life, in heaven, their rewards will be justified, many times over. One wonders how many contributions were kept secret and passed on mysteriously with them, attributing to our loss. Life takes many turns—this is one of the most clandestine to me. For till it's my time, I will never know.

The Old Mountaineer

A thousand years ago high on a bluff
Sprouted a seed in ground barren and rough
It had anchored its long, deep-seeking roots
Down in the crevices as rocky boots

Scorched by many fires and crushed by the snows
But battered old limbs took no fatal blow
It survived nature's harsh, rigorous test
Our ancient Juniper out in the West

No storm has ever budged it where it's found
As its hard muscled wood swells from the ground
Indians wove cloth from its shredded bark
Birds still eat its seeds as if in a park

If it could talk I wonder what we'd hear?
What if it could walk, would it still be here?
Withstanding hardships it's always been free
The old mountaineer stayed for us to see

Dorothy B. Fairfield
Merrill, OR

[Hometown] San Antonio, TX; [DOB] October 17, 1931; [Ed] some college; [Occ] homemaker; [Hobbies] sewing, quilting, painting portraits, spinning wool, weaving, poetry, sand casting, genealogy, leather craft, collecting rocks; [GA] a great husband and our four children

I am a twelfth-generation American, middle class. I have been dabbling with poetry since I was fifteen. During my eighty-three years, I have tried many hobbies and enjoyed them all. Poetry makes me feel good when I create something from out of nowhere. I never know what will suddenly appear from my pen. It surprises me. That is what makes it so much fun.

There Is a Place...

In memory of my first husband who died in 1997

There is a place...
    Where disease is unknown—
Or wars, hatred, violence or tears
    To scar the hearts of the
Tired souls.

There is a place...
    Where all are free to the light
And know the truth
    Where all questions are answered
Beyond belief
    And all are at eternal bliss
And content
    To spend eternity
Knowing nothing but
    Love.

Mary Ann Shelton
Huntsville, AL

[Hometown] Brooklyn, NY; [DOB] December 19, 1942; [Ed] high school graduate; [Occ] cosmetics—Mary Kay; [Hobbies] singing, dancing, writing; [GA] singing at the recital hall in Carnegie Hall

At age twenty-three, I married a military man. He was in Vietnam for a year shortly after we were married. We had two children and were assigned to places such as Ft. Bliss, Ft. Hancock, Ft. Leavenworth, Germany and the Panama Canal Zone. We returned to the states after President Carter signed a treaty to close out the Zone. My husband took sick after a fall, and within a year he was gone. After five years, I met a man and had a second chance at love. We met at a beauty salon. He thought he needed to look younger, so he was dying his hair. We eloped and were married by the Justice of the Peace. After a year, we were married in the Catholic church. We now live happily in Huntsville, AL.

The New Frontier

The spirit of Man is like the loftiest bird
Freeing Man from the shackles of kings:
The next frontier is the true frontier
Freeing Man from old war by its wings.

The spirit of Man can unleash a song
Sweeter than any heard before:
"We're free at last! Free to be!
We are no longer slaves to war."

L. J. London
Shaker Heights, OH

Journey to Splendourland, *my fantasy/sci-fi novel updating* Alice in Wonderland, *is available at Page Publishing, 1 Penn Plaza, Suite 6289, New York, NY 10119. Writing is more than a hobby; it is a message from an author to future generations: its value and impact will be revealed through time.*

Ripples

Drop a stone into a lake;
it disappears, is seen no more,
but circling ripples continue moving
until they reach the distant shore.
Human life is but a handbreadth;
it disappears, is seen no more,
but rippling down through generations
are deeds of those who've gone before.

Lord, I pray my life is worthy
to be remembered when I'm gone
for standing firm in faith and hope,
secure in Jesus to whom I belong.
I pray that future generations
will follow the path that I have trod,
walking close beside the Savior
on the road that leads us Home to God.

Leila Williams
Bozeman, MT

[Hometown] Bozeman, MT; [DOB] November 3, 1924; [Ed] high school; [Occ] retired legal secretary; [Hobbies] crochet; [GA] received an award for Outstanding Achievement in Job Performance in 1988

At an early age, I memorized long story poems and recited them for Christmas programs and community gatherings. This sparked my love of poetry, and I've been writing my own since then. In researching my ancestors, I learned that some were instrumental in the formation of this great country. I realized I am reaping the benefits of freedom and liberty because of their actions. This inspired me to write "Ripples" and to live a life worthy of the example they set. From age seventeen to sixty-six, I worked as a legal secretary and now enjoy retirement years reading, crocheting and visiting with my large family and many friends.

The Golden Years

These are the golden years
They say when you grow old
But I can't figure out
Where is the gold?

Of course you'll need glasses
Without you can't see
Things aren't the same
As they used to be

Your hearing is not good
But pretend it's okay
So then you have to ask
What did you say?

Your teeth fall out
And so does your hair
The color has gone bye-bye
Now that is not fair.

Sitting in your easy chair
And you try to get up
That's when you realize
You're not a young pup!

Don't believe these years are golden
For goodness sake
I found out it isn't true
The gold is all fake!

Joanne Bone
Apple Valley, CA

[Hometown] Kansas City, MO and Leav, KS; [DOB] October 3, 1936; [Ed] did not finish high school; [Occ] housewife for many years; [Hobbies] painting, gardening, sewing and writing; [GA] raising four good kids

I wrote one poem long ago about my mother's tragic death. Other than that I always helped my kids with their poems for school. But after my husband's death, I had a lot of time on my hands. Writing poems and my painting helped me through the tough times. I wrote "The Golden Years" one day while watching TV and they were talking about the golden years. So I answered back, "Where's the gold?" I always liked Erma Bombeck's sense of humor.

Grace & Todd

Little Gracie doddle
Little Gracie Pie
You're our junk food junkie
'Cause it puts you on a high
We go out to watch the Guineas
and talk to them awhile,
and ask them how they're doing,
and see they're doing fine.
You liked to give Jonathan an apple
when we went for a ride.
But now he is in Heaven,
so we can only sigh.
You wanted to hold Uncle's hand
when he was in a hospital bed.
It was so sweet
I just had to shake my head.
You looked into his eyes
and he looked into yours.
You were both communicating,
but never saying a word.
We found a little kitten
and isn't it so odd
that you insisted
his name will be Todd?

My love to Grace & Todd
From your MiMi

Sandy A. Kint
Orrtanna, PA

[Hometown] Orrtanna, PA; [DOB] September 27, 1945; [Ed] eleventh grade; [Occ] stay at home; [Hobbies] riding four-wheelers; [GA] beat breast cancer in 2011

Grace is three on December 13, 2014. She is my great-niece. I take care of her just two hours a week, but we are together for holidays and Saturday evenings. She is so sweet. I just had to write a poem for her.

80's Baseball

We've talked about retirement and watched others do the same.
They cry at their press conferences that they can't still play the game.
Some can't admit the failure that their body puts them through,
as the skills that often thrilled us slowly bid a sad adieu.

The mind remains a steel trap of special plays and exaltation.
If the body could do what the mind still can, we'd play now with great jubilation.
That's what I would wish for you, Dad, that you could just go out and play—
make long throws from the outfield with no pain to block the way.

You would sprint to second smiling that your swing didn't hurt a bit
and your legs felt so good you already knew—next time up you'd bunt for a hit!
When all your friends are in Heaven, just waiting there for you
with a glove and spikes just your size and a chant of "Let's play two!"

I hope you let me tag along like when I was so small,
and we can share our love again for the great game of baseball.

"Moody, you're up!" Happy Birthday, Dad

David Moody
Weatherford, TX

[Hometown] Azle, TX; [DOB] October 9, 1949; [Ed] school of hard knocks; [Occ] retired; [Hobbies] hiking, fishing, writing; [GA] not yet!

I wrote this poem for my dad's eighty-fifth birthday (hence the title). Though we sometimes struggled with our relationship in our sixty-three years together, we always had baseball as common ground. Dad passed last year at ninety-one. So, if there's baseball in Heaven, and many of us hope there is, I'm sure that Dad is on the team!

Thoughts

these thoughts I can't speak
these songs I can't sing
these words I can't form
my head jumbled and distracted
the baggage I can't say makes my mouth like cotton
arid and heaving for an oasis of truth
thoughts I can't word
for the letters have abandoned me
but you wouldn't have understood them anyway
the words are smothering me while I try to sleep
the kiss of absolution so very far away
stranded in the dark
memories comfort me
but they are also my dispute
hope gives me mercy
but they keep me up
when the nights grow deep
dreams are what I grasp for
but they come so swift
and stay so briefly
love is my antidote
but is also my poison
keep me asleep for I am lost
in a sea of trepidation
keep me awake and I will forever be
kept in the forest of the chaotic

Rebecca Frey
Red Bluff, CA

[Hometown] Red Bluff, CA; [DOB] June 26, 2000; [Ed] ninth grade; [Hobbies] writing, photography; [GA] getting my writing published

I've always had an interest in reading and writing, ever since I was able to. Living my everyday life with an anxiety/panic disorder and depression, writing and poetry have always given me the road out to peace. This poem expresses how I feel in my life, and how it's affected me. Some days are harder than others, but I am making it through them one at a time.

Favorite Memories

Things that touch my heart:
Frosty mornings and sunlit days,
Twilight's purple haze,
A humming bird zipping by,
The shimmering wings of a butterfly,
Slashing streaks of lightning in a summer sky,
The colors in a far-off rainbow,
The startled flight of a doe,
A whippoorwill's cry at noon,
A wedge of wild geese flying across the moon,
The haunting smell of lilacs in the misty spring rain,
The lonesome cry of a midnight train.
These are some of my favorite memories of long ago.

Wilda Downing
Marcola, OR

[Hometown] Marcola, OR; [DOB] July 29, 1931; [Ed] high school graduate; [Occ] homemaker and rancher; [Hobbies] reading and swimming

I am eighty-three years old and have lived on a cattle ranch for sixty-four years. My husband I were married fifty-eight and a half years when he died of cancer. I also manage all of our timber ground. We had three daughters, but one is deceased. The other two are both college graduates. We have two granddaughters who are both veterinarians. And, last but not least, we have a ten-year-old great-granddaughter.

The Room Is Full of You

This room is full of you, as if you just left and will return.
You are gone forever.
Your footsteps seem to be softly treading down the hall, I know you are not there.
You did not tell me that you were leaving.
There were no goodbyes.
There was so much more to share and do together.
Aloneness encircles me it is my newest enemy.
Visiting me regularly at every meal and in everything I try to do.
Who will I share the start of day with and evening starlight?
As time goes by I will find a way to build a new life.
Now, missing you is a new pain so intense my spirit and soul hurt.
For every day the room is full of you.

Jo Etta Brown
Gardnerville, NV

[Hometown] Gardnerville, NV; [DOB] June 14; [Occ] retired corporate banker; [Hobbies] travel, volunteering; [GA] recent election to Executive VP Alliance for Retired Americans, Washington, DC

Several of my poems have been printed in previous books of Eber & Wein. This poem is different, and so is this year. My husband of fifty years passed June 7, 2014. So I put my thoughts, struggles, and hopes in to this poem. Even while working in a competitive field, I found the time to volunteer, always trying to make the world a safer and more productive place. Now my energies are dedicated to the Alliance for Retired Americans. We deliver what we stand for, fighting for the protection of Social Security, Medicare and Medicaid, giving a voice to these issues that would otherwise not be heard. I have run for the Nevada assembly, now serving my second four-year term as an appointed Douglas County Planning Commissioner. If you want change or the protection of your community, you must get involved. If not, you have no right to complain.

Ode to Turning 75

When I wake up each morning
I thank God for being alive—
I thank Him even more,
Now that I'm turning seventy-five.

Where have the years gone?
They seem to pass too fast—
When I was growing up,
They seemed to last and last.

Now the older I get,
The faster the years go by—
When I stop to think about it,
All I can do is sigh.

Then I shake myself to reality,
And remember the life I've had.
Thinking only of the good,
And forgetting about the bad.

So, when I wake up each morning,
I will continue to say
Thank You, dear God, for being alive
And giving me another precious day.

Carolyn B. Poole
Covington, TN

[Hometown] Covington, TN; [DOB] August 3, 1939; [Ed] one year of college; [Occ] childcare giver; [Hobbies] writing and reading poetry, sewing; [GA] saving my dearest friend's life

I am so thankful to be alive and have loving family and friends. While I was raising my children, I helped working mothers raise theirs. One mother and I have been friends for fifty-two years—I went to Arkansas to see her recently and found her very ill. I called an ambulance to take her to a hospital. She had four blood transfusions and many antibiotics. She and her family thank me for saving her life and staying with her while she recovered. Now, when I wake up each morning, I thank God we are both alive.

My Other Mother

On the day that we first met, I could see
that you weren't really crazy about me.
You wondered if your son had a clue
what he was getting himself into.
A divorcée with a child must have seemed…
a little wild and not exactly what you dreamed.
It must have been the icing on the cake
when your son's name my daughter did take.
I knew from the very start
that you were a woman with a generous heart.
I felt that in time we would be
as close as mother and daughter could be.
Over the decades, we've had our ups and downs.
I'm sure I was the cause of many frowns.
I'm writing this so you can see
what a wonderful gift you gave to me.
A woman who raises a son alone should be praised.
I want you to know what a wonderful man you raised.
And if I could have chosen my other mother,
I would not have chosen any other.

Dianne Mulcahy
High Springs, FL

[Hometown] St. Petersburg, FL; [DOB] December 29, 1952; [Ed] some college; [Occ] self-employed; [Hobbies] quilting and needlework, restoring books; [GA] being happily married forty years

I want to thank my first grade teacher, Mrs. Anderson, and fifth grade, Mrs. Fisher, for teaching me not to be afraid to express myself with words. When I read and studied E. E. Cummings, I realized I could write different than other people and still have something good.

I'll Always Love Only You

When I met you so long ago,
You were the greatest I'd ever know.
The love we shared was the best.
We later started our little nest.
All the wonders of you linger still,
I'm so very thankful they were real.
I close my eyes and can feel your touch.
Those visions now I love so much.
Your lips were so very soft,
Your kisses remain in my thoughts.
You hair was the color of spun silver.
When I ran my fingers through it, I would quiver.
On the pillow you slept at night,
Your body was warm and felt so nice.
I can see your face, the one I adore;
And grieve so much because I can't have more.
I watched you as you left each and every day
God knows how much I missed you when you went away.
Letters we share I keep them still.
The love we had was so real.
You listened to others and turned your back.
I needed you so, for what I lacked.
The pain I felt you never knew;
Because you had found someone new.
My life was shattered that awful day;
When you wed another what could I say?
Deep within you'll still remain in my heart,
With the love I had for you from the very start.

Happy LeCornu
Tampa, FL

[Hometown] Tampa, FL; [DOB] April 10; [Ed] high school; [Occ] lead shipping and receiving manager; [Hobbies] painting, writing, gardening; [GA] winning souls to Christ

I was employed at the local college for some time. Working with young students was refreshing. I then went to work for an engineering firm as their bookkeeper. Later the Lord called me to work at The Salvation Army's Divisional Headquarters in Florida and I am still working. I loved helping others, and with The Salvation Army there were many opportunities to assist others. I enjoyed doing things for underprivileged children, i.e., giving them opportunities to learn skating, ice skating, horseback riding, all sorts of arts and crafts, dancing and performing in front of adults—especially learning who loves them above all. I have been writing stories and poems for many years. Words just flood my mind.

Build Me a You

Build me a god,
One that's shiny and new,
One that's everything to you.
Build me a river,
One that's clear and blue,
Teaming with life anew.
Build me a tree,
One that's sturdy and tall,
One that will bend but never fall.
Build me a life,
One that will walk and crawl,
One that can lead them all.
Build me a heaven,
A better place to strive for,
A place where there's more.
Build me a princess,
One to rule over the land and sea,
One with the bluest eyes with which to see.
Simply build me more,
A better place to be,
A better world for you and me.
And this home we shall share,
And in this home all shall care,
And we will love because we dare,
And we will love because love is so rare.

Nathan R. Barrett
Orrington, ME

[Hometown] Bucksport, ME; [DOB] March 15, 1985; [Ed] high school graduate; [Occ] full-time father; [Hobbies] mountain biking, writing, being a dad; [GA] my little poet

Sometimes we don't realize we are falling until we hit the ground. All of this has been me trying to stop the free fall. My daughter is the reason I wake in the morning and what I think of when I lay my head down at night. Everything I do, I do it for her.

It's Wonderful to Be Free

I will follow the road God made for me.
I answered when I heard His call.
I said goodbye and I left it all.
I could not stay another day
If my parting has left you empty
Then fill it with memories of joy
A laugh we shared,
A kiss, a hug, our friendship.
All these things I too will miss.
Don't be burdened with sorrow.
I wish you sunshine and a
Rainbow tomorrow.
I enjoyed good times,
My good friends,
Mostly a loved one's touch.
Do not cry for me.
Lift up your heart and share
With me every rainbow
The future brings.
God needs me now.
I will forever be free.

Sheila Evans
Forest City, NC

[Hometown] Forest City, NC; [DOB] January 23, 1963; [Ed] some college; [Occ] home health care; [Hobbies] poetry and beading; [GA] my children

I was inspired by a teenage girl. She said I was her angel. I just happened to meet her one day. Her parents were not connected to her. She had a poor life without love. She died September 2014 at the precious age of fifteen. It made me so glad that I took care of my children. My worst fear was them being taken from me. I have had a hard life, but my greatest wish was to be a good mother! My children are everything to me. I am so proud of them.

Words

I write and speak with limited words.
My speeches are short and terse.
You see, it is not necessary
To be wordy and perverse.
Many talk and write unending.
Deep into boredom often sending
May a listener with him time pending
Listening for the subject ending.
We talk endless and without stop
Expecting others them to prop
With a conservative attention to our say
When we want the subject to be dropped.

We talk, we chatter, dragging without end
Thus words why so many we offend.
The subject and data doesn't matter
When people realize we're filled with chatter.
Words spoken can be so nice
So long as we speak, thinking twice.
Before we bore even the best listener
Who might have good advice.
So when you are ready with your speech
Stop a moment to think,
Would such words to us appeal
If the subject has no interest nor zeal?

Larry K. Verley
Boerne, TX

[Hometown] Riverton, WY; [DOB] May 1940; [Ed] BS, University of Wyoming; MBA, Michigan State University; [Occ] retired; [Hobbies] volunteering at church; [GA] success in military and courses

 *Eber & Wein Publishing*

Just Do and Believe

Whatever God commands you to do, do it.
Those who trust God do nothing in vain.

Willie Easter Jr.
Dallas, NC

[Hometown] Dallas, NC; [DOB] October 27, 1963; [Ed] Gaston College radio and TV production; [Occ] shipping, wrapper, RSI; [Hobbies] animation, animator, writing; [GA] finding God

I write to satisfy my continuing hunger for knowledge.

Looking for Dulcinea

Love, they say has gentle manners,
and life is not so lonely as it seems;
No love ought to be unhappy
when it is frank and pure as in our dreams.

Love and brightness go together
and make this scramble all worthwhile;
if this be true which we are told,
then where is my dear one who will beguile?

Love is a God and he must know,
and knowing, pity wretchedness like mine;
somewhere between Heaven and here
is an angel who'll make my life divine.

Marion Hays
Vacaville, CA

Poets Forever Sail

Poets sail into ports, some arriving, others departing,
With countless souls happier! Enlightened, joyous voyagers! They have sowed seeds to grow.
While ships sail proudly on, old sailors and new sailors, they sail on the
seven seas—they are inspired or discouraged by the lands,
Their head forever bent over poetry, for they never miss an opportunity to
verse; their compasses always point North;
An army of poets, a world of verses, a sworn duty to
curse the land and sail the oceans of imagination!
Their glorious fate, to carry the soul, through all experiences!
emotions, tribulations, like a ship in a storm,
They sail on like Columbus, on a voyage to America
Each poet-sailer, a macrocosm unto himself,
With the spirit of God's poetry in us all:
The Wordsworths and Poes and Whitmans of latter days,
leading on to greatness, with the orbs and suns,
Of their days, but ghostly things in a greater purpose,
all poets see a heaven they are sailing toward.
Spirituality, the great unknown, the hidden aspirations,
Since the dawn of time,
ideas of justice, love, ethics and immortality
which overwhelms lesser minds.
To earn riches for the soul, not the pocket,
To go where no poet has gone before,
By day or by night, to scale the highest peaks
And say it is good, it is right they wrote in hindsight.

Lonnie Bailey
Pineville, WV

[Hometown] Pineville, WV; [DOB] January 13, 1957; [Ed] Regents BA degree (Concord College); [Occ] custodial agent, writer, poet; [Hobbies] running/walking competitions, songwriter; [GA] possible role in finding a planet (Alpha Centauri)

Author of twenty-one books, with poetry also included in 147 anthologies. My songs are included on ten CDs released nationally by Hilltop Records. Articles/letters can also be found in newspapers, especially The Register-Herald *of Beckley, WV. This poem, "Poets Forever Sail," reveals my ongoing attempt to demonstrate and encourage, new poets and poetry of all subject matters. Most of the time only the poets themselves will "appreciate" what they write. Don't give up; keep writing, keep dreaming.*

Me

One never sees,
One never hears,
that silent warrior
working for me.

Through life's tribulations,
I failed to recognize
all the wonders bestowed to me,
as I think of me, for me.

I lose my thoughts for prayer,
as I aimlessly wonder,
reaching and grasping,
at the mirage in front of my eyes.

What dismay have I brought upon myself
with these false idols of greed?
Which way do I go, left or right?
For the path no longer shows behind me.

Sitting silently alone in the dark,
I search the inner depths of my mind.
Never knowing what is imagination or real,
could I have lost my inner soul?

What am I to do now?
I keep asking the person inside of me.
Crying out of the depths of fear,
I see the bushes wrestle in front of me.

Yet they stop and no one appears,
I should be afraid, yet calm has come over me.
In that stillness, I feel regenerated,
as I come to know my Father is with me.

Richard Butler
Monee, IL

[Hometown] Chicago, IL; [DOB] August 1954; [Ed] associate's degree; [Occ] management; [Hobbies] golf, bowling, writing, fishing, traveling; [GA] doing what most others never thought I could

I am just a simple poet with simple words and meaning for all to enjoy. I am inspired by life and living it.

An Evening in June

It was an evening in June
The moon up above was full
The fragrance of the summer flowers
Floated on the light wind

The man and the young lady
Sat on the porch and talked
Of loneliness, and singleness and friendship
They were growing to care for one another

He was a poet of sorts
And she was a gifted artist
He had never married, not by preference
She was still single, by her own choice

She was a discerning Christian
And had discretion and virtue
She was faithful to the Lord
And to the service of the church

The man had three main goals
To be a strong Christian as he should
To find a career and a young lady friend
He hoped this lovely young lady would be the one

Charles Andrew Campbell
Montgomery, AL

[Hometown] *Dallas, TX; [DOB] October 18, 1948; [Ed] BS in Bible and social science, computer science senior college, junior college; [Occ] sheltered employee 1975–1980, Goodwill Industries; [Hobbies] writing, reading, photography, making and sending greeting cards; [GA] in 1959 I was baptized into Christ for the forgiveness of my sin becoming a Christian*

I grew up in Texas and Alabama, and have spent most of my life in Montgomery, AL. I was blessed with two wonderful parents. They took me to the church where I learned the Bible and was able to associate with faithful Christian people. My father died in 1988 when I was forty, and my mother died in 2005 when I was fifty-seven. After Mother's death I inherited a life estate, which I had thought meant that my mother wanted me to live in the family home until my death (which they did). Now, at age sixty-six, I have been told that I need to start thinking about moving to a retirement community. It seems that my funds have a nine-year window left. They are to sustain me for the rest of my life, and they feel that was my mother's intention rather than my mother's intention rather than my owning and living in the home Mother willed to me and my sisters. Evidently they feel that I was mistaken all these years as to my mother's wanting me to live in the relative comfort of our house on Bridlewood Drive.

41

Daddy and the Miner's Lunch Bucket

Nigh into late afternoon shadows we played
A gathering of small children, open space and a glade
We were a flock of sheep, a bevy of summer birds
Time passed—mothers called—not one of us heard

Suddenly, I heard what I wanted to hear
Far below on Country Ridge, a sound coming near
It was expected and I ran to top of hill
In the exciting moment, everything else became nil

I opened gate—a Model A came through—a Ford
Car stopped and I jumped on running board
An arm came around my waist, holding me tight
I perched there safe and secure 'til home came in sight

Down I jumped and Daddy called to me
"Here I have something for you as always, you see"
A double-decker lunch bucket he handed to me with gleaming eyes
I opened top deck and there—a small wedge of apple pie

A grown-up now I remember Dad's wrinkled neck—the back
Always filled with coal residue—even after a bath
I will always ache with a yesteryear memory of him without fail
And remember tidbits of love left over in a miner's lunch pail.

Helen Koontz Harrison
Springdale, AR

Aging

Aging ain't for sissies
The tradeoff is really a plot
For its sole purpose is to take from you
Every young part you've got.

It really is quite sneaky
The way it creeps up on you.
First time you take notice
Is when it's really new.

First, things begin to happen
As the skin begins to sag,
Then crowfeet and the bedraggled look
Make you feel like you're a hag.

This is followed by loss of breath,
Perhaps a stroke or two
And from there on, its "doctor time."
And he doesn't know what to do.

So he recommends a medicine path
Perhaps a pill or two
Then call him in the morning
If you make it the whole night through.

But this is life, you have no choice
So go ahead and play the game
For in the end it doesn't matter
We all end up the same—*dead*

Robert E. Brock
Hampton, VA

[Hometown] Hampton, VA; [DOB] December 23, 1937; [Ed] college graduate (two-year AA);
[Occ] retired US Army; [Hobbies] writing; [GA] not yet accomplished

Tribute to Clara Feldman

Born in Argentina
On the twenty-first day of May;
Chaikele, Mama Clarita,
Only loving things about her
Those who knew her
Can say.

Clara got married and continued her life
In Arequipa, Peru.
She raised three beautiful children;
All became physicians too.

Unfortunately, one son passed away;
Willy was his name.
After that for the entire family
Nothing was exactly the same.

Two of her children, thank God, are still here;
Efrain and Raquel;
Six grandchildren and two great-grandkids;
All who loved her well.

I had the chance to meet her;
To sing with her a happy tune.
However, now, I miss her so;
She passed away in June.

To her children she taught the values
Of generosity, integrity and love.
Clara was like an angel,
A true gift from above.

Sharon Chazan
North Miami Beach, FL

[Hometown] North Miami Beach, FL; [DOB] February 8, 1950; [Ed] bachelor of music, master of music; [Occ] teacher; [Hobbies] writing poetry; [GA] being part of the Dora Wasserman Yiddish Theatre

My Parents Are No Longer Alive

My father and mother are no longer alive
So my existence becomes a gloomy and chilly winter
I engrave my parents' images deeply in my memory forever
In order to remember their merits in giving birth and nurturing

I am still indebted to the whole human race
And busy and tired day and night making my living
I wish and wait for a safe and peaceful place
In which everybody treats and supports one's parents
With heart and soul

There may be high Heaven and vast Earth
But they can't compare to my parents' great love
I am like a little abandoned child
Who has no more father and mother in this earthly life

I embrace my natural predestination in silence
My parents don't know my lonely heart's sentiments
I earnestly envision for their souls a perfectly happy time:
We'll surely reunite with each other in the after-life...

Minh-Vien Nguyen
San Francisco, CA

[Hometown] *San Francisco, CA;* [DOB] *January 18, 1940;* [Ed] *Pedagogy School and military academy;* [Occ] *former literature teacher and army officer;* [Hobbies] *listening to music, watching sports;* [GA] Vietnam: A Nightmare War *(1991)*

I have been writing poetry since 1960. My favorite subjects are love, humanity and war. My poems have been published in the National and International Library of Poetry anthologies. I was elected into the International Poetry Hall of Fame in January 1997. "Poetry is the flower of mankind, artfully beautifying human life, this poetic flower that belongs to a person's heart and soul blossoms finely in the garden of humanity day and night."

Fleeting Angel

Lost in the sunlight flooding one's sight,
reaching up to a place one doesn't belong,
station steps above one's current position,
soul cannot take the pressure and weight,
anticipation grips this heart tightly,
caged like a wild animal seeking its escape,
mind stuck in a loop on playback of false realities,
forcing fantasies into one's head endlessly,
words escape when they are needed most,
saving this body in the end from overwhelming heat,
one last gasp to see that one beautiful sight,
an angel in flight these last fleeting moments,
welcoming smile to soothe the pain coursing in the veins,
high from a perch one will never reach in this lifetime…

Matthew Wilsman
McHenry, IL

*[Hometown] Wonder Lake, IL; [DOB] January 20, 1984; [Ed] associate's degree; [Occ] help
desk technician; [Hobbies] cars, sports, hiking; [GA] holding Stanley Cup for hockey*

Eternal

Born for greatness, to be on top of the tops,
Searching for answers, my mind never stops.

I'll show everyone who ever doubted me
That I'm not just another worker bee.

I will create my own legacy
To show them that I was meant to be

And when I'm on top with nobody else around,
I'll lend a helping hand to those on the ground.

For what's success without anyone to share it with?
I will become the next great myth.

Michael Sanducci
Lake Forest, CA

[Hometown] Lake Forest, CA; [DOB] May 23, 1997; [Ed] high school; [Occ] high school student, Starbucks barista; [Hobbies] wrestling, lifting, reading; [GA] winning first place in the wrestling league

I am a high school student originally from Baku, Azerbaijan. Although I've only been on Earth for seventeen years, I have developed friends and passions that will stay with me until the bitter end. I love writing poetry and I've been published in multiple books before this one. I am looking to study law and work with big businesses.

Peace from a Shattered Life

You gave me peace from a shattered life
Concealed and left untold,
Never to be told;

Thought to be hidden forever
Never of any value.

You saw my shattered life in need of
A makeover,
And took time to think it over.

Suddenly I saw you care,
And I no longer had feelings of despair.

I cherished the moment I had been
Waiting to see,
When I saw you love me.

Jewelean Taylor
McKenzie, TN

[Hometown] *McKenzie, TN*

I like writing poems, when I know what I want to say and how I want to say it. I hope they are worthy of attention. I wrote "Peace from a Shattered Life" to encourage the brokenhearted. The future should not be determined by your past. Don't let the past hang over you like a shadow.

The Roses of Ginette

Fissure lines
Blunt hours
Crispness hours
Lively colors twisted around the sea
Ginette's smile
The lines fall off
Ladies and birds in the night entomb the lunar cage
Hours scattered through the night
Forests resound and our senses silent bells
In silence imploring look
Stars forestry
Legend of suffering
Balloons of rainbow parade and cover the horizon
Of living colors attractive tactful glances
The full moon hides your profile of fire
Ginette love of my loves
You echo the rose opening to the sun
The moonlight your face distorted image
Forest is emitted and illuminates our bursts
Your hand on my invisible lines traits
Touches the ideal flower
Onomatopoeia in cascade
Flowing worlds along my sadness
Woven forbidden music of rain
The wind sense contrary signals of the night
Silently perched cross
Ginette my dolor my spiral of hope
The smile lifter tranquility
We turn on us same on our crumbling desires

Jean-Max Calvin
Uniondale, NY

[Hometown] Uniondale, NY; [DOB] June 1, 1945; [Ed] BS degree; [Occ] retired

Untitled

Sawyer, my great-grandson
Adorable you are
Wee little hands and feet
You're perfect...perfect by far
Eyes so dark, they snap and dance
Rocking you is a treat

Joy you bring
Awesomeness too
Melting my heart, as only you can do
Everything about you still so new
Softly, a lullaby I sing

Eagerly I cuddle you
Resisting you can't be done
I love you...I really do
Cuddling you is so much fun
Kissing your lips so sweet
Snuggling you close, never far apart
Only you make it complete
Now and forever you'll have my heart

Love, Great-grandma Rhonda

Rhonda L. Redetzke
Bowman, ND

[Hometown] Bowman, ND; [DOB] January 6, 1955; [Ed] high school; [Occ] self employed and restaurant hostess; [Hobbies] reading, writing poetry and camping; [GA] my children

All though I've been self employed (selling Avon) for almost thirty-six years, I feel my greatest accomplishments are my children. I've raised three daughters, became legal guardian of three grandchildren whose parents are deceased, and have adopted another grandchild who is two years old. My life is very busy, and by the grace of God, I hope to continue having good health, so I can continue caring for my children until they are able to be on their own. My poem is dedicated to Sawyer, he is my first great-grandchild.

The Extravagant, Memorable Life

When I die you may choose to cry, but please do not wonder why
I was chosen to die. No one on Earth was designed to wonder why
We must surrender our lives to the unknown future of an eternity we
Can only rely upon as our enduring supply of true life, comfort,
Extravagant love, and most importantly true inner peace. Please
Do not cry for the memories lost between you and me but rather for
The memories you and I earnestly earned together as well as the
Memories I will now strive for through my eternity my soul feels
Free to fulfill, always remembering those unforgettable memories
I shared with you. As hard as it is for you to see me leave, please
Do not let your grief prevent and hinder the strength you need to
Make new, more meaningful memories by allowing the peace of my
Passing, I can truly feel for the first time, to overcompensate your
Painful thoughts and feelings of any regret for the abundant life
You were hoping for me with you I have once lived now restored in
My soul forever for you to feel joyful and rejuvenated about as our
Thoughts of love merge together now in your time of encouraging
Need and in my time of remembrance of you loving me endlessly,
Almost as much as I love you. With my peaceful passing I thankfully
Extend this deeply heartfelt message of love to help you build a
Stronger, more meaningful life of peace not only for yourself, but
Also for anyone else in need of a more soothing peace your
Extravagant love willingly provides.

William M. Darrah
Bloomington, IN

[Hometown] Amarillo, TX; [DOB] November 19, 1978; [Ed] associate of science; [Occ] food service; [Hobbies] dancing, singing, drawing; [GA] believing God is my Savior

I saw how the death of my mom's only brother deteriorated so much amazing love she so abundantly shared with all of her family. I became confused how someone so extremely loving as my mom could instantly become so deeply despaired in absolute loneliness with a family who deeply loved her still. Confusion quickly became inspiration to write this poem in honor of my Uncle John's death, which caused me to express much more love to my mom so she would know death is about embracing how deeply fulfilled in love she always is! Love always lives on...

Are We There Yet?

Flutterbys and puppy dogs
Bubbie's house of Lincoln Logs
And riding Big Wheels down the stairs
No wonder Mommy has gray hairs
Hangabers and benchie buys
Out in the yard catching fireflies
Fairy-dust angel wings in the snow
Oh, read me a story before you go
Diggin' for treasures buried so deep
All that I find I'll get to keep
Family vacations through Ohio
We gotta stop 'cause I gotta go
Two drinks of water before midnight
Tuck me in bed, but don't turn out the light
The Wiggly Wart'll get you when you won't fall asleep
So you better roll over and not make a peep
When I grow up I wanna be just like you
But, Dad, I'm afraid and don't know what to do
When I was young, son, I was just like you
You know what, Buddy, I made it through, you will, too!
Evel Bollweevel and Green Snickerdoo
Hand-painted cards that shout, "I love you"
Summertime's hot and the winter's so cold
We all did our best—we all grew so old
And we're wondering—are we there yet?

John E. Sherman
Baytown, TX

[Hometown] Baytown, TX; [DOB] July 27, 1948; [Ed] some college; [Occ] retired operations supervisor for a school district; [Hobbies] writing genealogy, family history, traveling and camping; [GA] forty-four years married to same wife, five children, twenty-five grandchildren and three great-grandchildren

I enjoy finding my ancestors and seeing who I am. I also am a songwriter. "Are We There Yet?" is an altered song lyric remembering things that happened when our kids were young. My wife and I like camping out in state parks and relaxing near lakes, holding hands, talking and watching the sun rise and set. I have been writing since 1965.

My Mary

She was born in Iowa
She now lives in Tennessee
This is where we met you see
We said our vows in Clarksville
I am a better man now
She is quite a country girl
This sweet little girl from Council Bluffs
Of this you can be assured
Her beauty is best described as wow
This beautiful girl from Iowa
She is my whole world you know
Danish by descent this beauty of mine
She will always be you see
My Iowa native in Tennessee
A widow and widower we are
And my oh my what a pair
The good Lord put us together don't you see
A matched set for all to see
I love my Mary don't you know
Of this I want all the world to know
I am hers and she is mine
This is forever you see
This vow made in Tennessee

Luther W. Moorehead
Clarksville, TN

[Hometown] San Angelo, TX; [DOB] August 10, 1928; [Ed] business administration; [Occ] retired US Navy; [Hobbies] fishing; [GA] Senior Chief Petty Officer

I was born in San Angelo, TX in 1928, the youngest of three children of Matt and Ola Moorehead. I dedicate this poem to my Mary, who inspired me to write these words of prose. I am a retired Senior Chief Petty Officer in the US Nay and retired Post Master in the US Postal Service. I am presently living in Clarksville, TN. I enlisted in the navy on February 4, 1946 and retired on November 16, 1967. I started as a substitute letter carrier in 1969 and retired as Post Master in October 1986. I am a proud Vietnam veteran.

September

At three o'clock tonight, the
second day of September,
a bird of happiness sang in my
heart, a song I'll always remember.

So to explain to you my darling,
this feeling of which is new,
I'll write you this poem, this
poem of hope for me and you.

How do you thank someone who's
taken your heart of sorrow
and given you the will to live
for now, today and tomorrow.

He has taken my heart
of so many pieces,
And gently put it back together
with soft warm tender kisses.

There has been no other who has
been so gentle and kind,
and if the Lord be willing maybe
someday he'll be mine.

But today I felt a happiness
that I've never felt before,
And maybe someday I'll find
it's just beyond the next door.

Donna M. Hedington
Burlington, NC

[Hometown] Bradley, WV; [DOB] January 19, 1953; [Ed] one year of college; [Occ] hairdresser; [Hobbies] writing, painting; [GA] being published by Eber & Wein last year in Across the Way

I am a sixty-two-year-old woman who wanted to find love in her life but never did. As you might say it wasn't in the stars.

Untitled

In the darkness,
  In the night,
    Shadowy thoughts block the light.
Light and dark,
  Trust and doubt,
    What is life all about?
With the dawn,
  Night will flee,
    Light reveals what hope can see.
Fight the dragon,
  Slay the foe,
    So that hate will cease to grow!
Right the right
  that you know,
    With all the mercy you can show.
Shout out loud,
  Blow the horn,
    Personal truth is finally born.
Hate and sorrow,
  Want to dance?
    Instead, give love a chance.
We are light,
  And we are dark,
    Revelation begins with just a spark.

Carol Welty Roper
Chugiak, AK

[Hometown] Duncan, OK; [DOB] June 16, 1950; [Ed] BS in food and nutrition, graduate of art instruction schools; [Occ] retired dietitian, currently: writer, illustrator, artist; [Hobbies] reading, painting, gardening, knitting, flying, fishing, gourmet cooking; [GA] rearing five wonderful children to adulthood with a loving husband

People of the polar regions have an intense relationship with light and dark. I'm guessing phrases like, sunny disposition and cabin fever, were first spoken by someone who lived with sunlight almost all summer and darkness most of the winter. The duality is significant to each of us because our thought life dances with both light and dark moods and their acts of expression. This poem is my way of saying it is wonderful to embrace the revelation that light and darkness are necessary for a meaningful life.

Marilyn Belonged to No One

She was a beautiful woman
Every man's wish
She was so much woman
So voluptuous

The way she shimmied when she walked
Men lost their minds
They tried to buy her
She was just that fine

Marilyn belonged to no one
Only to herself
Marilyn belonged to no one
To no one else

She had tons of charisma
An abundance of charm
She led a mystic life
A glamorous one

Somewhere — beyond
she still exists
She remains an enigma—
Intricate

Marilyn belonged to no one
Only to the stars
Marilyn belonged to no one
Now she is a part

Myles Wallace
Chicago, IL

I love reading and writing poetry. Poetry is the light of life.

Scratches in the Sun

Green eyes like saucers caught my eye from the cage—
an orphan dropped off at the shelter.
Just one hug and a second later, fate deemed me her mother.
I brought her home in December—her first holiday décor.
She took off like a driver in the Indy 500—
proudly smacking each ornament to the floor.
To this gray and white inspector life was one big, toy mouse,
butt wiggling at the speed of sound, plotting the perfect pounce.
Pupils lost in their sockets, the sun's first ray on the carpet,
digging wildly, as if for gold, trying to make it larger.
Sprawled out and soaking up the sun, enjoying massages and hugs.
Eyes mere tiny slits as we'd coo, "Who loves scratches in the sun?"
For fourteen years through good and bad, she was always by my side.
She was our precious girl, our companion—our friend and our child.
They said her chest cavity was filled with fluid—
nothing more they could do.
Dear God, how do you say goodbye to someone who's part of you?
We had ten more days of quality time; I did not leave her side.
Her body grew weaker—no mice, no sprawls—
she was telling us it was time.
We told her we'd always love her and this was not goodbye.
We told her to follow the light—and wait for us on the other side.
It's been a year since she left us to cross the Rainbow Bridge—
my heart still weighs a ton.
Now the first morning light floods my eyes with tears
as I remember, "scratches in the sun."

Patti Downey
Rhinebeck, NY

[Hometown] Rhinebeck, NY; [DOB] May 31, 1960; [Ed] BA in psychology; [Occ] administrative assistant; [Hobbies] dancing, kayaking, hiking, writing; [GA] getting my bachelor's degree at fifty years old

Since I was a young teen, I have always gotten through rough times by expressing myself on paper. This poem is a tribute to my beautiful Lindser-Kitty whom we lost just a year ago at fourteen years old. She was our baby and meant the world to us. We lost her well before her time. I wrote this poem to share the precious life that she gave us and to keep her forever alive in our hearts and memories.

Just a Dream

I'm fading all I can see
is black in front of me. I'm
falling all can see is darkness.
I'm fading faster, faster please
wake me. Is this just a dream
or am I really falling? Please
someone wake me from this
terrible dream.
I feel as if I'm losing
everything and I'm losing
all I've ever known. Lord
please catch me before I
fall any farther, and save
me from this terrible dream.
I hope this is only a dream.

Tracy J. Hill
Joshua Tree, CA

[Hometown] Juneau, AK; [DOB] August 1, 1962; [Ed] graduated from the twelfth grade; [Occ] caregiver; [Hobbies] writing poetry; [GA] having my work published

When I was a little girl, I would daydream a lot, funny ones and scary ones. You could say I'm a dreamer. So that's why I wrote this poem, letting everyone know it's only a dream.

The Beauty of Life

The beauty of life is
The start of your creation
When you came from the womb,
And the beauty of life
Is even more special
When you can look up
To the sky and see
The stars as well
As the moon,
The beauty of life is
Even more special when
You can look towards
A loved one and see
Their beauty in view,
The beauty of life is
So powerful you see for
All to enjoy,
A beautiful remedy
Of life, love, and
The endurement of
All human beings.

Ivory Louise Fleming
Buffalo, NY

[Hometown] Buffalo, NY; [DOB] September 2, 1948; [Occ] housewife; [Hobbies] cooking, reading, poetry, writing; [GA] to write my own book

Hello there! My name is Ivory Louise Fleming. What's inspired me the most to keep on writing poetry is the violent death of my youngest son. He used to tell me to start back to writing poems when he was just a young boy and I used to say to him a lot of people don't like poetry because they feel as though if it doesn't rhyme, then it doesn't make any sense. I taught him that it's not so. It just has to be meaningful and that's the beauty of all poetry.

To My Dearest Husband, Don

How do I love thee? Let me count the ways.
What is it about you that I could brag about for days?
You are my sun—you give light to my life.
When you are away my days are filled with strife.
You are the rock upon which I rest.
You are ever constant and keep me at my best.
You are dear, dependable and true,
Endearing traits that make it easy to love you.
You have always been by my side
To help me through high and low tide.
Your able assistance and smiling face
Have always helped me to win the race.
Forty-eight years together as man and wife
Have made me realize that our entire life
Has really been an accomplishment — it's true
For all this time I've really been in love with you!
Thank you, dearest husband, my sweet
For giving me a life that's complete.
With special caring and a special love
Our marriage was made in Heaven, blessed by the Above.

I will always love you deeply!

Virginia Fuhr
Oviedo, FL

[Hometown] Pittsburgh, PA; [DOB] March 17, 1936; [Ed] BA in journalism; [Occ] high school and grade school teacher; [Hobbies] reading, writing, knitting, traveling; [GA] living in England for three years

I have truly enjoyed my life. My family was very supportive and my years of education were inspirational. Meeting the man I was to marry holds a special place in my memories. We met at two picnics. He had reenlisted and was leaving the next day. He asked me to write. Letter writing began and grew serious. When home on leave he proposed. I accepted. We married October 1. He left the eighteenth for England and I followed in November on the Queen Mary. We had forty-eight wonderful years together!

No Idle Gift

Do not think that time is but
An idle gift to us from God
Each and every day should be
Used to full capacity
If not through toil, but certainly
Spread His gospel, urgently
Each one of us, must do God's work
Orally, or by the written word
Toil through labor, many fold
Try to reach the young and old
Learn God's word, and fill your heart
Then teach your learning, do your part
Keep the cycle turned with love
Nourish, of the miracles He gave
Keep His wonderment alive
Help each spirit to arrive
Into God's paradise
Nothing that we do or say
On His behalf can ever useless be
Big or small, or in-between
To God, each effort means the same
Just as long as we do not
Waste away what we begot
Like freedom, speech and time
All these gifts are most sublime

Ute Dahmen-Burns
Kerrville, TX

[Hometown] Cologne, West Germany; [DOB] January 16, 1940; [Ed] high school; [Occ] beautician;
[Hobbies] writing, making doll clothes; [GA] finding God, writing a book not yet published

Between Two Worlds

There will be another dawn, another sunset on the shore,
between two worlds, and onward to the fore.

Time so fleeting; still, then gone.
Tracery scenes of trees and snow,
misty roseate settling sun,
darkly delicate silent woe.

Between two worlds of murky haze,
rapture clear that soon is gone,
the world of vague desire,
the world where all retire.

Sailing on in turbid night,
all knowledge now is past.
A bitter hope, a shallow world,
endurance not to last.

One so dearly missed is here,
two souls in life are now one heart.
Darkness falls then comes the fear,
between two worlds, then we part.

Sailing on the ship of being,
transits on to endless light.
Two new worlds now I'm seeing,
O wondrous shining in my sight.

Thomas L. Reiderman
Akron, OH

[Hometown] Akron, OH; [DOB] March 4, 1948; [Ed] college degree; [Occ] retired; [Hobbies] photography, art, writing; [GA] getting a poem published

I am a retired State of Ohio worker who enjoys photo and art projects, as well as writing poetry. Most of my poems are inspired by nature, the seasons, and feelings. I am most attracted to the change of seasons for poems—the awe-inspiring, natural world stirs my feelings to inspire me to write.

September Storm

It was stormy
October in September
A storm to remember
power was out
trees were down
high waves hit the shore
and threw the boats about
the neighbors' large maple
came down like thunder
and covered the yard
like a blanket
they were lucky
the tree didn't hit the house
A September storm on 9-11-14
a storm to remember

Aneta C. Schloemer
Sturgeon Bay, WI

[Hometown] Sturgeon Bay, WI; [DOB] January 15, 1949; [Ed] high school; [Occ] art teachers assistant; [Hobbies] reading, gardening, hiking, note cards, pastels; [GA] published book of poems

When I came from Poland at age ten in 1959, I started writing poetry at age thirteen. I enjoyed expressing myself in poetic form as soon as I acquired enough English skills. Right after high school, I went to University of Wisconsin, Milwaukee, where I studied American Literature. Now I write poetry that is inspired by local events that people can look back on. Since age thirteen, I also had great interest in photography and finished a course in it in 2001 from New York Institute of Photography. I combined my two loves and published a poetry book illustrated with my photos.

Why, Why, Why?!

I remember going to church fifty years ago
Praying for my mom and dad to forget their woes
I'd kneel and pray and cry: Why, why, why?!
Why can't we be happy?
My younger brother, sister, and I
Like other families who laugh a lot
'Twas not us—we cried a lot
My dad drank to excess every day
At meal times we'd stay out of his way
We were all so very much afraid
As all he did was rant and rave
The day did come when it all stopped
I hit my dad over the head with a crock
He was choking my mom and I saved her life
My dad apologized and started a new life
And we all lived happily together for the rest of our lives
Good and bad memories I have
Bad I try to keep out of my path
Memories are more precious than wealth you see
And God does keep a watch over me
My family is now all gone
And I keep ready to meet each dawn
No more crying around anymore
Cheerful, cheerful, cheerful me

Rita M. Krieger
Ponte Vedra, FL

[Hometown] Blairsville, PA; [DOB] September 14, 1929; [Ed] Conemaugh Valley Memorial Hospital School of Nursing, Johnstown, PA; [Occ] retired registered nurse; [Hobbies] writing stories, poems, and books; walking; reading; piano playing; [GA] raising six children: five boys and one girl, all born in seven years ('56 to '63)

I have six children and seventeen grandchildren whom I love to babysit and visit. I started to write stories after my husband left. "I can shake off everything if I write—my sorrows disappear—my courage is reborn" (Anne Frank—April 5, 1944). I am busier now than I was when raising six children, and I love it.

The Merry-Go-Round of Love

Love is like a merry-go-round.
Round and round and up and down.
It begins when a child opens his eyes;
It ends when an old man dies.

Little children are smitten with puppy love;
Pure and simple; white as a dove.
Teenage love is full of pain;
On again, off again, like the rain.

   Like a merry-go-round; round and round; up and down.

Long-haired men and women fall in love madly;
Feel six-feet tall and handle it badly.
Older couples find the years fading;
Falling in love means they're not aging.

Silver-haired seniors need one to share;
Always to love, never to compare.
From the cradle to the grave;
Finding true love is what they crave.

   Like a merry-go-round; round and round; up and down.

Love begins when a child opens his eyes;
It ends when an old man dies.
From the cradle to the grave;
Finding true love is what they crave.

Ruth Takano
Amarillo, TX

[Hometown] Amarillo, TX; [Ed] some college; [Occ] retired printer; [Hobbies] writing poems and songs, gardening, crossword puzzles; [GA] being a mother

As a senior citizen living in Amarillo, I have written many songs and poems—ninety as of this writing. I started writing as a young girl and did not pursue it again during my busy years. I have one daughter, Carol, who lives in Austin. I have worked over thirty-nine years in the newspaper field as a proofreader, linotypist and reporter, which I loved and which taught me so much. I also enjoy being employed as a school cafeteria manager for a number of years. My hobbies are writing, crossword puzzles, sewing, gardening and visiting old friends.

Growing Old Together

Sitting side by side
Into memories they do glide

Memories of
Dark hair and bright eyes
Walking hand in hand under moonlit skies
The lean college days
Cooking Spam in how many ways
The Navy years he flew off into the wild blue
They knew "Our Love Is True"
A healthy baby boy
There is no greater joy
The beautiful granddaughter
Love and adoration she did spur
With silver hair and eyes a blur
They remember that first date
As they celebrate anniversary fifty-eight

Mary Ann McKinney
Hanford, CA

[Hometown] Oklahoma City, OK; [DOB] December 25, 1937; [Ed] AS in accounting, AS in home economics; [Occ] retired bookkeeper; [Hobbies] travel, bicycling, sewing, writing; [GA] becoming a mother

I enjoy writing poetry and short stories about growing up an only child in a loving family and the pride I have in my husband of fifty-eight years, our son Mark, and granddaughter Quinlan. I flew an airplane solo at fifty-three, rode a bicycle 63.5 miles over hilly terrain at seventy-one and backpacked two fifty-mile trails in Sequoia National Park. My husband Don and I spend many summer vacations bicycling through different states or flying our private airplane to visit family. Our most memorable vacation was driving the Alcan, camping each night and celebrating Mark's fourteenth birthday in Alaska.

Light My Way

Full moon shining bright
Mysteries of the night
Light my way in the night
That I will see the light.

Day light morning bright
Guide my eternal light
That I will see my future site
That leads me down my path at night.

Betty R. Patterson
Goshen, IN

[Hometown] Goshen, IN; [DOB] September 21, 1948; [Ed] laureate certificate, Stratford Career Institute; diploma, Goshen High School; [Occ] retired; [Hobbies] writing, sewing, walking, homemaker

Colors Drawing Us Closer

The journey is it, but the end still matters.
The destination is our guide, the image in our mind of how life is supposed to go.
Year by year, we twist, we turn, to fit the figure—
That view in our dreams that we see so clearly in the distance
Like a picture hanging on a wall, rooms from where we stand,
Our portrait waits, as we photo and frame all the glimpses of the goals we tried to gather—
Even those draped in darkness and those in shadows shaded by the light, are reflected
In our eyes, like mirrors, as we never lose focus of the vision that has always been in our sight.
For even at night, it shines in the moonlight, showing us the way
When we were lost and traveled astray, hoping beyond hope
That we would be able to touch it, someday.

Kathleen O'Neill
Levittown, NY

Pair-O-Dice

We bought a ranch, oh so nice
And we named it Pair-O-Dice
We were young sixty years ago
But time passes fast as we all know.
What do you do when you get old
And just don't want your acres sold?
It was here we raised our children three
A source of pride for their dad and me!
Riding horses, welcoming each friend
It seemed the good times would not end.
But our family grew up and moved away
And then two came back to stay!
We gave them acreage at their request
But woe is me, we kept the rest!
Grandchildren came, and grandchildren went
Great-grandchildren from Heaven sent!
One granddaughter lives in the original home
Her children visit me, but just on loan
I'd love to give her the land, but me oh my
The others might start up a hue and cry
Because they might want that land to use
So how can we be fair, divide and choose?
Trying to decide, we lose much sleep
When others quarrel, it makes me weep
I think it wouldn't be bad to be so old
But we just don't want our acreage sold!

Myrtle Batsford
Trumansburg, NY

[Hometown] Trumansburg, NY; [DOB] April 8, 1926; [Ed] high school graduate, life; [Occ] office worker; [Hobbies] reading, swimming, children; [GA] teaching children to swim

I have self-published three books of my poems for my family and friends. After I retired from office work, I did childcare for friends, which I enjoyed thoroughly. At eighty years of age, I babysat for my great-grandson. I loved holding and caring for a tiny baby again. He is eight years old now, and his sister is six. I also cared for her when she was born. To my joy, they still visit when their mom and dad are working and school's out.

Ophelia/Frozen

There she lays face upturned
upon the path;
Visible in the moonlight.
The thought of disturbing
her seems almost profane.
Her eyes half closed; hair
that once curled
around her face
Lays beside her scattered
on the gravel.
Pieces and chunks of
cement curls.
Her face hauntingly beautiful
Fallen and broken from her
place amongst the roses.
She once added beauty to
the garden.
Now her place stands
forlorn.
And the roses still
bloom in rank profusion
As if all were the same.

Minerva L. Padilla
Arvada, CO

[Hometown] Arvada, CO; [DOB] April 5, 1932; [Ed] BS in speech corrections, MS in education; [Occ] speech and language specialist; [Hobbies] painting, writing, poetry and prose; [GA] raising my family: son, US Navy twenty-two years; daughter, teacher;

My full name is Lillian Minerva Padilla. I never use "Lillian," my mother's name. I was born in "Tornado Alley" in North Texas. I received a bachelor of science degree in speech therapy from Texas Woman's University in Denton, TX. I have worked in California, Texas, and Colorado, retiring from Jefferson County schools as a certified speech and language specialist. I have a master's degree from Midwestern University. After retiring, I studied counseling at the master's level at Colorado Christian University. I carry ordination from my church. I have a small garden outside my sliding glass doors. The patio extends to the garden. A beautiful face molded from cement hung on the garden fence. One day she was gone. My husband had moved her onto the path. She had fallen and broken. Hence, my lament for her beauty in the garden.

Easter Morning Butterfly

I stood in my kitchen window,
My heart sinking among despair.
Hope cannot be gone.
My spirit is still here.
Unsure if God was with me,
My eyes gazed outward.
And inward my thoughts ran wild.
Chasing elusive answers.
My soul, my mind
Came into focus.
As movement caught my eye, outside
Among my flowers was a tiny vibrant butterfly.
It looked like a rainbow, a bit of sunshine.
Dancing in the breeze it fluttered by.
With energetic ease.
Entranced by this miracle suddenly I knew
That God would gently guide me through.

Pamela L. Binette
Beebe Plain, VT

[Hometown] Beebe Plain, VT; [DOB] August 1982; [Ed] liberal studies; [Occ] self-employed; [Hobbies] snowboard, piano, gardening, seeing thirteen shooting stars in a night

I am not just interested in writing, I am a writer. I write all the time and have not yet been confident enough to have the urge to surge the minds of readers yet. I have to write in order to keep my mind from analytical overlay, or backed up brain functions of emotion, ideas, perspective, and ambitions. My mind leaks from my best friend the pen. Onto paper ink floods lines as if I am a waterfall with half of a rainbow that is never ending. I have never written with a complete purpose of benefit for finances or fame. However, individuals who come across me in such shocking applause, I will never get used to that. I have been writing for as long as I can remember. As a child I would mark symbols with my purple Crayola crayon. Anywhere I left my purple mark was a special place for me that I felt with words I didn't understand. The purple lines, dots, and shapes were a representation of my existence at that time and my ability to creatively record life standing still. A gift from God, my survival tool, defense mechanism, and talent I want people to share. I want to be known for amazing works, not working to be amazing.

Plastic Bag Adventure

I saw a plastic bag floating
along in the wind. It was puffed
up and it was rolling and tumbling
just like a person would, end over
end.
First, it would go one way and
a puff of wind would carry it
another way.
It was peaceful and entertaining
all at the same time.
What a glorious way to spend
a few minutes watching a plastic
bag float around like it was
having fun.
Then it got caught on a twig
and all the fun came to an end.

Peggy W. Shuping
Salisbury, NC

[Hometown] Salisbury, NC; [DOB] June 28, 1939; [Ed] twelfth grade; [Occ] mother and housewife; [Hobbies] crochet, painting ornaments, gardening; [GA] poetry published

I had a knee replacement and I was resting on my front porch when I saw the bag, and it inspired me to write this poem. My poetry is a gift from God; it just comes naturally. I am a wife, a mother of three, a grandmother to one grandchild, a mother-in-law to three. I have a busy lifestyle.

Panacea IV

Peace be unto every one!
May noble deeds in battle exist no more
That quite as well as it seems
We love one another but with lies, guns and outer riches
In daylight and nighttime we crouch that lead to deception.
Virtues and values to share are better more than ever
As we forgive and swear each other to live by
Just like today is the time for that inkling.
Universe expands as man begins to move with empty open arms
And as much as victory remains in peril if minds and hearts
Are in retaliation; O, democracy when do you (con)serve but
The 'legions' that prey its 'wanderers' with false kingdom and
Annihilation with leaders and followers from mosques,
The synagogues and temples that soon 'will not be left unturned?'
For the holy Church shall reign in the kingdom of God is at hand!
Jihad and war alone are pricey, but nothing
For it only destroys both humanity and the wanderers
Ironclad and xyloid men and women
With silverspoon or not, it doesn't matter
For everything, yes, time is sure:
Man returns to dust, and if man doesn't change
Like the dead
Zions, anti Church and unbelievers remaining outside the Kingdom
Will go to desolation as mourning weeds;
Or conversion to truth; for with God nothing is impossible
With pantuns and alphabets to abide.

Diomedes D. Dalde
Astoria, NY

The Curse of Old Age

My mind is strong but my body is weak,
the fountain of youth is what I seek.
Five or ten more years would be so neat,
but all I have is swollen feet.
Getting old is no great fun,
the other way I'd like to run.
I have so much I'd like to do, get a job, go back to school.
In my brain I'm still eighteen,
but in the mirror it's sight unseen.
Old and gray with sagging skin
is now the shape that I am in.
Don't look to close at me today,
just remember me from yesterday.
When I was young and full of dreams,
to go on forever so full of steam.
Not caring about what came tomorrow,
I had no time for tears and sorrow.
I lived for only the moment of fun,
from one sunrise to down of the sun.
And now I count the hours in the day,
no more to run and laugh and play.
For now I'm old and weak and gray,
hoping to make it one more day.

Eleanor Metheny
Brookfield, IL

*[Hometown] Brookfield, IL; [DOB] March 1, 1935; [Ed] ninth grade; [Occ] retired; [Hobbies] poetry
and three great-granddaughters; [GA] our family*

*We never had a chance to go on cruises or European vacations. We did not have enough money, but I never
missed a thing. I had the love of my four children, seven grandchildren, and three great-granddaughters,
so my life is complete.*

A Butterfly Called Hope

Fleeting and fragile, she offers beauty, serenity and peace
Each flare of her wing, the downcast now hath reason to sing!

This way and that, she caresses the air and sky, looking for a place
To land, safe to abide

She weaves in and out, her long ribbon behind
Touching the earth, freely, flying so high!

Up, up in the air, she offers glimpses; up there, of days to come
So perfectly paired!

Grab on, her flight doth declare, grasp tightly, goodbye,
Oh, ode to despair!

Fluttering and weak, she begins each day
Gaining strength, in each and every way

Lifted high, higher and higher, she carries bouts and syndromes
And puts into place, doubts and fears
And all her despisers!

How lovely your face, beautiful Hope, of all I dream, wish for and adore

On this flight, nurtured and held, in a cocoon, of soon will I soar!

Delicate and free, Captured by one, home forevermore
Will I lovingly be!

Connie Quintana
Canon City, CO

Why art thou cast down, O my soul? And why art thou disquieted in me? Hope thou in God: Psalm 42:5. This is dedicated to my husband, children, and you.

Visions Appeared

From eternity
they came, in unison by the dozen they marched.
His departed ancestors appeared.

In bodily floating shadows
they posed themselves before me,
to make their purpose known.

For lying on the bed, their beloved son laid.
"We've come for him that is suffering,
fighting dead on that bed," a father's voice demanded.

A whisper was heard, "He is my son,"
the mother's voice interrupting, impatiently, the sister's voice.
She cried out, "Can't you see? He is suffering,
eternal rest he needs, for life and peace
on this earth is no longer his."

Attempting to halt their marching forwards
with both arms outstretched, a trembling voice,
I pleaded crying, it's not his time to die?

Then, thunder roared, as raising, lifting their beloved
unto the spirited world, before me, as I gazed
up to the skies to a shroud of clouds
fading away!

My brother is here no more!

Ursula L. Bennett
Alburquerque, NM

[Hometown] Ponderosa, NM; [DOB] August 20, 1933; [Ed] BS in criminology/correction, AS in nursing; [Occ] retired law enforcement lieutenant; [Hobbies] writing, reading, traveling, fishing, hunting, horseback and motorcycle riding, construction; [GA] raising my ten children to be Christians and professionals, visiting and walking upon Jesus's footprints in Jerusalem

Visions of my dead ancestors appeared to me to foretell, prepare me for the death of my brother, whom I loved dearly and died thirty-three days after their vision appearance inspired me to write this poem. I am an eighty-one-year-old mother and great-grandmother who was raised between two centuries by my grandmother. I changed my medical profession to law enforcement. Being a nurse, I couldn't help my daughter survive from death from a drunken driver's head-on automobile accident. I'm an emotional writer, using visions of the beyond or realities of life that come to me, subconsciously as in this poem.

Can't You Slip Away?

The days are long
When you're away,
I want to see you,
Can't you slip away?
I wait for you to come,
Day after day,
Can't you slip away?
Our love is so strong,
We know each other's thoughts,
Can't you slip away?
I need your arms around me,
Feel you close to me,
Can't you slip away,
Just once more?

Brenda J. Regan
Egan, LA

[Hometown] Franklin, TN; [DOB] November 26, 1947; [Ed] high school, but did take home school as medical resection; [Occ] mother, homemaker; [Hobbies] walking, writing, making things; [GA] getting to put my poem in a book

I am the mother of two boys. I was born in Tennessee in 1947 and joined the military in 1967 for five years. Now I live in the country (Egan, LA). I've been writing since I was sixteen years old. I love putting words from my heart down for others to see.

His

His circuit crosses at the bracelet
As he passes by measuring the length of it
He is pulled as he travels by their net
Keeping his circuit forever within

As he travels back out passing by Ki
He marvels at his majestic work
Done as only he can, he will decree
A destiny for Ki he sets for all eternity

For time immortal is born unto him
A universal Lord his destiny shall be
As we bow, singing praises and hymns
An everlasting kingdom and of his glory

Mendle E. Harshman
Ohiopyle, PA

[Hometown] Ohiopyle, PA; [DOB] March 15, 1948; [Ed] graduated high school, two years studying carpentry; [Occ] maintenance man at the Fayette County Area Vo-Tech School for twenty years; [Hobbies] riding bike, gardening; [GA] helping others when I can

I'm first a small-town country boy from the Appalachian Mountains here in Southwestern Pennsylvania. I really liked my job as a maintenance man at the school and getting to know some of the students. They were very entertaining and amusing at times. The only thing that interested me was the Sumerian people and cultures. So, I read every book written by Zecharia Sitchin and found what I was looking for. My research is far from being over. Poetry is really not my thing; but something happened that I can't explain and I wrote over 250 poems. I wrote all of them down in a journal for keepsake.

A Season of Peace

The heart is the bearer of the soul
The Spirit lives within
Time surrounds the inner sanctum
As quiet fills the space between
It is the season of peace on Earth
Good will toward men
A starry night
A young girl's birthing
A son is born
In a manger laid
A son obeys
Terror rages
Death
Life again
God saves
Peace is in the heart
Not in the world
Peace flows like a river
Filling the space between
Only God gives peace
No one else can
We have peace plans
God has peace

Lee Hedstrom
Robbinsdale, MN

[Hometown] Norway, KS; [DOB] September 30, 1950; [Ed] BS in Religion; [Occ] morning stocker; [Hobbies] reading, sculpture, writing; [GA] writing my latest book of poetry

Service for the King

His call
Go ye into all the world and preach the gospel to every creature
baptizing them in the name of the Father, Son and Holy Ghost.
Go and make disciples of every tribe, nation and tongue.
Go till all have heard the news from My own word. Go till they have
become disciples in My name. Go and proclaim the good news; bearing My name.
Shout it on the hilltops, sing it at the shore; till the inner cities
are crying more! More! More!
Till all the nations have heard; proclamation of the mighty good
news of the Lord Jesus Christ.
Go!
The call is given!
The call is urgent!
Will you go?
Here am I Lord; I'll work for thee; I'll labor Lord that souls be set
free from the prison house, free from shame; I'll bring glory to Your
holy name!

Ann Mae Roberts
Fryeburg, ME

[Hometown] Fryeburg, ME; [DOB] January 19, 1941; [Ed] Bible college; [Occ] minister, full gospel;
[Hobbies] jewelry, music, embroidery; [GA] marriage

My life is spent caring for others, whether in ministry, the word of God, caring for the sick and infirm, giving
counsel to help others. I am a musician, play several instruments as well as sing publicly in concerts. I enjoy
writing, find it a joy and quite a sense of accomplishment; whether it's sermons, poetry, short stories, biblical
stories for women and children's stories as well. I enjoy life immensely and look forward to every day.

Rules

Rules
Rules
Practical
Practical
Rules are here
Rules are there
Rules are everywhere
Good rules
Bad rules
Practical
Practical
Rules adopt: don't adapt
Rules adopt: don't adapt
Squeeze them in your brain
Rules
Rules
One and only
Only one
One in the secret compartment of my heart:
"Do unto others as you would have them do unto you."
Golden

Mary Fichter Schmitt
Venice, FL

[Hometown] *Manchester, NJ;* [DOB] *February 4, 1943;* [Ed] *BA in English, secondary education;* [Occ] *teacher;* [Hobbies] *writing, reading, cooking, collecting perfume bottles;* [GA] *raised two outstanding sons and taught hundreds*

Shakespeare, Keats, and Byron are among my favorite British poets. Walt Whitman and Emily Dickinson are also treasured American poets. There are many novelists and poets who inspired me to write. One college professor also encouraged my writing. My teaching career presented the opportunity to impart my love of literature and writing to many children in elementary school, high school and college. My husband's career move afforded me the opportunity to teach in Alabama, Wisconsin and my home state, New Jersey. The writing lab at Raritan Valley College allowed me to mentor students in all levels of English courses. My poem was inspired by superfluous rules in our society. Perhaps we forget the most universal rule of all: "Do unto others as you would have them do unto you."

Parents' Legacy: Sharing

From childhood, my Pa had shown what *sharing* is:
He'd stop a bare-footed vendor of fruits and veggies
With paper and pencil, her dusty feet he'd trace,
With instruction to see him the following week.

He'd cut a branch of our acacia tree
Then shaped it to a pair of wooden shoes
Flapped with strips of sack-cloth to fit the toes
When given, the vendor would jump and yell with glee!

My Ma also had a way of *sharing* her talent
She'd buy 3 lbs of meat each market day
She'd cook adobo, calderetta, barbeque and lo mien
Come Sundays, her 4 siblings would enjoy free buffets!

With those *sharings* imprinted in my mind—
When married to an equally open-handed man
Gladly, we'd help and *share* our limited funds
With kin, neighbors, friends and deserving ones.

Now, with 50 years of married life
We can claim having helped 24 professionals
Nurses, lawyers, engineers, teachers, accountants
Who now have uplifted their own family lives.

With 1000 pairs of donated schoolkid shoes
Entrusted to us by our parish church
To six village grade schools in the Philippines
We distributed the shoes to excited and happy kids!

Francine T. Savellano
Jersey City, NJ

[Hometown] Buguey, Cagayan, Philippines; [DOB] April 26, 1936; [Ed] BS of literature in journalism; [Occ] retired, currently a Eucharistic minister; [Hobbies] traveling, fishing, reading and serving the Lord; [GA] 1999 Grand Marshal, PDOC Parade & Festival, Passaic City, NJ; 2012 New Jersey Parents of the Year

My poem was inspired by the mercy mission my husband and I had undertaken in the Philippines— distributing one thousand pairs of shoes to bare-footed school children in six remote villages of Cagayan and Ilocos Sur, Philippines. Unfortunately, during the week of our mission, typhoons "Luis," "Mario," and "Neneng" hit the areas, saddling us with gusty winds and heavy rains. But with God's mercy, we were able to withstand the inclement weather and accomplish our mission safely and successfully.

Imagine Me

Imagine me
From the land of no pedigree
In torture my conception germinated
Lurking in obscurity my demise the lubbers targeted
Out of ignorance gullibility raptured the tenderfoots
That compelled infantility to pursue the minds of the neophytes
At the crossroads two fledglings emerged together
Nothingness the gain for the rookies to gather
Aiming at the innocent with their first-class death arrows
Grace abounded to the feeble out from the hands of the tyros
With love the shadows of my ancestors became bright
And that made the kindness of my lineage ignite.

Raymond Obeng
Waltham, MA

[Hometown] Nkawkaw, Ghana; [DOB] March 24, 1978; [Ed] doctor of education in progress at Northeastern University; [Occ] assistant program director; [Hobbies] volunteering, research, and watching movies; [GA] completing a doctoral study

"Imagine Me" reminds me of the sadness poured on me the day my grandma disclosed to me how my dad, the then-basic school teacher in a Ghanaian Catholic school, lured my mom (who was by then my dad's student) to rape her. The rape, precipitating my birth, poured on me scars too difficult to erase in our community. Indeed, born out of rape to a young school-age daughter of a poor farmer and widow, I was whipped by the vicissitudes of life at the very early stages of my journey. But with dint of hard work, and humility to God and to my grandma and mom, God turned my captivity around. I am now renewed, refreshed, and blessed. Though I seem to ridicule my dead father and my living mom in this poem, as they attempted to abort "that" pregnancy, I want to take this opportunity to thank all, especially my grandparents, who continuously offered me their wings on which I flew to make me who I am today.

Photo Essay of a Life

Every life, long or short, is a photo essay of sort.
At first, a rudderless baby the Divine endows,
Clay to be molded in rain, sun, and clouds.
The toddler chasing chickens in a hurry,
Clipping the kitten's whiskers in a flurry.
Crabbing from a dock bait in tow,
A freckle-face kid with arrow and bow.
The young man in the white Impala,
Racing through life, a jaguar on the run,
So cool, so handsome in the sun.
Then slowly a man, a boy no more,
Ready to tackle endless chores —
A son, a brother too,
Husband, father, more to do.
Deft hands made dented cars like new.
Abundant talents, a Renaissance man,
Welcoming every diner to his place,
Greeting them with a smiling face.
Walking his daughter down the aisle,
Seeing his baby grandchild smile.
Every issue, challenge met,
Each new triumph, no regrets,
Each new day to savor dreams,
Time has colored all life's schemes.
Age too is a frame of mind—
A page to ponder, explore and find.

Illene G. Powell
Myrtle Beach, SC

[Hometown] Oyster Bay, LI, NY; [DOB] December 4, 1945; [Ed] BA in English, St. John's University; MA in humanities, Hofstra University; [Occ] retired

I grew up in Oyster Bay, NY and currently reside in Myrtle Beach, SC. I was employed as an account executive for a daily newspaper, weekly newspaper and radio stations for most of my career, but secretly longed to write in any capacity. Working on Long Island and here in South Carolina has been fascinating. I enjoy swimming, riding my one-speed bicycle, and travel.

Pathos and Passion

If I were to write about the many faces of the government,
And the pandering, I would leave the pretty words with
Shakespeare and the Renaissance.

If I were to write about the humility and the sacrifice of
Jesus Christ, I would write a satire about Nietzsche and his
Superman.

If I were to write about vanity and shining mirrors, I would
Write about Cupid and his conditional love for the beautiful
Psyche.

If I were to write about the folly of zealous devotion, and the
Dangers of ideology, I would write a discourse about the death
Of Achilles.

If I were to write about the perils of freedom, I would write
About the bravado of Icarus.

If I were to write about creation, I would take Darwin from
His fish….and start all over.

Lawrence Colvin
Colville, WA

[Hometown] Colville, WA; [DOB] May 14, 1945; [Ed] high school; [Occ] retired; [Hobbies] hiking, taking pictures, poetry; [GA] second place in a national poetry contest

I once thought the world was my oyster, until I found myself working in an apple orchard in Omak, WA. While there, I heard many stories of deprivation and survival. Working with the people society often looks down on, I discovered that my hopes and dreams were no different than theirs. Because serendipity was holding my hand, I found a treasure of knowledge and inspiration for my poetry. Though I never found that elusive pearl, I went back to the orchard for six more seasons.

Love Apples

They brought to you, dear loved one,
The young tomato plants
To watch their fruits grow and ripen,
Hang firm and red, inviting.
You could not stay to see them
Change color and mature,
Joy in their delicious taste,
Juicy, sweet love apples,
I pluck them as you would have,
Slice them,
Imaging you are here,
Salt cellar in hand

Mary Ann Dalbey
Minneapolis, MN

[Hometown] Minneapolis, MN; [DOB] August 25, 1925; [Ed] high school and some college; [Occ] teacher's aide with special education students; [Hobbies] writing, sketching, reading, Scrabble

In my junior-high years, I had a creative writing teacher who mentored and encouraged me and others to read good poets and write. Thus began seventy-five years of writing poetry, and what a joy it has been.

Infernal Storms

Who throws these bolts of lightning
From heavens down to earth?
These bolts that mar the souls of men
A primal fear since Mankind's birth.
What cause or anger have the gods
To inflict this pain to some
Thrown down upon a chosen few
Causing strife, their sanity undone?
Relentlessly they seek their prey
These barbs unleashed with malice.
Each day these storms intensify
Leaving souls insensitive and callous.
Unlike Longinus's spear thrust
Into the chest in search of life,
These lances pierce into the soul
Causing pain, anguish and deadly strife.
Or is this assault, to each within
Repercussion, the tragedies of war,
Dark memories, implanted deep
That maim men to their very core?

James P. Grigg
Danvers, MA

[Hometown] Danvers, MA; [DOB] June 18, 1946; [Ed] high school, USMC; [Occ] retired; [Hobbies] photography, poetry; [GA] raising two sons

I started writing while in the Marines in Vietnam '66–'67. After leaving the service I went on a long hiatus from writing. I worked as a carpenter for forty years, raising a family, with no time for writing. Two years ago my VA counselor advised me to write poetry for therapy. I decided to write about the Vietnam veterans and tell their stories. Some are mystery and others are the stories of many veterans who told me their experiences in Vietnam.

Summer Day

That summer day I sat beside him. The car
Jostled our shoulders and hips into a gentle
Rhythm...touching...not touching. All sounds
Faded...all voices...all music.

I remember how his hair curved perfectly above his
Ear and meandered down his neck. The tan ripple of
His arm tempted me to run my finger up the blue vein
And rest at his heart. My senses deserted me.

No words passed between us. No promise for tomorrow.
The car jostled us along to his destination. He went
His way. That summer day disappeared, blending
Into others. My heart was mute.

It's funny isn't it what we choose to remember?
After all these years, I still savor that summer day,
That splendid day, that forever time with its
        Thrill of first crush.

Judith Ziegler
San Rafael, CA

[Hometown] San Rafael, CA; [DOB] August 21, 1942; [Ed] college graduate, BA in 2004; [Occ] retired; [Hobbies] bicycling, hiking, water color painting, reading, writing and singing; [GA] fifty-three-year marriage, five children, eleven grandchildren

The lovely thing about retirement is that I can be busy when I want, and on days when I feel like it, I can just smell the roses. My poetry writing began in the early 1980s while working forty hours a week. It consisted of a rhyming style at that time. When I began college in 1990, my favorite class was Poetry and Short Story Writing. After that, I began writing free verse. My poem was inspired by my first big crush at the age of fifteen.

Anthem

On a beautiful fall morning, the words of Sunday's
anthem leaped, live and full-born,
from the mouths of the small choir.
"Holy, holy, holy," the twelve voices sang, clear and strong,
the harmony close and true,
lifting the worshiper to a huge, sparkling place
he'd never been before,
a vast upper region under high, lofty arches,
the music holding him there
in comfort, without fear, without thought,
in tears,
until the anthem slowly subsided
and he was, once again, seated quietly in the pew,
his tears already drying on his lined face.
How is it that a pocket choir can pack power
to lift ten times its own vocal weight
in such secrecy?
How is it that a little church on the corner
can become a huge cathedral on the square,
and no one notice?

Robert Skeele
LaConner, WA

[Hometown] Columbus, OH; [DOB] March 4, 1927; [Ed] BA, Ohio State University, BD, Yale Divinity School; [Occ] retired college dean; [Hobbies] writing, reading, walking, baking; [GA] a long, happy marriage

After seven years serving two congregational churches in Minnesota, Bob became involved in college work, which took him and his growing family from Maryland to New Mexico to Vermont over the next twenty-seven years. In 1987, Bob and his wife moved to LaConner, WA, only too happy to settle down in one place. Eventually Bob became facilities manager for a nearby museum, a part-time position he held, off and on, for the next nineteen years. Since the death of his wife in 2012, Bob has continued to write and enjoy the benefits of small-town life.

Leaves in Motion

Leaves flowing slowly to the ground
Falling so gently—not a sound.
Making a covering for the grass
Red, orange and yellow—a creative mass!
Some make mounds great big and bright
Others just scurry out of sight.
As the wind begins to blow
They flip and turn—their colors glow!

Jeannie W. Webster
Oklahoma City, OK

[Hometown] Mountain City, TN; [DOB] February 13, 1951; [Ed] piano major, University of Tennessee; [Occ] retired from private piano teaching; [Hobbies] stained glass and fused jewelry artist; piano—composing, arranging, and performing and recording CDs in my studio; writing poetry; [GA] sharing my creative/artistic abilities with others

My roots go back to East Tennessee where seasons flourish and nature abounds. Family ties are cherished. Time has yielded change, but sweet memories are everlasting. I have always been a devoted pianist through study, performance, teaching and composing. Inspiration to "note" simple heartfelt poetry began in the '80s. I further express myself as a stained glass and fused jewelry artist. Music, poetry, art and a profound belief in Christianity encompass me daily. I am further blessed by my husband Mike, my two wonderful daughters, three awesome grandsons, and two gorgeous cats.

Silent Tears

For what might have been
But can never be,
I cry silent tears.
When life presents problems
That seem unsolvable,
I cry silent tears.
When loved ones silently
Leave without saying goodbye
I cry silent tears.
When we arrive at the
Destination God has promised
There will be no need
To cry silent tears.

Millie Kolp
Ashland, OH

*[Hometown] Ashland, OH; [DOB] April 7, 1924; [Ed] high school; [Occ] homemaker; [Hobbies]
music, gardening, poetry; [GA] living ninety years*

*As a widow of nearly twenty-five years, I have cried many silent tears. Sometimes we don't seem to
fit in this puzzle called life. Count your blessings and remember the sun is always shining someplace.*

Dancing with Dolls

Electric Mind Symphony: swaying to the tune
of his own autumn psychosis.
Yet in the summer field among the blazing sunflowers,
dancing with dolls, 'napped from loving arms
into the grasp of one Moonstruck.
Not of love, nor of sound mind.
Invincible, or so he thinks, and the doll—invisible,
for his sight, and in his eyes only does she dance.
We've observed his ways, and I've eluded his hold
but the doll is fragile, mild and trusting.
And she weeps for her loss as he calls her tears
a valley of sorrow.
Adorned full in black and gray of ash
his hair kindled, flowing and flickering crimson
he waltzes with the unseen porcelain.
Her eyes of glass and tears of pearls
pleading to cease, but his clock has yet to chime.
And all this time we perceive from a looking glass:
A strange distance—
and behold a single presence dancing alone
naked, in human guise at the midnight hour
in a sea of flames.
He will be there always, but not so the doll;
for one day, my faith will hold her hand.

Alex J. Sowder
Somerset, KY

[Hometown] Somerset, KY; [DOB] 1984; [Ed] high school, Lighthouse Christian Academy; [Occ] writer, poet; [Hobbies] collecting card decks, keeping a journal, swimming; [GA] seventh grade talent show—third place playing guitar

I've always enjoyed poetry with mystery that has emotion. The inspiration for my poem was an experience with sprinkles of imagination. My life hasn't been very positive, but I rely on faith to get me through. In the poem it is offered to help avoid the dollnapper, as it helped me from his grip on my mind a few years ago. Faith has great power over fear and negative feelings. Although I was released from this grip in 2012, it tries to come back. When it does, I pray and say, "Faith over fear."

Drowning in the Dark

I've been trapped in this dark
I've been trying to break free
Shadows clouded my spark
There's no light I can see

It's dragging me down
Into the dark depths
I feel I may drown
I'm losing my breath

No hope for escape
Hope withers and dies
It's sealed my fate
No one hears my cries

It's black as night
No help will come
It's snuffed out the light
Darkness shrouds the sun

No one can hear my desperate screams
Trapped in dark and dismal dreams
Shadows consume the fading light
Give up, give in, it's not worth the fight.

Rio Johnson
Kenosha, WI

[Hometown] Kenosha, WI; [DOB] May 30, 1987; [Ed] BA in theatre; [Occ] clerical support, administrative; [Hobbies] reading science fiction, writing fan fiction and poetry; [GA] earning my black belt in Tae Kwon Do

I've always loved to read science fiction. I've always had a book in my hands and my head in the clouds. In 2007, I was devastated with the harsh reality of a bipolar disorder diagnosis. This poem was inspired by the depressive moods I've been subjected to. I've suffered greatly and there are many times I've wanted to give up. This mental illness will lie to you and make you believe that death is the only way out. Don't give up or give in. Keep on fighting the dark because you are not alone. It is worth the fight!

Ol' Blue-Chipper

He returned to the setting of battles past, knowing this was his final time
to visit the lush turf, the grid in his domain of honor and glory combined.
Distanced from combat, this rugged veteran, by two score and five years;
he gazed contemplatively at the huge crowd, as he brushed away the tears
while recalling, back in the day, when he achieved a life's worth of fame
by donning a helmet and jersey forty-two: ol' Blue-Chipper was his name.
His wheelchair now perched perilously over the tunnel the gladiators trod,
"Grant me one more battle, another scrimmage!" his head bowed to God.
The clickety-clack of cleats on harsh cement regaled him with storied ties
that raised 'ol Blue-Chipper's head, as if to eminence he again would rise.
But he glimpsed downward at his spasmed hands, now his ultimate shame,
once vise-like grips with supple fingers: beefy fists pounded out his claim.
His useless hands rested on legs now still, paralyzed from the major event,
as Gray-Beards avowed "what might've been" were it not for that accident.
He was a genuine Blue-Chipper, a legend, to which the record books attest
that of all the runners down through the years, he was indisputably the best,
with moves you can't coach into a kid, and speed you can't learn from man.
He was the whole package: indomitable, brutal—on top he'll forever stand.
The years rightly pass and erstwhile memories fade, as new players emerge
from the pack, with skills and thrills to make crowds cheer, to sound a dirge
for our warrior of yore, battle-scarred and worn, who beat the best in his day.
He came back a final time, to escape the name and entomb the fame his way,
and watched each play with mournful eyes, no matter how intensely he tried.
Fans that day can solemnly say, they were there when ol' Blue-Chipper died.
So, it was decreed by those who agreed, that his jersey of gold and royal blue
be posed at his school for all to view, and nobly retired ol' number forty-two.

John M. Morrow
Mooresville, NC

[Hometown] Mooresville, NC; [DOB] October 24, 1949; [Ed] Sorth Iredell High School, Mitchell Community College; [Occ] distance learning advisor, Career Academy Tech School; [Hobbies] writing, football, NASCAR, fishing; [GA] one of my newspaper columns was printed in the Congressional Record

As a newspaper columnist, I wrote about everything from sports to politics to family. After tutoring students in my home, I became a teacher assistant at Shepherd Elementary School, helping students read and write. The next logical step was distance learning advisor with the North Carolina Virtual Public Schools. Inspiration for my poem came from my life. While I was an all-conference running back in high school, I suffered a paralyzing spinal cord injury two days before my senior year began. Blue-Chipper is part truth, part fantasy, and part desire regarding how I would like my life to conclude.

Winter's Fishing Hole

A circle cut out of a frozen lake,
Looks exciting to a grandpa
   And his young helpmate.
They're all bundled up, from head to toe,
As they trudge along
   Over the ice and snow.
Fishing poles in hand, a sandwich or two,
Steaming hot chocolate
   And marshmallows to chew.
They sit each on a stool, then patiently await,
That familiar tug that says—
   "It took the bait!"
A jerk on the pole, a spectacular sight,
A fish out of water, and onto the ice!
   The two trudge on home,
With their fish and their poles,
But more than that—
The Memories they hold!

Mary Jo Urseth
Ridgecrest, CA

[Hometown] Lisbon, ND; [DOB] December 29, 1931; [Ed] master's degree in education; [Occ] retired teacher; [Hobbies] music, sports, writing; [GA] raising four children

Being raised in ND as part of a large and closely knit family, I learned to appreciate the value of an education and the work involved in being successful at whatever one chooses to do! My own four children and nine grandchildren are very dear to me, and I only hope that I have instilled in them the love of family and life that I have.

Bring on the Rain

When things aren't going right
When I feel pain
My mother is in Heaven
Her tears bring on the rain
She always told me
"You're on your own
Though you will never be alone."
Mother is in God's hands
I'm in Mama's heart
It's the love of a mother
Sending all of her rays of love from up above
She calls it sunny days
Al Gore calls it climate change

Marilyn Blackwood
Kalamazoo, MI

[Hometown] Otsego, Kalamazoo, MI; [DOB] August 15, 1945; [Ed] twelfth grade; [Occ] old; [Hobbies] making people smile; [GA] my grandchildren and children

Only love is good when you give it away.

Shem Creek

I cannot wait to walk once more
Where dolphins swim and egrets soar
Where marshy blades of grass can grow
And fiddler crabs might touch your toe
As shore birds rise above the sand
And rolling waves lap free
I watch the glistening rays of sun fall gently to the sea
Where golden hues of evening come to set on another day
Grand shrimp boats dock with their catch
And for the night they stay
So as the morning's misty breeze dances across my face
It is here that I shall walk once more
Among its tranquil grace

Karen M. LoCicero
Mt. Pleasant, SC

[Hometown] Mt. Pleasant, SC; [DOB] July 17, 1948; [Ed] AD, early childhood education; [Occ] teacher's assistant; [Hobbies] reading, writing; [GA] teaching, marriage of forty-one years

After working with teachers and students for over twenty-four years, I developed a great appreciation for poetry and writers of all kinds. My students always taught me so much about life and learning. This poem is about a beautiful section of the Charleston, SC harbor. It is nestled in a small area of Mt. Pleasant known as Shem Creek and once you have seen it you will not be able to forget its peaceful charm.

I Tried Him

Giving my life to Jesus was the best thing I've
ever done, for all my battles and strifes I have
won. He's always there to protect me, and
to keep me from all harm, just thinking about him
keeps me cozy and warm.

If you have problems and can't find your way,
just get on your knees, he'll teach you to pray.
Don't worry about these worldly things, they
will all pass away, but the love God gives to you,
it's here to stay. So wherever you go, and
whatever you do, always remember it's God
who loves you.

Frances Earl
Chattanooga, TN

[Hometown] South Pittsburgh, TN; [DOB] September 9, 1936; [Ed] eleventh grade; [Occ] retired from the Holiday Inn after thirty-five years; [Hobbies] reading, writing, singing, walking, helping people; [GA] to love God, others and myself

I was born in a small country town. I had nine brothers and there were six girls. My father was a minister and a chef. My mother did crocheting and sewing. She made dresses and clothes for us girls. I learned to read and write my name before I started school. I got very ill once, I prayed and gave it all to God. He healed me and I wrote this poem.

Stood Up

It was your idea to go on a third date,
not mine.
Honestly, I didn't care either way,
but I said okay.
That morning I told you when I was
leaving and you said fine.
You waited to stand me up until I was on
my way.

You said, "It's too tough."
Do you realize how hard it was for me to
come meet you?
All you did was blame me for everything
until I said enough!
There were things you did wrong too.

All you did was pick a fight.
You didn't care you almost cost me
my rides to my job.
Be honest, you just wanted sex without
any commitment, right?
Even though you stood me up, I'm moving
on and leaving a slob.

Abigail Hucker
Chester, PA

[Hometown] Landenberg, PA; [Ed] BA in mass communications; [Occ] self-advocate leader for PA Education for All Coalition; [Hobbies] writing, playing my drums; [GA] being able to entertain others through TV, radio, newspaper segments, interviews and my poetry

The Beauty of the Kind

I with everything;
My life without pain.
You with nothing,
And nothing to gain.

Why should I be allowed to see
The beauty of the kind,
When others, even eighty,
Since birth have been blind?

I have food aplenty
To avoid an early death,
While others without a morsel
Starve upon their final breath.

The earth I hold in my palm,
The soil of many lands,
Others never know or feel;
Others with no hands.

Why am I, the least deserving,
Freely given the best,
When the worst there is
Falls upon the rest?

Charles O. Rand
Springerville, AZ

[Hometown] San Francisco, CA; [DOB] April 19, 1939; [Ed] BA in English; [Occ] retired juvenile probation officer; [Hobbies] archaeology, reading; [GA] DVD of my archaeological work

My wife of fifty years, Christina, and I live in a small mountain town in east central Arizona where I spend my retirement years uncovering a prehistoric habitation site. I am a poetry lover since childhood who has always been blessed with a life filled with the natural and human beauty of the earth. I have been given every possible blessing while most of the world of humanity has nothing and suffers greatly.

Galloping Home

Think about waking
Think about eating
Think about walking
Think about loving
Think about sleeping
Think about dying
Think about Jesus...

Think about Jesus
Think about dying
Think about sleeping
Think about loving
Think about walking
Think about eating
Think about waking...

Think about you
Think about me
Think about Jesus...

Dedicated to the Soldier
who died in Afghanistan.
The Marines stepping ever so lightly
bringing him in his flag-draped coffin
back to the U.S.A.

Eleanor A. Tingelstad
Fergus Falls, MN

[Hometown] Pelican Rapids, MN; [DOB] February 17, 1933; [Ed] finished tenth grade; [Occ] housework, babysitting, factory; [Hobbies] writing poetry, sewing baby quilts and embroidery; [GA] received poetry gold medal of excellence from Poetryfest

I saw the Marines carrying the flag-draped coffin of a soldier who died in Afghanistan. I thought of his family (loved ones) because I have soldiers in my family. My dad was in World War I. Two brothers served in World War II and came home safely to us and five children waiting for them. They both were wounded. Three brothers served in peace time: one drafted and two who joined the Air Force. I have one brother remaining and one sister. I am thankful!

Autumn Is Here!

Autumn is here, nothing to fear
Halloween hoot, trick-or-treat loot,
A sudden wind, night chill not still,
Coles, "Autumn Leaves," Suddenly reprieves,
Whitman's "Green Leaves," we will believe,
Geese up above, sing songs of love,
Sparrows tweet-sweet, trees blown leaves fleet,
Soulful crow's caw, good treats in store,
Autumn is here, go get some beer,
Winter coats and gloves, warm up by stove,
Whistling train, delivers grain,
Faint rays-sunlight, Thanksgiving bite,
Christmas will come, you sing, I'll hum,
New Year in rear, another year,
Autumn is here, baked apples dear,
Reindeer will prance, such grace to dance,
May ice or snow, sudden sleet flow,
Football in play, turkey today,
Autumn is here, the feast endears!
A pumpkin smile, his secret guile.

Michael Berger
Amagansett, NY

[Hometown] Amagansett, NY; [DOB] January 22, 1945; [Ed] MA; [Occ] retired history teacher; [Hobbies] writing, lover of music, classic movies; [GA] my life's quandary: "to be or not to be."

Thank you for the opportunity to present my work! Life amazes many of us, I am caught by the natural beauty of nature, which abounds in all seasons. A distance of both the nature and spiritual wonders as well, we find more questions than answers in terms of fighting the puzzles of life together in an understanding and intelligible flow. Sometimes, what we know can be beyond our ability to relate or even understand. It is in what we cannot understand and attempt to interpret which is the matrix of poetry itself!

Cross Winds

Feeding fish
Diving birds
A bell buoy
Waves breaking on the beach
All restful and lulling
Tidal pools where water flows
I walked along the shoreline.
Shells were glistening in the sand.
Warm breezes blew across my face.
I thought of you and your love of the sea.
A seagull flew and startled me.
It was wild, beautiful and free.
I felt you there, and I felt your touch
Where the winds blow across the sea.
Stay here and walk with me
Always in my thoughts.
You are harbored there.
Though the cross winds blow...
You will not go.

Marilyn Shavender
Virginia Beach, VA

[Hometown] Virginia Beach, VA; [DOB] February 22, 1938; [Ed] BS degree; [Occ] retired teacher (forty-three years); [Hobbies] playing my piano, writing children's books; [GA] teacher of the year:

I was reading teacher of the year three times. I published one poetry book, Marsh Winds: A Sentimental Journey. My daughter passed from this life some years ago. She was a beautiful auburn-haired gal. She gave us three beautiful girls whom I love dearly. I wrote this poem about her.

November 22, 1963

November 22
Fifty one years ago
Our president was shot
The one we all loved so

He was hit in Dallas
I do not know why
The minute he was hit
I broke down to cry

My son said Mommy do not cry
What can I do?
How do you tell a three-year-old
What is really true

He was a good president
But never had the time
To prove what he could do
To make our country fine

Little John saluted him
As he did pass by
That will never be forgot
No matter how I try

He is resting peacefully
In our Father's hand
We must not forget him
For America we stand

Kayla Kimball
Blue Earth, MN

[Hometown] Waupaca, WI; [DOB] September 6, 1940; [Ed] some college; [Occ] worked at an electronic plant for thirty-two years; [Hobbies] writing poetry, doing Sudokus and volunteer work; [GA] raising three wonderful sons

I was diagnosed with MS at the age of twenty-seven. After I turned sixty, it became quite hard for me to do many things physically. Writing poetry kept my mind sharp. I also receive much enjoyment and relaxation. I write poems for birthdays, anniversaries, to say Thank You, and any other special occasions.

A Kaleidoscope Season

How very utterly mesmerizing autumn can be,
Such dramatic overtones and wonders to see.
Once greenery surrounded each and every turn,
Now softly nature has the hot summer adjourn.
The trees begin a fascinating journey of change,
Colors burst forward with a variety of range.
Brilliant reds and toasted oranges suddenly alive,
Soft browns whisk in the mix trying to survive.
A season with a paintbrush of endless colors,
Leaves complete with previous season's flowers.
Such a journey of wondrous beauty to walk through,
Each step makes everything around seem like new.
One should venture through this picturesque place,
Carefully taking in every moment but not in haste.
Even the wild flowers of various golds and purples
Accent the scene and work their magic so boastful.
Oh season of powerful beauty please don't leave,
As there is so much more to see and believe!

Kathy O'Connor
Mahopac, NY

I am a retiree now living in Mahopac, NY. Writing poems was my escape from the world in high school. I enjoyed making magic with words. Then I put down my pen to concentrate on family and friends for many years. My heart was totally broken when I lost three loved ones to cancer, so I began to write again to help my grieving. Writing poetry again helps to not only heal heartbreak but to see the blessings around me.

Back in Time

An expression, statement,
of a return to a time ago,
the past once lived in,
lived through on ways to
new beginnings adventures.
Back in the day, a travel wish,
to revisit people, places, things,
recapture special moments in
memory, history, to augment,
heighten, enrich, give credence
to the present path in life.
Dreamscapes of childhood,
family, the way things were
when naiveté, innocence,
initiated spontaneity, laughter,
a love of the moment and day.
Turn the clocks back an
hour to capture the last hour,
incarcerate, in case you missed
an important moment, chance
to get it back, grab it and
take it with you, sprinkle
the lost upon the found.

Ronald M. Ruble
Huron, OH

[Hometown] Huron, OH; [DOB] July 4, 1940; [Ed] PhD in theatre; [Occ] retired college professor; [Hobbies] writing; [GA] my family

I was fortunate to have elementary, junior high, and high school teachers see in me what I did not, the ability to create. I started writing poetry and short stories by the time I was eight years old. My school friends and I acted out the stories at recess, on the playground. Through the years, I have often looked back to those endearing, challenging, naïve times when the spirit of adventure, romanticism, ruled supreme in my head. "Back in Time," allowed me to go back, reminisce, smile over tender times.

The Good Old Days

Sends a tingle
Down my spine
As I go
Back in time

Raindrops
From the sky
Glittering like jewels
Passing by

Sunlight
Warming the sod
Where you can
Speak with God

Hunting berries
And picking wild flowers
By
The hours

Through green pastures
And over a rocky hill
Sounds of voices
Are present still

The good old days
Are now gone
Leisure ways
Replaced by hurry and rush days

Margaret Worley
Watertown, TN

[Hometown] Watertown, TN; [DOB] February 4, 1960; [Ed] graduate of literature; [Occ] salesperson; [Hobbies] writing, hiking, reading; [GA] being published by a magazine

My poem was inspired by the old days. Just as the name "the good old days!" It tells how things have changed from forty to fifty years ago, when life was slow and at a less rushed pace than we are at today. It's a lot different than my last poem that was about the future and higher technology. I decided to time travel back to the past for this one. Life as we know it has made a big change from then. So, sit back and take a leap back in time for this one. May God bless all.

Tale of Love

Written with such emotion
Lived in such devotion
The tale of love is told

Two youthful lovers
Hidden behind life's covers
Together they've built a stronghold

Their growing tender connection
Brings no one any objection
They'll love even when they're old

In time they may say vows
Now they push away *hows*
Their hearts won't ever be cold

In a generation of risk-taking
Their love will be breath-making
Hearts of their symmetry will fold

Together they are one
On a journey that's just begun
Their tale of love foretold

Abigail S. Noble
Clinton, MO

[Hometown] Clinton, MO; [DOB] July 15, 2001; [Occ] student; [Hobbies] writing, reading, flute; [GA] being published

A small-town girl, poet and bookworm, I'm fascinated with history and the stories it brings to life. I refuse to believe that there is nothing left to discover. When I take out my notebook and pencil, it's as if a whole new world is waiting at my fingertips. With a family of six though, I'm never having peace and quiet, but I love them anyway.

The Homeless Soul

For them there is no warmth of the daylight to wait for,
no warm evenings to rest for the weary body,
suffering and pain is their only wealth in an unnoticed
world of flash and fast.
From sunrise until sunset they think alone,
from early morning until the dark of night, tears and a
broken heart their only friend. They see no hope, no footprints
in the sand, no one reaching out with a helping hand.
Alone and cold they wait in the darkness for the judgment day
and they wonder, is this the hell I had to pay?
Guilt, depression, hurt and loss fill the airways of today,
some would say, but gratitude, faith and hope are here to stay,
I say. When someone is filled with doubt and fear, be the one to
give them cheer, when they just can't take a stand, be the one
with that helping hand. In the play of life, it is our roll, to reach out
and save the homeless soul.

Thomas Dutcher
Breinigsville, PA

[Hometown] Milford, NY; [DOB] September 23, 1948; [Ed] business marketing, management; [Occ] operating manager for Direct Media USA; [Hobbies] golf, writing, sports; [GA] learning to express my feelings

This poem is all about the hard times, the rough times, the sad times that many of us have gone through. If you are fighting depression, sadness or fear, help is very near. My book Words for You (U Know), *a collection of poems by me, starts out thanking my wife for bringing me out of that dark spot. I have been in many of Eber & Wein's publications, and I hope my words have helped others.*

My Dad

As you can see, this poem's to be.
It's about my dad
who meant the world to me

Strong and kind, he made mistakes.
This is true, but was a better
person than me and you.

Cancer came, changed our lives,
as nothing would be the same.

Never complained, although in pain.
Fought this battle without gain.

His body once strong and healthy
now lay frail. Eyes shined and
bright, now stare out the window
awaiting his flight.

Sky so blue, clouds so white
all of a sudden we saw guided light.

The Lord took his hand and said
"Come with me, away to
Heaven's promised land."

Dyan R. Ramos
Milwaukee, WI

Storm

As my dreams lay as dust upon my bedroom floor
I think about the flowers springing up so full of life
Stretching ever upward to the heavens
Out my window as my last raindrops fall, I see the glass rainbows
Shattered upon the ground
As I lay here in the remains of my day, I reflect...do you see, God?
Do you hear, God? The emptiness, the bitter emptiness.
A shell, yes that's what remains...
As I look to the West, it's coming, oh God, it's coming
The cold harsh reality of winter
Perhaps the last storm of my life
Horses of death and destruction
Faceless rider on the storm
Are you out there?
Do you hear me?
Into this house I'm born, into this world I'm thrown
Outcast, hurt, abused, robbed, my child life lying dead upon my face
The cold black reality of winter is creeping in
Suffer the little child to come unto me...Dear God, if it's possible
Remove my life so I suffer no more
The end is near, I can feel the cold fingers of death
Creeping upon my little heart
Father—no words, just sorrow, emptiness
Forgiveness? Can't find it in *me*...God?
The storm is upon me, winter has settled in my heart
So I see no light, just darkness, is it so wrong to want to feel the warmth
Of a mother's arms about me? Hold me tight, only you can fill this barren void
Yes, the flowers are all dead, the cold reality of life

Charles W. L. Flick
Bowling Green, OH

[Hometown] Graytown, OH; [DOB] February 23, 1954; [Ed] twelfth grade; [Occ] retired mailman, BGSU; [Hobbies] woodworking; [GA] being a loving father

I wrote this after sitting at a railroad crossing—I wanted to kill myself. It was a hard time in my life. I believe God spared my life that day. Now, several years later, I do some preaching. I gave my life to Christ on March 4, 1994. I now live for Him.

Going Girls

Dream of granddaughters
At night when lie in bed

I am worried about
What is in their heads

No suspicions that
It's not something good

Wish it were all about
cooking and food

They accomplished scholars all
Athletes who push the wall

I push rosary beads to bead
That they can readily see

Culture of their age flowing
And they not choose girls going

Mary Ann Carrico-Mitchell, RN, BS
Campbellsburg, KY

[Hometown] Louisville, KY; [DOB] August 1, 1937; [Ed] RN, BS, scholarship winner, graduate of University of Colorado; [Occ] retired; [Hobbies] art, poetry, prose, quilts, published six books of poetry, maintains nine acres; [GA] published in Journal of Pierre Teil Hard de Chardin

Discussion of the movie, Gone Girl, evokes these remarks. I spend much time in prayer, writing, conversing and listening about the state of affairs of our nation. The distress I feel at the onslaught of drug scenarios, evident lack of parental supervision, and feeling sadness for our youngsters. The productions of Hollywood show a considerable lack of concern for the ethics of their productions, the influences of productions on our young and an overwhelming smell of creativity which appeals to a low standard and the reaping only of monetary value. Thank you.

The Difference

The difference between your being here
And not is that it is hard to keep up
Appearances. Daily routines leer
At us even though cooking meals like soup
Changing dietary needs from skim milk
To whole milk saves ourselves for
The rest of the difference. No silk
Sheets for us but the reclamation chore
Sharing, we made the best team of caring
Thought we would be helpmates forever
Heaven came for you with a new calling
You said you had a new job to do wherever
God sent you since you appreciated His Creation
We miss the humble, compassionate, thoughtful
Husband, father, man who stood for his nation
Knowing the difference we are ever mindful
Grieving, grinding forward walking in your shoe
Doing what it takes to prompt proliferance
Life is not the same without you
Your greatest theme is to make the difference
You stood up for us, by us, loving and loyal
Defending us, smoothing over interference
Helping us meet goals through tough toil
Now it is our turn to make the difference
How earnestly we begged you stay
Your company was next to Jesus's

Joan Mays
West Brooklyn, IL

[Hometown] West Brooklyn, IL; [Occ] horticulture; [Hobbies] writing, music, pets, weather watcher; [GA] family

Writing poetic words in the modern age is a great privilege and acts like balming salve ointment to the mind. Although my roots began in Indiana, I settled near West Brooklyn, IL to write, acknowledge family, and be inspired by the scenic beauty of nature. Circumstances cause me to put incidents to pen. Reciting at poetry slams in Urbana, IL coffeehouses as extracurricular Illinois State University English studies was immensely enjoyable. Other verses include "Songs to Save the World," "Rock Your Way to Heaven," and "Cinder Road," tales.

Palm Springs Air Museum Volunteers

They come to serve day after day
Some backs are bent. Their hair is gray
They seldom speak of what they did
So long ago when they were but kids
But they are the ones who took the sky
With hostile fighters slashing by
And some were with that hardy band
Parachuting into foreign lands
And still there are some who knew
Strife at Tarawa and Peleliu
Some say they're heroes—maybe so
But there's one thing that they all know
Here at home and many foreign lands
Their rows and rows of crosses stand
And you can visit near and far
To be just where the heroes are

Everett L. Price
Cathedral City, CA

[Hometown] Cathedral City, CA; [DOB] September 28, 1922; [Ed] MD, DO, DNB; [Occ] retired; [Hobbies] music, woodworking; [GA] fifty-two years of medical practice

On Sept. 29, 1940, the day after my eighteenth birthday, I enlisted in the armed service. I had heard our president state, "I hate war! My wife Eleanor hates war, therefore there will be no war!" I am sure that anyone who read of the events that were happening in Europe was aware that someone would have to stop Adolph Hitler. Growing up in Kentucky with a reserve officer as a father, I had obtained considerable skill in the use of firearms and I wanted to fly. Many times during the next five years, while I was flying fighters and commanding forward fire control teams in the Pacific Theater, I remembered something my mother had told me many times. Be careful for what you wish for. When the war ended, I went to medical school with the help of the GI Bill and practiced medicine for fifty-two years. After retiring, I volunteered at the Palm Springs Air Museum and am now the Director of Visitors Service. I have written many verses, some of which reflect the fact that during the last part of WWII, I was given the thankless task of writing letters to families of kids who would not be returning home.

Imagination

Using our imagination, we are demonstrating a cognitive ability, act, or
power, of forming mental images, thoughts, ideas, or concepts of objects
or things that have not been sensed or experienced previously, or
of combining or recombining the products of past knowledge simultaneously.
Something new, original, inventive, or inceptive is created by the mind,
and the outcome may be in some way beneficial to mankind.

Imaginative thought can be used in pretending, fantasizing, wishful thinking,
daydreams or dreams, where we can go anywhere, be anyone, or do anything
according to any possible or hopeless scheme or theme.
We might use it to recall, reminisce, or relive a past experience, for its
own sake, with or without it having any relevance, significance, or
meaning interrelated with a current consequence.

In everyday life, or in scientific or nonscientific disciplines, imagination
plays a crucial role in supplying us with possible answers, to hypotheses,
theories, concepts, notions, plans, designs, projects, or purposes we ponder.
It allows us to detach ourselves from the real, objective world in order to
reflect, contemplate, and deliberate, about conceptions, impressions,
and speculations of anything in new, creative, or diverse ways to assimilate.

Imagination permits us to use our mental faculties formatively, aesthetically,
and freely, allowing us to interpret, understand, and appreciate degrees of
imaginative thought, from extreme fantasy to rigorous problem-solving effectively.
It tends to be the most beneficial, advantageous, and rewarding to humankind,
when imagination is used with an open mind!

Peter O. Peretti
Chicago, IL

[Hometown] Chicago, IL; [Ed] PhD in psychology; [Occ] professor; [Hobbies] reading, book clubs, bicycling;
[GA] teaching and research

Wind Blows

Can you see wind
Can you search wind
Can you touch wind
Can you taste wind
Wind blows
It blows and blows and blows
over little houses big houses
rattle rattle rattle roof top
Wind blows
You can't see wind
You can't search wind
You can't touch wind
You can't taste wind
Wind blows
It blows and blows and blows
over low hill high hill
makin' little Daisy dance Daisy dance
Wind blows it blows and blows
None be said behind wind
there God!

Loranie Bates
Milwaukee, WI

I am a housewife, raising eight kids and giving a helping hand to teenage kids as well. I worked at Salvation Army Rehab. I loved working there because it allowed me to share love with others. At rehab, there was a certain young man who had great respect for me, but later I learned shocking news: the young man was a prison escapee from Indiana. As shocked as I was, somehow I don't regret I shared good words with him. I was mostly inspired to write poetry by Silas, AL, "small country" where I was born. The natural beauty of Silas interested me to write poetry at night in the Silas Big Country House. I'd lie in bed and listen to wind blow over our tin roof.

War

Battlefields laden with soldiers
Rifles and cannons blaring so loudly
Killing all part of a day's work
War...why? I ask so profoundly.

Young men and women leaving their homes
To take up residence on foreign lands
Leaving loved ones behind, to don armored vests
With true grit and dirt and bloodstained hands.

War...a game of backyard childhood play
Enticing to young eyes on wide screens
In reality no game at all, just bloodshed and death
Is the only real scene.

The bravery of these young men and women
I certainly do not question
But the leaders of these courageous young warriors
Need to learn a serious lesson...

If only peace could be their first thought of choice
Then war would definitely take a back seat
Listening and planning a peaceful solution...
Oh God, if only, if only...I repeat!

Geraldine McCusker
Williamstown, NJ

[Hometown] Williamstown, NJ; [DOB] August 27, 1946; [Ed] graduate of Peirce Junior College; [Occ] retired administrative assistant in the nursing department of a New Jersey hospital; [Hobbies] writing and reading poetry, painting, traveling, cooking Italian food, and water aerobics; [GA] my forty-six years of marriage to my husband Edward, my three children, and my five grandchildren

Besides my love of family, I enjoy writing and reading poetry. Since my retirement, I find that my poetry gives me relaxation, and can take me in any direction that I would like to go. Six years ago, I wrote this poem, "War," after reading of the deaths due to the Iraqi conflict in the Middle East. I wrote this with a very heavy heart. I feel that war is something that definitely should be the very final outcome after all avenues have been exhausted.

Romancing the Bar...or the Pirate's Lair

On the edge of the old French Quarter,
there's an ancient and crumbling bar.
Both blacksmith and pirate's headquarters,
as LaFitte traveled near and far.

At night in the dark interior,
the candlesticks flicker and glow.
The reflection in all the mirrors
make a mesmerizing show.

Back in a shadowed corner,
a piano plays soft and low.
The crowd drifts in through open doors,
like a moth to the flame they go.

Sitting way back by a window,
we watch the people go by.
As the sultry night breeze caresses
across our skin like a sigh.

Hands touch on the old, wooden table.
Eyes twinkle like candlelight.
We sip our drinks in contentment
and savor the sounds and the sights.

I feel the ghost of the pirate
still lingers in his lair.
And long ago laughter echoes
in the humid New Orleans air.

Janet Sue Deckard
Texas City, TX

[Hometown] Galveston, TX; [DOB] June 16, 1953; [Ed] associate's degree in applied science; [Occ] retired computer operator; [Hobbies] reading, writing, traveling; [GA] forty years married, my wonderful daughter and grandkids are the best

Being born and raised on Galveston Island, I've always felt an affinity with New Orleans for many reasons. Both cities are historical treasures on the Gulf Coast. Both cities were also home to the notorious privateer who roamed the gulf, Jean Lafitte. Galveston has the remains of his 1817 built home called the Maison Rouge. New Orleans has the old Lafitte family's blacksmith shop, built around 1730, which is now a bar. True to its original form, it still has no electricity.

It's Still You, Lord

It's still You, Lord
We lift our hands in praise
It's still You, Lord
You saved us by Your grace
There's no other way
It's still You, Lord
It's still You, Lord
We glorify Your name
It's still You, Lord
We shout and we sing
It's still You, Lord
We trust and obey
It's still You, Lord
We worship and we pray
There's no other way
Yes, Jesus still S-A-V-E-S
It's still You, Lord
Jesus, oh Jesus, come to Him today
Trust Him all the way
Jesus, oh Jesus
Yes, it's still You today

Doris Cox
Tunnel Hill, GA

[Hometown] Dalton, GA; [DOB] July 21, 1950; [Ed] North Whitfield High School; [Occ] textile Shaw Plant 81, thirty-six years (2015); [Hobbies] restoring toys, riding my bike, reading God's word; [GA] having my birthday poem published in Across the Way

My life is simple. I work in a carpet plant: Shaw Plant 81 in Springdale. I love my life and my desire is to share God's love in poems and songs. God gives me strength. My friend made book markers with my poems. I share them with everyone. This is what I live for. My favorite verse is Psalm 63:3. "My Lord Is Bigger Than Big" is one of my songs. To God be the glory.

Kaleidoscope Unseen

Colors, images, sounds dance on light
Paths and choices twirl before your eyes
Will you see beauty or pick the night
And the kaleidoscope spins

Colors, images swirl, then solidify as her dreams
Will you see them or go for pleasures of the flesh
So many brilliant choices, pick her bright beam
And the kaleidoscope spins

The right path is always the hardest to choose
Now flesh rules you, you're prisoner to the night
Maggots eat your soul while you choose to lose
And the kaleidoscope spins

Colors flash, plead, "Don't hurt her; let her go"
Darkness screams its need for power, money and flesh
Happiness and awe within your grasp, you see only your dark goal
And the kaleidoscope spins

Foolish man, she is the colors, your babes the light
You traded your honor for money and blight
You don't see beauty of family, of embracing warmth at night
And the kaleidoscope spins

She is free now and dances with colors and twirls
The schema of changing images, yours no more
Sparkling, twinkling, always swirling to be discovered
But the kaleidoscope spins for you no more

Virginia Diane Troxel-Spence
Loomis, CA

[Hometown] Loomis, CA; [DOB] July 13, 1951; [Ed] MA in education (ECE); [Occ] teacher; [Hobbies] gardening, choir, reading; [GA] raising my grandson alone

There is nothing more magnificent than a couple who truly see what they have. Alas, it has been my experience that most human beings search their whole life for that elusive something to fill the void in their life. They fill the void with sex, alcohol, gambling, and recreational pursuits. Sadly, the hole can never be filled with empty pursuits, only with the love and devotion of friends and family. True happiness that warms your heart on a cold night, and allows the soul to take flight comes from seeing the beauty that is hearth and home.

True Friends

When you have friends,
You know you'll never be alone
They'll come when you are in need
They're as near as any phone

A friend can help to cheer you
Whenever you feel blue
And when you need a favor
They are there to give to you.

Friends come in any color
They can be in any size.
It doesn't really matter
If they are girls or guys.

Friends love to share your happiness.
They comfort you in sorrow.
They give their hearts in friendship
And they'll still be there tomorrow.

So if you're feeling lonely,
You're down and out or blue,
You can call upon a good friend
They are always there for you.

Ruth Gombos
Madison Heights, Virginia

[Hometown] Bourbon, IN; [DOB] January 28, 1934; [Ed] high school graduate; [Occ] retired from Sears; [Hobbies] knitting and crocheting; [GA] marrying a good man and birthing four great children

I am the last of eight children. I was raised on a farm where I lived until I married. I graduated high school in 1952, met William and married in 1954. I had four children and when the last one started school, I went to work for Sears. I stayed with Sears until I retired after twenty-five years. When I married, I moved to Michigan. When I retired, I moved to Virginia. My husband and I have been married sixty years and still counting.

Jesus Christ

Jesus Christ came and sacrificed His life for you and me.
He was manifested in the flesh.
The shedding of his blood covers the head of all believers.
He lived here on planet Earth, in a world of sin,
So all could receive eternal life.
Jesus died on the cross for our sin—He was sin free,
But yet he suffered and died in order to redeem man.
His blood was shed on the cross for us all.
The cross, being a part of a Christian life.
God has predicated that all who walk in His footsteps—
Persecution will come upon them.
When Christ resurrected from death,
He won victory over death and hell.
Humiliation, trials and tribulation may come,
Strife may threaten our faith and hope,
But Christ will be with us to the end.
A Christian must take his cross and walk,
Behind our Lord and Savior Jesus Christ—
Which is the only way to reach heaven.

Fred Cato Jr.
Casa Grande, AZ

[Hometown] New London, NC; [DOB] January 2, 1945; [Ed] BS degree in criminal justice;
[Occ] retired military; [Hobbies] writing poems and lyrics; [GA] reading and writing

The Old Rag Rug

My mother's motto was save, save, save!
In case some day a path it will pave,
Just look at that over by the door
The old rag rug upon the floor.

Let's see now, this was a dress I wore in school
When we first learned the golden rule,
This red and white was my heart's delight
And I treasured it with all my might

This was a coat my mother wore
And it was really tattered and tore,
When she wore it I gave her many a hug
Till one day she said, "Oh heck, save it for the rug."

I wore this to my high school prom
You'd never think I came from a farm,
What memories it brings back—but let's hurry on
Or we'll be sitting up till dawn.

Every braid tells a story
To me as great as "Old Glory,"
It's a welcome mat right by the door
The old rag rug upon the floor.

Kitty Schafer
Morrison, IL

[Hometown] Morrison, IL; [DOB] November 29, 1916; [Ed] tenth grade; [Occ] homemaker; [Hobbies] just living now, but I used to model; [GA] being able to grant my dad's wish: taking care of Mom so a nurse didn't have to—no nursing home for her, no way

I've been a widow since January 2011 after sixty-one years of marriage. I live in the home we shared for thirty-five years here in a small Illinois town. Before that we lived in Chicago and Sun City, AZ, and we had a home a block from the Atlantic where we spent seven months of winter. This was after we lived here in Illinois where the winters are very frigid. Ormond Beach, FL was a heavenly place. We sold it and decided to be near a family of relatives, very distant ones. So many have gone to heaven. My poetry is mostly of true events. My little Japanese Chin keeps me agile. Also, I'm happy Mom was here with us and able to go to Heaven from her bed. For her last ten years, she was a joy and loved by all. She was never sick and lived to be 105 years old. The Florida sunshine was a tonic for all. Wading in the Atlantic was pure joy. Mom loved Florida, and we all waded in the ocean.

evening serenity

lavender twilight:
the outgoing tide carries
day's ebbing light out to sea

Margaret V. Savage
Winchester, IL

[Hometown] *Winchester, IL;* [DOB] *February 19, 1942;* [Ed] *college;* [Occ] *medical record transcriptionist;* [Hobbies] *writing, reading, music and piano;* [GA] *my first published poem*

I am a college major employed as an accredited medical technician until my retirement. I started writing poetry in high school. A few years ago I read my first haiku and was inspired to try writing my own. I'm intrigued by the pictures a three-line haiku paints. I've written about five hundred haikus thus far and am working on self-publishing some. I will continue writing as long as I have passion and good health.

At Last

When I at last am laid to rest,
my children born in pain and fear,
shall hold my memory dear.
And in the spring of every year,
flowers they should plant for the birds
and butterflies I've loved so dear.
And when the clouds of dark and fear appear,
may they have faith and courage to fight and persevere.
Until at last the winds of change appear and
know that the sun is always near.
And joy and laughter will appear,
as though they were waiting in the rear.

Maria P. Marrero
La Porte, TX

Yes, Ashley

In all my life I've never met a girl like her
that stirs up my emotions and makes me want
to give her all of my devotion.
Wise beyond her years. So young, so beautiful yet,
so strong. She brings me to tears. Yes, Ashley
Is her name never into playing any games. Her
will is strong so determined to make it in this
life she lives. No matter what you say,
whether you're joking or not, her will can't be broken.
When you see her from afar you just want to hold
her close and hold her near and protect her from
all harm, yes, you, my dear. To think of her in a
metaphor or a synopsis, take your pick, she is
a guiding light showing you the way through
unchartered waters to bring you into her safe
harbor from all harm. Yes, Ashley, she's the one.
She is a beacon of light. Always full of energy.
And always shining bright. Yes, Ashley, you will
live and shine forever, girl.

       Yes, Ashley

Lawrence D. Student
Cleveland, OH

[Hometown] Cleveland, OH; [DOB] June 2, 1969; [Ed] high school grade, college for CNC machining and tool and die; [Hobbies] working out, writing, photography, playing guitar, Harley Davidson motorcycles, my cars and trucks I own; [GA] my brother in life and my friends that I've grown up with and had all through my life.

I have seen it all and have done it all. I can't believe I am still alive. I've always been an artsy kind of guy—into playing guitar, into music, photography, my writing. This poem I wrote is for a girl I have known for some time now. She is, I guess, my muse. She helped me through a dark time in my life. If it wasn't for her, I wouldn't be here today. So I dedicate this poem to her and only her. Ashley, thank you for everything, girl. Words can't say enough about you and how much I appreciate you and your friendship. I will always be there for you, Ashley. Take care and be safe.

Dust on Old Pages

Dust on old pages
Of books well read.
Old school rooms
Where young minds were fed.
Desks with inkwells,
Blackboards with chalk,
Hallways to higher learning
Many footsteps did walk.
Recess and playgrounds,
Four rooms with walls,
We shared our youth
Running up and down halls.
Words and numbers filled our lives
As young hearts were fed
On the dust of old pages
From books well read.

Nancy E. Tayman
Akron, OH

[Hometown] Akron, OH; [DOB] March 11, 1946; [Ed] high school; [Occ] retired; [Hobbies] reading, writing, painting

I retired after many years working in the business world. I have always enjoyed reading poetry, especially Walt Whitman and Robert Frost. I recently had my fiftieth high school class reunion, which brought back memories of early school days. I was raised in a small town in West Virginia, and those memories reminded me of that four-room school house where my education began—my inspiration for this poem.

Ivy and Brocade

The mask is exquisite,
A work of fifteen years.
I painted it to show false love,
And to hide my tears.
I call this mask "The Charmer."
One smile, and you're sold.
Would you ever guess that my heart
Isn't truly made of gold?

The mask remains unbroken,
Though it's cracked over the years.
I painted it to show false hope,
And to hide my fears.
I call this mask "Beguiler."
It does as it is told.
Would you ever guess that I don't
Truly fit the mold?

Amanda N. Moore
Stuart, FL

[Hometown] Stuart, FL; [DOB] March 30, 1998; [Ed] high school senior; [Occ] student, artist, writer; [Hobbies] painting, sketching, writing, singing, divination, brooding; [GA] cleaving my soul into fifteen separate identities—take that, Voldemort!

I am a relatively young kid who acts more like an ancient, jaded immortal. I draw, paint, sew, and craft jewelry, though I view art as a necessary ritual rather than a fun hobby. I float amongst the clouds with my mind fixed permanently in space. I adore literature, computer games, and studying abnormal psychology and ancient languages. I can read and write Nordic, Pictish, and Egyptian hieroglyphics. I battle valiantly with severe scoliosis and dissociative identity disorder. My poetry delves deep into emotions that are universally experienced—and universally concealed.

Don't Always Assume

Don't always assume life is rosy and nice.
Before you do anything bad,
think once or twice.
Don't always assume life's sunshine and beaches.
Sometimes it hails,
like rock hard peaches.
Don't always assume if you try you'll fail.
Sometimes you'll stumble,
fall and flail.
Don't always assume, you'll never succeed.
Sometimes you might actually exceed.
Don't always assume your goals are not in sight.
They just might not be as bright.
When we get older it seems,
The most important things weren't always our dreams.
Growing up we all just consumed,
everything was just all always assumed.

Rose Rodgers
Titusville, PA

[Hometown] Townville, PA; [DOB] age fifty-two; [Ed] high school diploma; [Occ] CNA, housekeeping; [Hobbies] flower gardening, crocheting, canning, grandkids; [GA] my family, raising them all to be good

Will You Marry Me?

Long ago a young man in love
Had asked his girl to be his bride.
She was shy but loved him so.
And she answered with a glow.

Her answer was "yes," he was so proud!
They set a date and made some plans,
For their wedding day must be grand.
There was much to do before they wed.

Times were hard, money was scarce.
There was a gown to sew, a veil and a dress.
The young man had his work to do,
Plus building home and furniture, too.

Time passed slowly, but only to them;
Each day brought a new chore at hand.
They worked each day on what was needed.
All came together, as time was fleeting.

Then one day all was completed.
A home, furniture and other things needed.
Quilts were made and linens too.
And all was beautiful and brand new.

They took their vows with all their hearts
And promised forever never to part.
Their life was good, rich and full,
Just like they planned as they built their world.

Sandra L. Towne
Gordo, AL

[Hometown] Tuscaloosa, AL; [DOB] November 11, 1944; [Ed] one year of college; [Occ] homemaker, caregiver; [Hobbies] quilting, corvettes; [GA] three wonderful children

I've always written poems. I never kept them, just wrote for fun. I was born and raised in the south. As I've grown older, many of my childhood memories bring me pleasure. So, the majority, of my work is based on the reflections of those wonderful "good old days." I now have a collection of poems and I read them from time to time. They always made me laugh or smile. My aunts, uncles, grandparents, and cousins were, and are, so dear to me. Hope you enjoy this poem. It's about my paternal grandparents.

The Carpenter

The dusty shop, which smelled
of fresh-sawed wood,
Found him creating something good.
He showed signs of age in his
Dust-covered clothes, as his
Gnarled hands were creating,
Sawing and notching.
They were forming something sad,
But important.
Something to remind us all
How someone suffered.
It was formed from a tree,
No longer alive,
Yet it's there year after year,
Reminding us of the story,
Of its resurrection like he was.
Each year when I see it,
I'm reminded of the man
Who loved His Savior and his church,
Also his family.
He cared, was firm, but gentle,
Showed respect and love,
My dad the carpenter.

Darlene K. Lannholm
Galesburg, IL

[Hometown] Galesburg, IL; [DOB] September 13, 1937; [Ed] high school graduate; [Occ] retired retail department manager; [Hobbies] camping; [GA] in 1972, I was in the book Outstanding Young Women of America

I've lived most of my life in Galesburg, IL, mother of four children and a stepdaughter, plus many grandchildren that I love most dearly. I am also retired and do a lot of volunteering, so I'm very busy. The poem I wrote is in honor of my dad, a man who loved his family, his work, and his church. His hobby was carpentry, wood used straight from the tree, he made wagons, doll buggies, chalkboards, furniture. We all have things he made, but the most beautiful is put up in church each year: a wooden cross.

Time

Where is there no tomorrow?
Today, for yesterday's
Tomorrow is today.

Where is there no tomorrow?
Yesterday, for yesterday's
Tomorrow is today.

When is there
No a.m. or p.m.?
Midnight, for 12 midnight
Has no a.m. or p.m.

When is there
No a.m. or p.m.?
Noon, for 12 noon
Has no a.m. or p.m.

Yesterday, today, and tomorrow,
A.m. and p.m.
This I did not borrow,
My thoughts are new.

Alfred Elkins
Bronx, NY

[Hometown] Bronx, NY; [DOB] September 16, 1946; [Ed] BA in history and English; [Occ] retired proofreader; [Hobbies] writing poetry, reading history; [GA] marrying my wife, Ethel

I have been retired since 2012. Now I have more time to write poetry and read history, my hobbies. This book is the forty-sixth anthology I have been in. It is also the fifth time I have been in a Who's Who in Poetry anthology. From 2001 to 2008, I was in Who's Who in America. I am a member of the American Historical Association and the Academy of American Poets. I currently reside in the Bronx, NY with my lovely wife, Ethel.

Through the Eyes of a Child

So here I am awake but not heard.
Only heard by cries and laughter.
Have I tried reaching out?
Yes, many times.
I see my mommy and daddy,
and my brothers and sister.
"Oh my she's beautiful,
the radiance in her cheeks,
the red rose blush,
the peach lips,
and her dimples.
Hailey you're so beautiful."
I bring forth the love, the purity, the strength
and the bond of a family.
The purity of love is in the air,
and
the strength to protect our loved ones.

Laura M. Keifer
Amsterdam, NY

[Hometown] Amsterdam, NY; [DOB] December 12, 1988; [Ed] high school; [Hobbies] writing, poetry and fiction books; [GA] my poetry

I have read children's and teen books to gain knowledge of what they want to read, so I can write them a book that handles everyday situations. Some of my poems are based on the books that I am writing. My poem is based on when we come into the world and we are just figuring how to see and hear. This poem is inspired by my cousin Hailey who was born in 2012. She lost her mom to cancer. May she rest in peace.

Give the Devil Her Dues

The devil is a bitch with an icy-hot kiss
She'll spin you around
Throw you down
Break your nose with a rubber hose
Make you kiss her toes
Pull out your eyes, but no surprise
Tie your tongue with a rope of dung

The devil is a bitch with an icy-hot kiss
She will break your head with a pipe of lead
She will bury you in a bed of ashes
She will make you kiss her two asses

The devil is a bitch with an icy-hot kiss
You will say you were my partner
She will say you were never my partner
You were my slave then
You are my slave now
You will always be my slave

The devil is a bitch with an icy-hot kiss
Give the devil her dues
Forever and ever.

Dennis Kane
Buffalo, NY

*[Hometown] Lackawanna, NY; [Ed] one year of college; [Occ] retired meat cutter;
[Hobbies] reading, writing, sports; [GA] seventy-one years*

Inspired by Charlie Daniels Band's "Devil Went Down to Georgia"

Our Love Was Always There

Remember the day of our wedding.
We were the perfect pair.
We never had a worry.
Our love was always there.
But the years passed by so quickly.
We didn't have time to look back.
Now we are older and wiser.
Our children we raised to obey.
The days of our lives are filled
with joy and laughter.
As we enter our lives' final chapter,
our love remains solid.
Our lives we've shared.
Today we are here, tomorrow,
the hereafter.
We will meet again someday,
my love.
I will wait for you there.
With rose petals and dew
we will join together anew.
Our lives we've shared, a journey.
Now we join together completely
as we meet to enter eternity.
And together we will live forever,
my love.
Remembering our love was always there.

Sandra B. Tremblay
Plattsburgh, NY

[Hometown] Plattsburgh, NY; [DOB] June 22, 1956; [Ed] two-year college degree; [Occ] file clerk; [Hobbies] reading, biking and computer classes; [GA] to be published by you

Mama

Five feet tall in stature,
Ten feet tall by nature.

Always meeting her family's needs,
Never shirking her household deeds.

Washed the clothes the old-fashioned way
But lived to see an automated day.

Was always there for each grandchild, newborn,
And packed lunch for the aluminum worker each morn.

Sewed beautiful clothes for the one still in school:
"Shoulder seams are even" was the rule!

Learned music from her sister at an early stage,
And didn't forget it, even in old age.

"To be a teacher, set the example," she said;
Her example was mostly quietly led.

Gave up her fruitful life at age ninety-seven
And has now heard "Well done" in her home in Heaven.

Helen Cunningham
Alcoa, TN

[Hometown] Alcoa, TN; [DOB] January 19, 1926; [Ed] high school grad with on-the-job clerical training; [Occ] retired record clerk; [Hobbies] embroidery, have created pinecone wreaths; [GA] won two state of Tennessee spelling competitions, 1990 and 1994

My poem is about my mother, who was my dearest friend. I worked thirty-eight years during World War II, helping to win the war. My mother would have the evening meal ready each night for thirty-six of those years. The last two years she had suffered a heart attack, but recovered, and we had nine years together after I retired. We are all "teachers" by the example of our lives. She encouraged me in this way when I entered the work world. The "music" refers to an antique pump organ in the home. Later, we were able to buy another one.

Looking Through the Eyes of Jesus

Look through the eyes of Jesus
See what he sees in you.
Then you will know why he paid the price
Of showing his love for you.

Feel through the heart of Jesus
The love that cares so deep
Then you'll know why He loves us so
To pay a price so steep.

Speak through the words of Jesus
The words he wants you to say
Then you'll hear his voice in power
In everything you say.

Connect through the spirit of Jesus
With your soul, your heart and your mind
Then you'll see your blessings are many
In the new way of life that you find.

Donald B. Perlinger
North Huntingdon, PA

[Hometown] North Huntingdon, PA; [DOB] August 20, 1940; [Ed] high school; [Occ] retired paint contractor; [Hobbies] carving, drawing, riding my trike; [GA] walking with Jesus

My love for Jesus is where my poetry really took off! I can't take credit for any poem I write because Jesus inspires me in my heart and my mind. I just write what he gave me. Once, while writing out a check to pay a bill, I stopped and started to write a poem about a neighbor who was dying of cancer. I read it as my hand wrote it and never had to change a word or line. It's such a great feeling when you ask the Lord to use you, and He does. Thank You, Jesus!

The High Towering Mountains

High in the mountains across the hills
Come the lonesome sounds of the
Whip-or-wills

A cool gentle breeze fills the air
As a peaceful solitude fills the
Air everywhere

Streams flow down the hills as they
Continue to flow
Onward and onward into the wilderness
They go

The bold eagle spreads his wings and
Flies
As he soars up to touch the beautiful
Blue sky

Oh, so peaceful and such a delight
To see
The high towering mountains and all
Of their beauty.

Bobbi Jo Hager
Ozark, AL

[Hometown] Clarksburg, WV; [DOB] August 19, 1954; [Ed] over fifteen years; [Occ] disabled army veteran; [Hobbies] art, poetry, song-writing, painting; [GA] Who's Who in Poetry

As a child, I loved reading the literary works of Emily Dickinson and Edgar Allan Poe. I always wanted to be a published poet. I have been writing poetry since I have been eleven years old. I am married to Richard M. Hager and I have two children, Jeremy and Julia. I have two grandchildren, Ginger and Ewan, who are the loves of my life! I spent over twenty years and eight months in the US Army. I was an air traffic controller, and I traveled a lot. Writing poetry is one of my greatest achievements.

Emotions

Emotions run deep when you cannot weep,
Tears form but do not flow,
Just a release of them would be slow.
Sun is shining, beautiful weather,
Only thing missing, we're not together.
Almost two years since God took you home,
I still have the feeling of being alone.
I'm not alone, for the Lord is with me,
Holding my hand, guiding me through each day.
Yes, lonely, but there are things to do,
Sharing with others, not about me and you.
God gives each of us blessings every day.
We just don't always see them that way.
Trials, tribulations, joy and peace,
They are all His blessings for each.
He loves all His creations, big and small,
From grass so green and trees so tall.
Sunshine, rain, spring, summer, winter
and fall—God is the creator of all.

Shirley Flaharty
Odessa, MO

[Hometown] Odessa, MO; [DOB] April 22, 1934; [Ed] twelfth grade; [Occ] retired; [Hobbies] reading, writing, crafts; [GA] sixty-one years married to same man I loved and eight grown children I love

With all the poems I have written, they seem to be brought from within on emotions, which is why this poem started that way. Losing my husband in 2013 has been a struggle emotionally, but there are happy days, fulfilled days, and very active days. The Lord is with me, and my church family, along with friends, my children, and extended family, are very supportive and caring. I am very blessed.

Highland Spring

Witness a golden glow—dawn and rising sun
the blackbird sings a song of welcome to spring
welcome—oh how long I've waited for thee
o'er yon brae scotch pines wail in the wind
a lilting love song to his sweet bonnie lass
notes float on the breeze both near and far
ever o'er the brae into the swale and beyond
view white clover's return to the meadow
animals of the field graze on the fresh clover
with heather and broom in bloom—perfume sweet
clumps of bluebells in the field magically ring
scotch thistle seem scattered—stand on guard
flying bees buzz, are working collecting precious pollen
after a long gray winter days—sun finally appears
bringing hope—warms the cockles of the heart
the return of highland spring is a song of hope
a joy to celebrate—God's blessed sun
as I plead to the sun to lengthen its stay
as the setting sun roams o'er the heather
soon fades into night as we bid thee farewell
to dream eagerly for another golden dawn is
God's highland dawn in the sun

Stuart Gibbons
Salt Lake City, UT

[Hometown] Salt Lake City, UT; [DOB] March 24, 1943; [Ed] high school graduate; [Occ] retired, handicapped—lost my legs to diabetes and now it's taking my eyesight as well; [Hobbies] writing, listening to music and viewing paintings from which I get inspiration for my poems

I was born and raised in New Zealand. I wrote a lot back then, when it was considered we were a crazed people. So I was quiet about my hobby, poetry. It was not manly enough. Over the years I have burned much of my writing. The reason being, I just got tired of my efforts I judge as poor. My neighbor who is an English teacher says I'm in a class all my own when it comes to writing. She frequently uses my work in her classroom. As a father, I helped raise a family of seven boys, a great responsibility. I am widowed twelve years now. It's a lonely life without my Lujuana by my side. Although I am a proud grandpapa of nine little ones and one on the way.

John Walling

The lilies lay in the valley below.
That's where all the military go.
Today they laid John Walling down.
Six feet under, in the deep ground.
Military was John's calling.
A family tradition for the Walling.
He fought the battle so long.
He made the list so strong.
Today they laid down John Walling.
Six feet below, military following.

Kathy R. Hughes
Sudan, TX

[Hometown] Sudan, TX; [DOB] November 20, 1958; [Ed] BS in elementary education; [Occ] retired; [Hobbies] crafts, sewing, gardening; [GA] fulfilling my desire for a college degree

I have always had a strong respect for the military. I admire and appreciate all the work they do for this country. If it wasn't for them, our safety would be jeopardized.

Four Seasons

1
Nature springs to life
Hatchlings rejoice in the nest
Sweet spring is singing

2
Lengthy sun-burnt days
Hot and sultry in the shade
Summer advances

3
Glowing leaves falling
Pumpkin piles await carving
Autumn shares bounty

4
Stout trees stark and still
Dozing through the icy chill
Winter grips landscape

5
Dour winter gloom gone
New shoots bask in smiling sun
Nature springs to life

Mary A. Gervin
Albany, GA

[Hometown] Columbus, GA; [Ed] MA in English; [Occ] retired university professor; [Hobbies] writing, reading, singing, working crosswords; [GA] seeing my students place in writing competitions

I am a native of Columbus, Georgia but settled in Albany after college graduation. I recently retired after over thirty years as a college professor and writing consultant. Mother of two adult children and grandmother to three grand girls, I spend my spare time writing, reading, and singing. The poem was inspired by daily morning walks around my neighborhood.

Autumn's Colors

Let me paint you a picture
Of God's work in the fall,
See the leaves turning colors,
See the joy of it all.

There's yellow, gold, and red,
There's orange and rust,
The green has left the trees,
Leaf peaking a must.

As I drive to and fro,
There's painting ahead,
Each tree is showing its color,
By the beauty, I'm led.

Children discovering their leaves,
Spread all over the grass,
Amazed by their bounty
Counting, by each lad and lass,

Now you've seen the picture
I'm taking in my mind,
Discovering nature's best
With each leaf I find.

Patricia Stevens
Standish, ME

I am a retired special education teacher. I enjoy poetry, reading, and collecting antiques. I enjoy anything to do with ballet. That's my "cup of tea."

My Little Doxie

He doesn't mind
if you're homeless
or rich
He doesn't mind
if he eats food
off the floor
or in a dish
He is always there
for me
when I'm happy
or sad
He will never
hurt me
or tell me lies
For I can see
the love in his eyes
He will love me
with his dying
breath
and be my
best friend
until the end
He is truly
my faithful friend
my love, my dog
Weenie

Corena M. Elmer
Elk River, MN

[Hometown] Sauk Rapids, MN; [DOB] April 15, 1961; [Ed] some college; [Occ] CNA, first responder, published writer; [Hobbies] reading, exercise, taking care of the sick; [GA] awards at work for my great passion of taking care of the elderly

I have always loved dogs; they have their own personalities and they have unconditional love. Friends may fight, marriages end, but, with a dog, his love never ends. My parents, Richard and Janet Abfalter, of Sauk Rapids, MN, have always taught me to respect animals and to always respect the elderly. Mom and Dad were good parents; I learned much from them. As you get older, you understand them more. So I would love to dedicate this poem to my mom and dad and also to Debbie Guerin, my sister in Christ.

God's Rainbow

Showers have ended,
the sun is peeking through,
a lovely rainbow arcs across the sky,
where will it end, I wish I knew.

Spring air is sweet and pure,
there is a calm so peaceful, it lightens one's heart,
a feeling of happiness gives radiance to the soul
and never allows our joy to depart.

Where does it start,
this heavenly hue,
could it be gentle pixies playing a game
or butterfly dust mixing with morning dew?

Some say Leprechauns know the secret,
but if there is a Pot O' Gold,
I'm sure they will never tell,
else the threat of leaving their fold.

Thank you God for this phenomenon,
Your heavenly touch is supreme,
as is Your follow-up sunbeam
and the calm it always will bring.

Mary Ann Messinger
Boise, ID

[Hometown] Boise, ID; [DOB] April 8, 1934; [Ed] high school; [Occ] retired housewife; [Hobbies] reading, writing, poetry; [GA] wife, mother, friend and office manager

After high school graduation, I enlisted in the USAF, basic training, then assigned to Mitchel AFB, Long Island, NY as a communications specialist, where I met and married my husband, Bill. This month we celebrate our sixtieth wedding anniversary. We have three children, four grandsons, four great-grandchildren, and one more on the way. We lived in Utah twenty-one years, eventually came to Idaho, started our mechanical contracting business, and have lived here thirty-eight years. I have always loved poetry. Many adventures in my eighty-one years contribute to my poetry, a wonderful journey this has been!

My Mother's Love

There is nothing more
priceless than my mother's
love.
She is there when I need her,
and sometimes when I
don't.
She is firm, yet gentle when
she speaks.
And when I become
angry with her, she
simply turns, smiles
at me and says—
I love you!

Carol L. White
Niles, IL

[Hometown] Niles, IL; [DOB] December 26, 1950; [Ed] two-year college degree; [Occ] retired; [Hobbies] writing poetry; [GA] enlisted in the Navy 1974–1977

Raspberry Jam

Many years ago
At about this time of year
I would go to my grandma's house
Grinning from ear to ear.
She had this raspberry bush you see
She would have me pick them
one, two, three.
I would bring them into the house,
She would make them into jam,
I would spread that jam on my toast
And say, "I love you, Gram."

Emma Taylor Walston
Roy, WA

[Hometown] Tacoma, WA; [DOB] May 4, 1995; [Hobbies] *writing poetry, photography;* [GA] *having my poems published*

I wrote this poem in honor of my great-grandma who recently passed away in June. She has been one of my biggest supporters in my writing journey. She has always encouraged me to follow my heart and dreams. I never got the chance to meet my dad's mom, as she died before I was born. Luckily, I had my great-grandma. She has helped me grow into the young woman that I am. She lived to be eighty-six, but she never showed her age.

Love

dedicated to my husband, James W. Marquette Jr.

A longing from the heart,
Love is a journey,
A search for the one you are meant to be with,
Finding many hardships in your way.
Love is an adventure,
A story ready to be written.
So many things are difficult to get through
While on your search for the one.
When you find them you will want to be with them forever
Like sakura flowers longing for the warmth of the sun.
I remember the way we were before you asked me out.
You would say a dirty joke and I would smile and giggle
Along with calling you a punk.
When we got together,
You promised to protect me and always make me happy.
I feel safe with you,
Like a young tiger cub together with its family.
We have been through so much together,
That I know that without you I would be a defenseless
Little girl trapped in the pits of darkness.
Trapped forever.

Sandra L. Marquette
Watertown, NY

[Hometown] Watertown, NY; [DOB] November 21; [Ed] Jefferson Community College; [Occ] student, writer; [Hobbies] arts and crafts, writing, video games; [GA] Poetry Nation member

I am a mother of a wonderful ten-month-old little boy. I have been married to my husband for just over a year. My inspiration for this poem was my relationship with my husband while we were first dating.

Frits Fate

Molly went online to date for a mate
But an alien got her bait as a date
From yonder gate, he pondered his fate
And debated whether to come to her gate
So back and forth he gaited, whether to be baited
That as her coffee-mate, this would be his fate
Yet she favored waiting only on his plate
So much that he, on his electronic slate
Asked would she abate to become his mate?
Oh yes, there would be no wait, to become his mate
Because as soul mates, they would have no hate
So they would mate at their final date
The wait was over, so he crated his freight
But going over, there was too much weight
And his offspring were almost too late
To see her seal his fate as she closed the gate
Now they wait on each other's plate
Serving such flavor there is no debate
Now her slating has no more baiting,
So she states to her mate, my life is your fate
But isn't life together now so great!

Frits Bax
Attica, MI

My wife Jan and I live in Attica, MI. For my marriage proposal, I wanted to do something different, so I proposed to her online in a poem. The poem and proposal were both successes. It inspired me to create more poems. Now writing poems is a challenge I enjoy. Here is a list of my poems: "A Proclamation of Love on the Net" (My marriage proposal), "Me and My Jan," "My Molly," and my most recent poem, "Frits Is My Name" (on page 68 of From a Window: Sights Unseen, *published by Eber & Wein 2011).*

Judging

Come my children and sit by me,
let me tell you a tale of being.
Judge not me by my lines and wrinkles
for each line is more than a crinkle.
They tell a story of life and dreams,
some came true and others scream.
Scream inside my spirit deep
and in fact may make you weep.

Alas, young ones life does not cheat
and this fate you cannot beat.
So never judge by a cover
look inside and you will discover,
nothing inside will ever change
even if a mind is deranged.
The spirit of life will always thrive
and through this our dreams will survive.

Dolores Kutzer
Erie, PA

[Hometown] Outer Banks, NC; [DOB] July 12, 1948; [Ed] BS, MS, PharmD; [Occ] professor of pharmacology; [Hobbies] working with stained glass, painting; [GA] being named Teacher of the Year four times

I have been a pharmacist most of my life, but English literature and writing are my true love. This passion has allowed me to incorporate feelings and compassion into my teaching. Most of my poetry reflects experiences that have occurred in my life. It seems that after I put these experiences into words, I have a better understanding of life and many times a burden has been lifted. I feel that writing poetry allows one to dig deep into their soul.

Saint Patrick

(AD circa 385–461)

Saint Patrick lived an exemplary life.
We've reaped the benefit of his extraordinary plight.
Born in Great Britain, father a deacon, grandfather a priest.
Kidnapped by pirates, at age 16,
Sold as a slave—his job: tending the sheep.
He spent hours each day, praying to God.
God spoke to him: "Escape to the coast."
And to the coast, he swiftly went,
And begged the ship's captain to take him aboard.
They took him on, to England's shore.
Patrick hiked 200 miles to his family's land.
Next, he attended the monastery at Auxerre, France.
After completing studies to become a priest,
He chose pagan Ireland, as a Missionary,
Using a shamrock to explain our concept of the Trinity,
God gave him the grace to perform miracles,
And the power to raise the dead.
For thirty years he baptized the Irish,
Converting them to one Faith.
His pledge was fulfilled, changing Ireland forever.
He died in Saul, Downpatrick, Ireland, March 17, 461,
Where he had built his first church,
And they declared him a Saint.

Catherine Dower
Holyoke, MA

[Hometown] Holyoke, MA; [DOB] May 19, 1924; [Ed] BA in music composition, MA in musicology, PhD in musicology; [Occ] professor emerita; [Hobbies] writing, swimming; [GA] Phi Betta Kappa or getting married at seventy

Catherine Dower, PhD. Phi Betta Kappa, is Professor Emerita of music at Westfield State University where she founded the music department and taught thirty-five years. She is the author of Puerto Rican Music Following the Spanish American War; Actividades Musicales en Puerto Rico, Fifty Years of Marching Together, 1952–2001, *biographies of harpsichordist Yella Pessl, musicologist Dr. Alfred Einstein, Sistine Chapel Codices in the Clementine Library of the Catholic University of America and is currently writing* Justine Bayard Ward: Renowned Music Educator—Patron of the Arts and Leader in the Restoration of Gregorian Chant *for the Catholic University of America Press.*

A Tribute to Our Mother: In Loving Memory of Florien Walden 1920–1997

A seat in our home is vacant, a voice we loved is still
Our mother is gone to be with the Lord to do the Master's will
Many hearts were saddened, many tears were shed
She is just away, she is not dead
She was a special angel, gentle, loving, and kind
The morning of December twenty-seventh she left us all behind
Days and months seemed to disappear
We're approaching the anniversary of the seventeenth year
A million times we will need you
A million more times we will cry
Sleep on, Mother, take your rest
God has proven to us He only takes the best

Doris Walden
The Rock, GA

[Hometown] Thomaston, GA; [DOB] October 17, 1952; [Ed] high school graduate; [Occ] retired textile worker; [Hobbies] writing poetry and photography; [GA] winning a poetry contest

I have always written poetry in my spare time. This poem was dedicated to the memory of our mother whom we loved dearly. She encouraged us to always do our best whatever we attempted to do. My family consists of three brothers, many nieces, nephews, and cousins, and countless friends.

The Hawk

The hawk is circling in the sky.
He owns the air above our land.
A hunter yes, a killer too,
A majestic shadow on the sand.

The yard hens they have no fear,
But give the devil his due.
They ease to low-hanging branches
And allow the drama to play through.

Much too heavy for him
To carry off the ground,
He looks instead for the smaller doves.
Their fear of him is oh so sound.

They gather in larger groups.
He can take only one at a time.
When the victim is found
There is no escape of any kind.

The others leave
Each in a different direction.
He is gone for now and so are they,
But he will return for another selection.

So the battle of life and death
Carries on each day.
There are those who will live,
And those who will go away.

Leanora Salmon
West Palm Beach, FL

[Hometown] Ft. Lauderdale, FL; [DOB] July 13, 1941; [Ed] high school, ballroom dancing; [Occ] housewife; [Hobbies] raising and showing rare poultry; [GA] a waltz with Fred Astaire

As a dance instructor, I met my husband. He came in for lessons. We fell in love, had two sons and moved to the country. It was here that I began my rare poultry hobby. The poem was inspired by a real hawk who is very much at home around here. I was president of our local poultry club for twenty-three years and I have been Chairman of the Poultry Tent at the South Florida Fair for the last twenty years. All in all, I feel that I have had a great life.

The Gloaming

The day long
dress
of an October
azure
blue
ebbs slowly
down
exhibiting
a cadmium orange
after image
evening fades
as expected
to become
a luna white
adornment
for the lamp black
diamond
bedecked
finery of night

Russ F. Housman
Arlington, VT

[Hometown] Sunderland, VT; [DOB] January 13, 1928; [Ed] DIP of fine art, MA and BS in art, doctorate, New York University; [Occ] semi-retired college teacher/administrator; [Hobbies] collecting antique Christmas ornaments; [GA] assisting children and adults with handicapping conditions

I have been a contributing visual artist with New York City galleries shows and representation for years. I, due to an accident, will not be back in my studio until next spring to continue the excitement of creativity. I have turned to poetry attempting to do with words that which I express with paint. I hope that I can offer another and conceptual view of what may even be commonplace to others, a creative, conceptual view utilizing similar but different receptual senses.

When Time Stands Still

When time stands still and someday it will,
I hope it stops wherever anyone wanted a thrill.
I bet there's a place in everyone's heart they'd stop,
A happy place that's just top notch,
A place where the warmth of your being rises way high.
With the brilliance of a peek of heaven that's in the sky,
When time stands still, and you look and people are all smiles.
That would be great if we could see eye to eye.
Through time, into all our own trials,
The marching of time wears us all down.
To escape into illusion may be the only life found.
We all have dreams, millions of dreams.
We are all like snowflakes, each of us dream a scene.
Never the same, never identical.
That thought says we're all on the same team.
What frequency do you think we'd all hear and see?
Man oh man, what an idea time that can stop!
What would we choose? Through the mist of moistured fog,
How far would we walk for that perfect pause?
Lifetime ticks on and on and on.
One day the sand in the hourglass pours out and beyond and gone!
Which life would we pick?
Maybe the future is the place we'd stick.
This idea is wonderful, don't you think?

Eleanor Pearl Atzert
West Palm Beach, FL

[Hometown] Belmont, MA; [Ed] high school, child management degree; [Occ] mother and grandmother; [Hobbies] poetry, arts, taking pictures; [GA] my love for people and animals

All my poems come out of nowhere. I get a feeling and the words come to me without me thinking or trying to rhyme—like when you turn on a faucet for water. You just jump up and write. That's when you know you've had help from somewhere else.

My Dream

I sometimes wish I was a butterfly
Fluttering and flitting across the sky
Sampling pretty flowers in their bed
Or the climbing honeysuckle overhead.

I know I should be thankful for who I am.
I just like to dream, when I have pen in hand,
God's greatest gifts begin to unfold.
And I can write things never before told.

But my wildest dream is to be a mourning dove
Softly singing a song for my one true love,
Perched high above in a grand oak tree
Hoping and praying Ron can hear me.

Just like the mourning dove mates for life
I swore by his death bed, I would stay his wife.
Now he patiently waits at the pearly gate
For the day I rejoin him as his mate.

Mary Hamner
Luray, MO

[Hometown] Luray, MO; [DOB] March 10, 1940; [Ed] high school diploma; [Occ] janitor for businesses; [Hobbies] bowling, crochet, sewing; [GA] female bowler of the year

When my husband passed, I started working for the public. I enjoy people from all walks of life. Most of my poems are inspired by memories of Ron. In bowling this year, I received the Northeast Missouri USBC Female Bowler of the Year award—Dist. 6, 2013–2014 season. I try to inspire people to express thoughts of beauty. My grandson Layne, fifth grade, and great-granddaughter, Hannah won awards in poetry at school recently. I am so blessed.

Decisions

Black and white—not grey again.
No decision from me means no vote.
I am dying and yet scared to death of the decision
I must make to live.
I stand bored in a safe, grey, womb-like world
living for others on the periphery of my life.
What if this and *what if* that my mind incessantly
ticks off the fears.
Who stole my courage, my dreams, and my beliefs?
I will surely lose myself if I let time and others
make another decision for me.
Decisions....................decisions.

Karen Clark
Alta Loma, CA

[Hometown] Rancho Cucamonga, CA; [DOB] November 12, 1944; [Ed] Sec. Credential and MA in fiber; [Occ] contract watercolor teacher; [Hobbies] mind games, dancing, karate, gardening; [GA] constantly overcoming my fear of lecturing in front of large audiences

My poetry is simply a diary. I write about experiences, observations, impressions, and intuitions as I walk through life. Most are about universal human experiences, some more personal. Writing allows me the opportunity to share with others and to clarify my own thoughts. "Decisions" is about a time in my life when I chose an easy path that was not "right" for me, but made everyone else happy. Decisions are not always black and white.

My Quiet Life

My lifestyle will bring no fame
But I do really like my quiet life
Go ahead, watch your ball game,
While I stay home with my wife.

Being retired from my old job burden
Now provides me the best of times
Let me fiddle in my backyard garden,
Even if the nasty bugs ruin my vines.

My quiet life you may call quite boring
But this is truly my simple heart choice
And you can go and get lost soaring
On a jet plane to the moon to rejoice.

I do not care what you do any day,
Go to Alaska hunting for wild deer.
I rather stay home drinking a beer,
Doing something trivial my way.

Hanging around home with my wife
I'm happy, has happy can be,
No dumb worldly desires for me.
Believe it or not, I love my quiet life.

Mariano A. Rivera
Maitland, FL

[Hometown] Maitland, FL; [DOB] December 8, 1940; [Ed] master's degree at Nova University for business; [Occ] retired computer manager; [Hobbies] poetry, prose, music; [GA] a happy marriage

I'm a Puerto Rican born in the city of Ponce in the year 1940. In 1963, I came to the University of Ohio to study chemistry. At college, I met my wife. We have been together for over forty-eight years. After a long career in computer technology, I'm now retired and living in Maitland, FL. My interest in literature, from early childhood to my college days, has always gravitated toward poetry, prose, and music. The poem reflects on my current retired life with my wife.

A Winter Evening

It's late Saturday evening, it's air time
Turning the dial, radio crackling a little
The dial button is the size of a dime
Through the air wave, sound of a fiddle

Settling down front row box seat
The old rocking chair, rocking to the music
Aged floor boards are creaking to the beat
Drumming the old Westinghouse with a stick

A parade of stars walking on stage
Theatre of the mind I could see
Or is it a book turning another page
This is where I truly want to be

Welcome to the Grand Old Opry
My drumming stick punches the air
Have my favorite star appear, I plead
As I keep pleading and punching the air

Sadly, the evening is ending
My parents calling time for bed
The battery is old and wearing
To the old Westinghouse, goodnight I said

Adding more wood to the box stove
Hoping it will last till morning
I hear a rumble from above
I know it, it's only Pappa snoring

Florence Richmond
Wauconda, IL

Roller-Skating

Roller-skating is fun.
I love roller-skating. In
the '70s and '80s I would
go to roller-skating rinks
and go skating in the rinks,
and I would skate to the
music. Now there are hardly
any more roller-skating rinks.
They have only a few rinks
left. Roller-skating is mostly
now a dying sport.

Eka Asante
Cypress, CA

[Hometown] Los Angeles, CA; [DOB] August 17, 1970; [Ed] some college; [Occ] actress, artist, poetry, writer; [Hobbies] arts and crafts, roller-skating, acting, swimming; [GA] when I got my high school diploma

I was born in Los Angeles, CA on August 17, 1970, raised in Buffalo, NY, and then we moved back to California. I am an actress, artist and poetry writer and my poem is inspired by my love of roller-skating and how I used to roller-skate when I was younger.

Joy's Son

Time suddenly exploded in my head,
Accelerating, like a tachyon,
at unimagined speed from start to finish!
There soon resulted, in my bursting brain,
A vision of time's end—it moved me fully,
It stirred each cell found in my protoplasm!
I saw myself there; Moses, Jesus, Buddha,
Along with trillions of other strange faces,
All living organisms that once flourished!
I knew, and grasped, each thought, each word, each movement
From the beginning, from the Big Bang's instant,
On all the worlds that ever had existed,
All their progressive metaphysics dramas!
I saw how all wills danced with satisfaction,
God's sons and daughters in grand throes of laughter
At being resurrected—their gifts stated
By that most stirring end-complexity;
Accepted fully, not like when they breathed!
Their viewpoints needed to form that strange newness
Called the next Cosmos; all force-mass then stirred,
And was reborn, through eon-brewed perspectives,
In something so profound it overwhelmed
A simple soul like mine—the vision faded—
But I've been changed; Joy's son, now, for I know
I am a note in that God-Symphony
We call the universe at this young time!

Tim Kruszynski
Riverdale, IL

[Hometown] Riverdale, IL; [DOB] September 21, 1949; [Ed] BS in psychology; [Occ] security guard; [Hobbies] writing poetry; [GA] having my poems published

I am the son of a steelworker and a housewife/caterer. In the Chicago area, that meant anyone in authority felt they had the right to exploit and brutalize me psychologically. Sadly, working-class people in Chicago are used to getting money and political needs met for the rich and powerful! My poem, "Joy's Son," is a message of hope for those abused by society in such a manner. Each person's mini-fate drama has a cosmic purpose, needed to complete all the possibilities of force-mass so God might fashion an eternal that is indestructible.

Thought

Thought would be an enigma
were it not for a familiar
individual persona and mind
and heart and power.
In our experience as children
some things were beautiful
some were not.
Thought made us who we are today
choices, even in play
influences of a myriad type
parents or parent or no
if we survived, even the onslaught of the mind
and lived to tell the tale
who would believe that God said no to suicide?
He would not be happy
and His plan was not finished
to tell any and all His Son
paid the terrible price to bring all to Him
forever in love and joy and peace.
So, I said, well, since I'm still here,
a miracle of life, send me and now you know why.

Elliott L. McQuay
Colorado Springs, CO

*[Hometown] Colorado Springs, CO; [DOB] June 8, 1949; [Ed] AS degree in broadcasting, computers;
[Occ] retired; [Hobbies] computer, writing; [GA] God knows me*

*As a dreamer, reality succumbs to my footprints. It was told I was seen seven years before I arrived. This
writing on thought addresses its design and creator, we his offspring, their experience with self-will, and
then, mine. In his disheveled uniform and many medals against the background of the universe, the creator
convinced me he'd lead me. He led me to Jesus, the Savior of the world.*

My Words with Jesus!

My prayer time is my words with Jesus, and it is a
privilege. Jesus, I need to thank you for that privilege of
prayer time with you. I know I can tell you my prayers and
not be afraid.

Jesus, I am sorry that I so often find excuses not to
say my prayers, and yet I want, and want more from you without
ever saying thank you.

Jesus, I know that you hear, but we so often forget that
it is your heart that hears our every word with love. The
Apostle Paul was right when he said we have ears, but do not
listen. We have eyes, but do not see. I think we are more
blind and deaf to the lies, than in seeing the truth.

Make a list of all the thanks and take them to Jesus.
Jesus, thank you for all the treasures of the earth you
have allowed us to borrow. Thank you for the heart that hears
our every prayer with love. Thank you for the yeses, but even
more the nos. Thank you for the cures of our hurts. Thank you
for my beautiful children, grandchildren, and great-grandchildren.

Did you ever think about your words with Jesus, and how
important they are to him? Well think about this the next
time you are having a word with Jesus, tell him that you love
him.

Next time you go before Jesus to have a little word with
him, know that his heart will be focused upon you with love.

I would be honored to wash his feet, and to hold on to
his hands. Often when I think about his feet and holding
on to his hands, I feel that smile of his lifting me to his
shoulders of Grace, and Salvation of his love and carrying
me.

Jesus wants us there!

Carol A. Miller
Washingtonville, NY

[Hometown] Washingtonville, NY; [DOB] September 18, 1942; [Occ] retired; [Hobbies] sewing and writing

*I like taking my poems and turning them in to counted cross stitch. This year I entered several, and this year
at the Orange County Fair, NY, I won four first, three second and one specialty ribbon. A Christmas gift won
first and specialty, and uncontrolled boat second. A Christmas gift got many praises.*

Finally October

The rain fell hard today
I stared at the sky
Letting the big drops hit me in the face
It was refreshing as the water washed my worries away
Finally! A change in season from summer to fall
The rain quickly dampened the last of summer's heat
Easing a blistering pain, to nothing at all

I looked back into the timber
Each branch glistened with a radiant spectrum of color
Smiling as soft rays of a setting sun waved me home
I could see
It too was glad to see October come

Cody Van Epps
Myrtle Creek, OR

[Hometown] Myrtle Creek, OR; [Occ] hook tender, Graf Logging Company; [Hobbies] hunting, fishing, alternative medicine

RIP, Daddy

My angel from Heaven,
With love in our eyes,
We will meet again when the time is right,
You taught me so much.
From the first day to the last.
I will miss you dearly,
But remember our times
Spent on Earth
Up to the day I watched you fade.
You held on till the end.
I knew you didn't want to go.
God called upon you
So you took His hand.

We let you know
That we always loved you,
So I'm sitting at this table,
Staring blankly at the world
And can't believe you're gone.
You are my daddy,
The one and only.
But I will never let this world replace you.
In the heap of trouble,
You're there guarding me and the rest.
I hope you are happy there, for I must go.

RIP, Daddy.

Stephanie C. VanHorn
Grandview, IN

[Hometown] Grandview, IN; [DOB] October 21, 1998; [Ed] South Spencer High School; [Hobbies] fishing, drawing, writing

I am still a student in high school. I've always enjoyed writing poems. This poem was made a week after I lost my dad, so it inspired me to write it. We were very close, and I think he would have been proud today.

The Season of Fall

You can see it coming;
The sun slips behind the plum colored dusk raising
the curtain for the harvest moon to glow.
Golden leaves falling from the trees like pirates gold
from their treasure chests.

You can smell it coming;
the earthy smells of dying leaves
on stocks of corn standing tall in the fields,
drained of their color. The scent of ripened fruit
falling from the trees and vines.

You can hear it coming;
Cicadas begin to silence
their summer songs, crickets no longer serenade us
as they did in the warm summer nights.

Yes, you can see it coming
as we watch the pencil colored buses
winding through the streets, silencing the summer sound
of children at play.
Shorter days, crisper nights, making a path for
Snowbirds to fly.

Joann Perez
Denton, TX

[Hometown] Minneapolis, MN; [DOB] February 17, 1940; [Ed] high school; [Occ] housewife, grandmother; [Hobbies] gardening, writing poems, reading; [GA] raising showing Basset Hounds and having one of the top female Bassets in the United States

I live in Texas and the summer months are so harsh that I welcome Fall with open arms. I love the colors and coolness and being able to work in my garden. This poem is only a hint of how I feel and what I see.

God's Gifts

God's gifts are many, not just a few
He brings us rain and sunshine
Ocean breezes and morning dew
We enjoy the season of rebirth
After winter has rested the earth
He gives us majestic mountains and foothills grand
Rivers, lakes and tiny Rills
He's blessed us with fall's colors bright
The moon and stars to light the night
He gives us His love unceasingly
As we do His will each day
We thank him many times in prayer
As our burdens He helps us bear
Looking on the beauty of sunset or sunrise
We see God's power before our eyes
Singing His praises our voice we raise
We have His love to light our way
As we show Him honor each and every day
Being grateful for His justice and wisdom grand
We are guided by Holy Spirit each day
As we truly try to follow His
Thus to be rewarded on Judgment Day

Lillian Merrill
Battle Creek, MI

[Hometown] Gaffney, SC; [DOB] July 24, 1934; [Ed] high school graduate; [Occ] food service and preparation; [Hobbies] writing, reading, studying the Bible; [GA] struck by lightning and still here

I had a general education. I worked in the food industry for forty-four years and six months. I started writing poems in 1994. I'm a Jehovah's Witness. I was struck by lightning at age four, married in 1955, and was widowed in 1998. I am a simple country girl. I feel God gave me the ability to write poems.

One Sweet Valentine

Do you ever have a day that's not quite right?
You want to cover your eyes and pray for night?
Go to sleep hoping tomorrow will be better
Then the mailman stops by and leaves a letter
It's a valentine, what a wonderful surprise
The words written inside bring a tear to my eyes
It's a sweet little card that says *I love you*
It brightens my day and turns the sky to blue

It's amazing, the power of a little valentine
It can change a whole day, leave the sadness behind
You can hear yourself humming a happy song
Your step will be a bit lighter as you skip along
It doesn't have to be fancy or even ornate
But those three words, *I love you*, makes it great
When it's from someone you've loved always
You'll wear a smile that could last for days

I've tucked it away in a very special place
Among my treasures that bring a smile to my face
These are things to read and enjoy when I'm older
Sitting in front of the fire when the weather's colder
So thank you, my son, you simply made my day
I love my valentine, there's nothing more to say
Except moms love these little surprises every year
It fills old hearts with happiness knowing you care

Shirley A. Miller
Mountain Home, AR

Our son lives halfway across the country from us, and we don't get to see him very often. When his sweet little valentine came, it turned a cold, dreary day into a bright, happy one. This little poem was my way of saying thank you and telling him that my love for him was returned ten times over. A little card can make such a big difference in a person's life.

Lost Memory

I wonder what's going on in your head?
You'll be changed soon all the doctors have said.
The memory will go and what's left behind,
Things of your past life will stay in your mind.
The present is the first time to go.
You can't read the clock and what it does show.
Words to explain are difficult to come.
You're no longer sharp and now appear dumb.

New fears appear and really concern you.
You can't solve problems or know what to do.
The lights are left on and drawers are not shut.
You try to do things as once you could, but —
Everything's hard and your mind doesn't work.
Movements are slow and you walk with a jerk.
Occasionally after a long nap,
Delusions confuse you leaving a gap.

Driving a car is definitely a no!
It's erratic, dangerous, going so slow.
Your life worsens as the days go by,
While leaving your loved ones wondering why.
Why did this affliction happen to you?
The man that you were is no longer true.
Yes, my love for you will always be there.
Still, I wonder, "Your memory is where?"

Sandra Kisler
Othello, WA

[Hometown] Othello, WA; [DOB] July 6, 1938; [Ed] BS in elementary education; [Occ] retired teacher; [Hobbies] reading, writing poetry, crocheting; [GA] mother to three successful children

Three years ago my husband was diagnosed with Dementia. It has gotten progressively worse. "Lost Memory" is about some of the difficulties in his life. We no longer do many of the things we enjoyed during our fifty-three years of marriage. We no longer travel to Maui or to our condo in California, two places where I have many happy memories. Writing poetry, not only about good times, but sad times too, gives me understanding and some peace of mind.

Waiting for Santa

Once again Christmas is almost here.
It doesn't seem possible it's been a year
Since last we heard Santa Claus call,
"Dash away, dash away, dash away all."

It looks like the rooftops will be snowy white
When Santa arrives Christmas Eve night.
I hope this year to hear each reindeer's hoof
When they land Santa's sleigh on my roof.

In the past when they came I'd be asleep.
And, I'm sorry to say, I heard not a peep.
But this time I vow, by all that's in me,
To stay up all night and watch the chimney.

So I sat myself down in my easy chair
And waited for Santa to enter there.
It was early so I closed my eyes a minute
Thinking there would be no harm in it.

Opening them again I was surprised to see
Gayly wrapped packages under the tree.
I looked at my watch, I'd dozed for hours.
I felt as foolish as Basil of Faulty Towers.

My strategy didn't work, I must confess.
I'll just have to wait till next year, I guess.
I'll have to make a new plan to catch him live.
Oh, did I mention, this year made eighty-five.

Leslie L. Newton Jr.
Cape Elizabeth, ME

[Hometown] Hartford, CT, but living in Cape Elizabeth, ME since 1966; [DOB] August 19. 1929; [Ed] general education including two years of college; [Occ] safety engineer; [Hobbies] golf, writing poetry; [GA] marrying my wife

I've been writing poetry for a great many years and have been published in many books including three of my own for family and friends. A great many of my works have appeared in publications of Eber & Wein Publishing and the International Library of Poetry. I have found writing poetry helps keep one's mind stimulated and provides much satisfaction.

Autumn

The colors so resplendent
Meticulous in detail.
Wonderment abounds
Like a fairy tale.

Enjoy it while it lasts
Colors so profound
Gaiety of spirit
Leaving us spellbound.

Colors on the hillsides
A quilt like no other
Artistry of nature
A shelter, a cover.

Wendy W. De Guise
Oronoco, MN

[Hometown] Oronoco, MN; [DOB] April 15, 1946; [Ed] two years of college; [Occ] LPN, daycare, paraprofessional; [Hobbies] knitting, reading, singing; [GA] my four children

I have always enjoyed poetry. I started writing poetry as a teenager. I was inspired by my dad. I didn't write as much when my children were small, but when I did, it was mostly for family and friends at Christmas. Now that I am retired, I have more time to write. Autumn is my favorite time of year and always takes my breath away with the lovely colors. So I wrote this poem about it.

You Are Invited into God's Family

Feeling out of place?
Different emotions, feelings,
You are invited into God's family!
Feeling out of place?
Different physical appearance or health condition
You are invited into God's family!
Feeling out of place?
Different clothes or customs,
You are invited into God's family!
Feeling out of place?
Different ideas, hopes, dreams,
You are invited into God's family!
Feeling out of place?
Different likes, dislikes, loves,
You are invited into God's family!
Feeling out of place?
Different strengths, weakness, abilities,
You are invited into God's family!
Feeling out of place?
Different place to live or lifestyle,
You are invited into God's family!
No matter what the differences are
When you turn to Jesus for forgiveness of sins,
You are forgiven,
And you always have a place in God's family!

Angela C. Michael
Mesa, AZ

[Hometown] Mesa, AZ; [DOB] August 6, 1979; [Ed] high school graduate; [Occ] childcare worker, housekeeper; [Hobbies] reading, writing, drawing; [GA] sharing God's love with others

I have a learning disability, still it does not mean I can't do anything. It just means I have to work harder and do the things. God has given me the gift for it accordingly to His plan for me. People are always telling me to be like everyone else or be like someone else. This inspired me to write a poem for anyone who feels out of place to always know they have a place in God's family.

Brothers All

Silly squirrel races to our front porch
And stares at me.
Chipmunks race to gather food
To hide away.
A bright sun glistens through the trees.

Brother crow circles
And has something to say.
Perhaps snow is on its way.

Lil' skunk slowly waddles
Along our path
Unafraid of tired Shih Tzu and me.
I guess all is okay
With our little world here.

Andrew Batcho
McAdoo, PA

[Hometown] McAdoo, PA; [DOB] November 13, 1945; [Ed] BA in English; [Occ] retired as of 2007; [Hobbies] writing poetry; [GA] serving in our US Navy

Born and raised in McAdoo, PA, I am a high school graduate of St. Francis, Andover, MA. I am a 1969 graduate of King's College, Wilkes-Barre, PA. I spent four years with the US Navy as a hospital corpsman. I had diverse employment as an elementary school teacher and principal, textile patternmaker, zinc casting worker, and forklift operator. I enjoy writing poetry, Native American Indian interests, being a religious education teacher, traveling, and caring for my Shih Tzu companion.

Except...When

I get along without you, very well, except when:
Morning comes, I awake you're my first thought.

I get along without you, very well, except when:
I hear a certain song; I think of you, my heart
flutters and I long to dance with you.

I get along without you, very well, except when:
A day goes by and I haven't heard your voice.

I get along without you, very well, except when:
I feel like loving you, and you're not around.

I get along without you, very well, except when:
A Sunday afternoon rolls around, and I long to
just sit outside, in your arms, read poetry
and be held and touched by you.

I get along without you, very well, except when:
Night falls and I want to lay with you, but you're
not here.

So I realize, I don't get along very well without
you after all.

Carol D. Brewer
Pomona, CA

[Hometown] Pomona, CA; [Occ] retired accountant; [Hobbies] urban ballroom dancing, and decorating; [GA] raising my daughter to be a good-hearted and loving person

I've always loved reading and writing poetry, especially poems of love and romance. I wrote my first poem in 1979.

The American Soldier

Listening to the news, as the president speaks
they'll be departing soon in maybe a week.
With the families all gathered, you hear the cries
as the men and women must say their goodbyes.

Their way of life becomes an American soldier
from the age of eighteen until much older.
They listen to the voice of Uncle Sam
a lot of their lives will soon be damned.

Over here we can't imagine what they feel,
some of the wounds that never heal.
Not only the ones from the battle
the feel of the rumble as the bombs rattle.

Sun beating down on the sand, how it burns
the countless men lost, make their stomachs churn.
Knowing them all, and calling them friends
waiting for the day that this will all end.

Going down the road, headed for home
when into view the faces of their family come.
Most with smiles, and some with frowns
the road they chose, tragedy comes down.

We must support them for all they do
when our flag flies with pride, we should too.
Proud of them for all they are
the American soldiers, who wear the scars.

Julie K. Thorpe
Rolla, MO

[Hometown] Rolla, MO; [DOB] September 19, 1965; [Ed] GED graduate; [Occ] sales associate; [Hobbies] spending time with my family; [GA] having my poems published

This poem was inspired by all branches of our military and their families. These men and women have the hardest job ever and make all sacrifices. They are the true heroes of the American people. I wrote this to show all my admiration and appreciation—that ordinary people do realize what they give up. I, for one, salute, applaud and thank each and every one of you for a job well done. I am proud to call you heroes.

Monogamy

The day has come for me to be with one
Giving up my freedom as a bachelor, along with the late nights of fun
Countless faces and myriad memories
No longer a gentleman thrown into the clubs, with one-night stand tendencies
It's funny how life portrays itself to be alone
We are all born to die, by ourselves in the same tone
A heart beat, which now skips to another person's melody
Love is for real? Is that what you're really tellin' me?
Why must I feel your pain?
Why do you hurt and throughout my body I feel the same?
Sometimes I wonder if there's truly another guy out there in this world like me
Who writes love poems and is not afraid to kneel on one knee
Honestly, I believe chivalry is dead
And some people envy the fact that I put my emotions out there to be read
I'm alive, well and full of passion
One life to live with uno heart to give, the ultimate transaction
Waking up to her by my side is the most incredible feeling
Ecstasy and euphoria, bursting through the roof of my membrane ceiling
Even in my roughest days I contrive to be the best man
Eventually I will be a husband and a father with the blueprint of a million dollar plan
I always dreamt of being an affluent human being
So I made a commitment to be betrothed with a kiss and a promise ring
I was so inquisitive about the theoretical principals of the pursuit of happiness
Until I prayed to God, who sent me an angel fulfilled with rapture and bliss
Monogamy, twined around a dreamer and a realist
Forever living a prosperous life, Mr. and Mrs. Perfectionist.

Artist Clay Jones
Fort Bragg, NC

[Hometown] Orlando, FL; [DOB] February 14, 1986; [Ed] BS in history; [Occ] student, military; [Hobbies] writing, running; [GA] deployment overseas in Afghanistan

My inspiration comes from my personal experiences. "Monogamy" was inspired by my fiancée at the time, Jewel. She was my future wife and the person that I wanted to spend the rest of my life with. All I can say is, "Love is an incredible feeling, and I wouldn't trade it for anything." I know that there is a true lady, future wife and mother of my kids out there in this universe for Artist Clay Jones! Besides love, my true passions in life are traveling, writing and running. I plan to experience every second and minute of life, everywhere in this world!

Evening Prayer

Thank You, Lord, for seeing me
    safely through the day
Thank You, Lord, for showing
    me the way
Please be with me all through
    the night
Lead me toward Your everlasting
    light

Carol Shurilla
Reading, PA

[Hometown] Reading, PA; [DOB] January 27, 1942; [Ed] high school diploma; [Occ] inspector at Ludens/Hershey Candy Company in Reading for forty-one years; [Hobbies] animals, especially cats, reading true stories, doing crafts, poetry; [GA] having my first poem published

My poem was inspired by my faith in God.

Honor

Honor the one who created
the world who created you to do what you do

Honor the one who created all
the world who created you and other people too

Honor your mother and father
for together through them you
were born created by the one
above from the one who created them too

Honor the person who taught you
in school to obey the rules
who created them to do what they do for you

Honor the one who is in authority
on your job so you will know
what to do and not be blue

Honor everyone and everyone will
honor you for what you do

Honor the one who created
you to be you so you can do what you do
God

Renita Love-White
Robbins, IL

[Hometown] Robbins, IL; [DOB] September 14, 1961; [Ed] associate's in liberal arts, travel and tourism, medical assistant, psychology, social work; [Occ] retired; [Hobbies] writing, poetry, plays and reading; [GA] to have a poem published with Eber & Wein for the first time and perform in a play with the theater group at church in September 2013 (the play was Crossroads, and I had a walk-on part, which was very exciting)

My name is Renita Love-White, and I reside in the Midwest. I am retired from my career in management in the healthcare field, which was very rewarding for me. I have currently four poems published with Eber & Wein, one of which is in a collection in their Who's Who 2013. I am very active with my church as a greeter, the outreach department and the theater group. I am very grateful for my association with Eber & Wein, because of their interest in me and my poetry. I have had the opportunity to have my poetry included in their poetry collection of published books they have completed over a period of time of four years. It is very gratifying to see my poems in print.

Nature

I watch the sunrise each morning shedding light on Earth,
A lone bird soaring overhead, a soft breeze blows.
A tiny clear stream flowing through a forest,
Butterflies clustering near beautiful flowers.

The ocean crashing on sandy shores,
Leaves changing from green to red, yellow or orange heather.
A light snow falling to cover land like a blanket,
Wild animals searching for food and shelter.

I watch nature change as we progress each day and night,
New roads leading to unknown, once serene areas in future.
The skyscrapers climbing to unthinkable heights,
All changing symbols of nature.

Faye Kendall
Williamston, NC

Teary-Eyed Dream

Raindrops falling on
Saddened face
Recalls the memory
Of a teary-eyed dream
Once forgotten
As the clouds go by.

But someday soon
We'll remember
The past of that
teary-eyed dream
Then as the sun
comes out
our faces smile
sweet and sincere
Until the teary-eyed
dreams will appear

Have you ever wondered
What it is like to die
It's just like a
fountain
They too will die
If you don't clean it
Then it will fade away

Just like our body
will not survive
If we do not protect it
From deadly things
Then we too will fade away.

Sherie P. Parks
Cedar City, UT

[Hometown] Cedar City, UT; [DOB] June 16, 1954; [Ed] preschool teacher for two years; [Occ] housewife; [Hobbies] crocheting, reading, poetry; [GA] being married to my husband

I wrote this poem years ago, but I decided I would send it in. I'm dedicating this poem to my sister, Marie Hayes. Her husband, Gary Hayes, was involved in a motorcycle accident in October of this year. He is doing well now.

Walk the Walk

Do you hear the words?
What do they mean to you?
To me they say—
Be strong, look up, keep going.

Be hopeful, be positive, be joyful.
As we walk the path of life we
Encounter all the twists and turns
On our way—
Joy, anger, sadness, disappointment.

How we cope is the answer to our walk
Do we give up? Become morose, withdrawn or
Do we stand up—forge ahead, take each day
And make it our own?
Do we have faith tomorrow will be better?

I believe tomorrow is always better!
"Hope springs eternal." Do your best
Go onward and upward—
That is walking the walk!

Josephine Ingalls
New Smyrna, FL

[Hometown] *New Smyrna Beach, FL and Waterville, NY; [DOB] March 10, 1932; [Ed] high school grad; [Occ] twenty years banking, fifteen years hospitality; [Hobbies] reading, sewing, gardening, writing, baking; [GA] I'm writing poetry and trying a short story*

This little poem comes from events of the past three years: the loss of two brothers, a beloved and precious mother, and my sweetheart of thirty-two years. I miss all of them. I try to honor them by walking the walk—that's life!

Listen Within

My teenage child, inexperienced, indeed not worldly wise—
If I were only perfect, it would be so easy to criticize—
Instead, I search for words, to touch your heart
Remember, one small wrong is but a place to start
Turn off the world sounds and listen to your soft voice within—
If you wonder, "Is this wrong?" and hesitate, it is, begin again.
For one positive step, turned toward right,
Could change your life and bring us both delight!

Virginia Embree Cole
Casper, WY

[Hometown] Casper, WY; [DOB] December 1929; [Ed] high school; [Occ] retired; [Hobbies] arrowhead and fossil hunting; [GA] I'm still working on it

I am a Wyoming adopted daughter. Originally, I was born at home, on a farm in Nebraska. My husband and I moved to wild, wonderful Wyoming sixty-six years ago and have remained here. It's our home. I am thankful for my husband and four delightful children. They have been a constant source of inspiration and material for my writings.

Suicide

Suicide's a selfish bitch.
It took a life so full and rich.
Bipolar claimed a victory,
Left those behind in misery.

The Tylenol and antifreeze
Finally brought you to your knees.
Warning signs were ignored
Never really struck a chord.

Questions you can never answer
Eat my soul just like a cancer.
My heart remains forever broke.
You did not even leave a note.

I hope that you can somehow see
The anger and pain you left in me.
My baby sister once so near
Has left me drowning in my tears.

Vickie Joyce Pauley
Patrick Springs, VA

[Hometown] Patrick Springs, VA; [DOB] September 6, 1955; [Ed] AAS in accounting; [Occ] retired payroll manager; [Hobbies] aerobics, cross stitch, cycling; [GA] thirty years of service to state of Virginia

After serving thirty years as a payroll supervisor for the state of Virginia, I have finally retired. I was diagnosed at the age of twenty-nine with bipolar mental illness. From a family of an alcoholic father and a bipolar mother, and five siblings, I live the curse of bipolar mental illness with my mother and three sisters. My first marriage of twenty-seven years ended in divorce after covering up my husband's alcoholism and keeping it all "together" for the children's sake finally became too much. I dedicate this poem to my baby sister who committed suicide a few months ago.

Florence

My daughter Florence passed away. This is what I hear her say:
Mom, don't cry for me. Don't you see? I am free! I am free.
Free as the breeze to do as I please. No one to hold me down.
No more troubles, no more strife—what a happy afterlife.
I fly around on the wings of a dove, sending you blessings, sending you love
From above: On the wings of a dove, I am in God's loving care—
It's beautiful there. I want you to know I am fine, I am happy, I am great!
I want you all to celebrate. I am watching from above…
And sending you my love…

Florence

Mary Rombout Andrus
Modesto, CA

[Hometown] Salida, CA; [DOB] August 18, 1939; [Ed] eighth grade; [Occ] cannery worker; [Hobbies] reading, making cookies; [GA] my poems

I was born in Modesto, CA, but was raised and went to school in Salida, CA. My poem was inspired by the kind and good deeds this young women did for everyone. She was a loving mother and grandmother, making cookies and baking cakes for the class. Florence was a very hard worker. I dedicate this poem to my wonderful daughter with all my love—the love of a mother.

Seasons Change

Fall is here, the leaves are down
The branches lone and bare
And as I stand in the silent yard
I feel at peace, no care

Then winter makes its coming call
Cold chill upon my face
Soft and silent snow does fall
Hiding nature's secrets, without a trace

Spring and summer beckon on
With hope and life reborn
And then time moves to fall again
When bright colors will adorn

It always seems amazing
That each season has its place
Each one makes me see
A world that has such grace

Donna Adams
Butler, PA

[Hometown] Butler, PA; [Ed] registered nurse; [Occ] retired; [Hobbies] painting, poetry; [GA] my children

Hearts Afire

Hearts afire
Loves desire
Reach your peak however high
Speak your truth, through the cry of blowing winds of change
Rearrange your space erase your doubt and fear
Hear the words inside your heart
Where the Holy Spirit lives, can you hear it?
Fly without boundaries
Live life to the fullest, free of chains
That bind you grind you, walk behind you
Remind me of how blessed I really am
Knowing Jesus is my friend

Rose M. Commisso-Lazzari
Roseville, MI

[Hometown] Roseville, MI; [DOB] March 1, 1956; [Ed] high school and some college; [Occ] mattress sales at Macy's; [Hobbies] writing, singing, gardening; [GA] living gluten free for seven years

First of all, I would like to thank God, my husband Gino, our family friends, and, finally, my nephew Lou Commisso, the pastor at the Life Church in Warren, MI. He is such an inspiration for this poem. Poetry for me is found through everyday life, moments and memories, both express feelings in the written word! I am happy knowing that I have touched someone's heart—that brings tears of joy and gives me inspiration to keep on writing.

Songs of Earth

Hear the trees sing praises to His name,
See the trees lifting their branches towards Heaven!

Hear the streams whisper of His goodness,
See them running towards His open arms!

Hear the birds sing Hallelujah,
See them join together with one accord!

Hear the thunder shout out His goodness,
See the lightning drown out the darkness!

Hear the rain chatter His name,
See the calm of His love flow down from Heaven above!

Hear the earth sing
See God's creation lift up the one true King!

Theresa L. Quarshie
Fort Smith, AR

[Hometown] Fort Smith, AR; [Occ] administrative; [Hobbies] photography, writing, outdoors

I have been writing since grade school. I'd write short stories and poems to help express what words could not express. I would write about my hopes and dreams and about my fears and failures. I write now to encourage and share the light in my life. God has given me grace and mercy when I have not deserved it. God has shown me that we are all gifts and masterpieces formed and created for a purpose! So now when I write, I share what He has shown me.

Open My Window

I wipe the fog from the window to see outside
trying to focus and keep my thoughts in line.
I see you but I can't hear you talking. What are you saying?
The thought keeps me watching, wanting and waiting.
Just open my window so I can hear!
Are you laughing at me or is that just something I fear?
Inside I scream please let me out!
I bang on the window and continue to shout.
I can't get your attention no matter how hard I try.
Can you see a reflection in the tears while I cry?
But nothing changes, in here I don't exist. I
don't understand, what did I miss?
Time can pass by in the blink of an eye
and my window is stuck but I continue to pry.
But my window won't budge, it's stuck, closed tight.
How long was I trying, how long can I fight?
In here the clock doesn't tick and the hand doesn't move.
Time has no meaning so what do I do?
Just sit here and wait for the feeling to end,
then open my window and be normal again.
So I ask myself how did I get behind the windowpane glass?
Who am I mad at, whom do I ask?
Please just open my window and climb in here with me.
I'll show you who trapped me...my epilepsy.

Tanya L. Salata
Millersburg, MI

[Hometown] Green River, WY; [DOB] September 26, 1976; [Ed] associates degree in medical administrations; [Occ] hunting; [Hobbies] homemaker; [GA] my children

Writing poetry has always been a way for me to express my feelings. Having suffered from epilepsy since 2012, I wrote this poem to show others what seizures feel like to me. It's never easy to live with a condition that changes your life, but, with the love and support of my friends and family, I'm staying strong. I hope to help others stay strong as well by inspiring them with my poetry. Remember you are never alone and stay strong.

Soldiers

Soldiers in the field, fighting night and day,
Longing for forgiveness, not knowing what to say.
Killing isn't easy, nor is living with the pain,
Knowing what you've done, a mind could go insane.
Watching as their friends get wounded in the field,
They protect each other, their body, as a shield.
Carrying the wounded, knowing some will die,
On a battlefield, you have no time to cry.
Freedom isn't easy, we really have no clue,
All they sacrifice, each day for me and you.
Judged by everyone, for doing as they're told,
Longing to go home to loved ones they can hold.
Don't be passing judgment on those who will endure,
Dying for their country, so *our* freedom is secure!
Say a prayer tonight, let them know they're not alone,
Pray each day until, they *all* are safely home.

Donna Goforth
Lincolnton, NC

[Hometown] Whitewood, VA; [DOB] February 10, 1965; [Ed] graduated with honors; [Occ] full-time mama; [Hobbies] movies, watching football, being outdoors, writing poems, spending time with family; [GA] being blessed by my two daughters

Most of my poetry comes from my life experiences or of things I've witnessed. I started writing with the birth of my first daughter, then continued since with my second, expressing emotions on paper that could say more of how I feel. My written collection of poems was created, through various stages of my life, covering sorrow, simplicity, comedy, darkness, and inspiration. I call it Simple Poems for an Unsimple Mind. If anything I write touches anyone in a good way, then I'll never quit. Just brightening an unsuspecting person's day makes it all worthwhile, one poem at a time.

The Flame

A spark ignites that he does not like
Tears swell in his little eyes
They sparkle in the dim light
Gathering him in my arms,
His lips begin to quiver.

The spark grows to a flame
Little fires shine out of his eyes
And travel through his tears.
I hold the screaming boy to my chest
Rocking back and forth.

The flame roars at us
I sink to the ground,
Hugging him tightly
Tears stream down our faces
Forming a small pool around us.

The roaring flame begins to flicker
His screams quiet as he gives me a small smile
I return the gesture as my heart flutters
His face is no longer red as I wipe away our tears
And he begins to giggle as the flame dissolves.

Leah Barr
Rochelle, IL

[Hometown] Rochelle, IL; [DOB] July 10, 1989; [Ed] Eureka College; [Occ] stay-at-home mom; [Hobbies] reading, gardening; [GA] my son

I have always loved to write stories about animals or characters that beat all odds. This poem was inspired by my son, who gets an idea into his head and sticks to it.

A Woman's Prayer

Oh God! who gave me
A woman's life,
A woman's heart,
A woman's tongue,
What wouldst Thou desire of me?
Oh God, who gave me
A woman's strength,
A woman's hope,
A woman's soul,
What wouldst Thou desire of me?
What is it that I promised Thee
I would do so long ago
When before Thy throne I knelt
With the love of Christ upon my brow?
Was it then that hope burned bright?
Was it then that I knew
I would bring the souls of men
Through another veil of eternity?
Was it then that I looked
Into Thy beloved face and said,
"Thy will be done"?
Oh God! Who gave me
A woman's life,
A woman's heart,
A woman's tongue,
What wouldst Thou desire of me?

Charlene Anderson Newell
Draper, UT

[Hometown] Price Carbon, UT; [DOB] July 31, 1938; [Ed] BA in music education with voice emphasis; [Occ] music teacher, choral and general music, private piano and composer; [Hobbies] published music composer, teaching, reading, singing; [GA] published ten-CD set of my original music, married fifty-four years, mother of twelve children, and forty-one grandchildren

I am an advocate of all the fine arts. I believe that the "true" history of mankind is revealed through the expressed feelings of the artistic soul. I was attending a music concert at the BYU many years ago when the words of this poem came into my mind. I had been pondering about the worth and value of being a woman. I came to the conclusion that every woman—and her compassionate, nurturing qualities—plays a very important role in the eternal plan of God, despite the constant redefining of the role of womanhood by the world. My husband and I have been married fifty-four years and have twelve children and forty-one grandchildren.

Mild Mischief

When the world seems flat,
and nothing is irreversible,
riddled by the mild mischief
of contradictions,
the moon is still significantly full,
casting deep purple shadows
that lines the jewelry boxes
in amethyst.
But treasures get lost on their own,
vanishing as easily as a dream.
Pushed to the edge of the world,
I step back quickly,
pretending not to fall or I may be
mistaken for someone else,
walking past bare trees,
a reminder of what was not to be,
knowing I must escape
to a world more circular
that appeals to the imaginations.
For if I were to see the same people
all the time,
life would be too ordinary.
Distortions draining my energies,
stretching out the longitudes,
crisscrossing the latitudes,
and I'm loving everything in-between.

Yvonne Gannon
Kaneohe, HI

[Hometown] Kaneohe, HI; [Hobbies] photography and painting

My hobbies, photography and painting, revolve around my writing ambitions that keep me focused on the world around me and are captured on canvas and film. In this poem, "Mild Mischief," you'll find yourself caught in a slight tilt of the earth, testing the nature of each individual. Is it the shape of the world, whether it be flat or round, that decides our fate? Though the unmistakable answer to the question, who am I, if I had to second guess, can readily be read in a smile.

Kylie's Prayer

Let me cast in my nets, Lord,
For just one more throw
Toward the bay's horizon
Once more before I go.

Another sunset at the bay
Over on the eastern shore,
Or at the place of my birth—
I'll not ask for more.

You created my sunsets,
I crafted from lovely wood;
If body and mind were able,
I'd continue to do so if I could.

I leave behind those I love
And those who have loved me.
My life is spent; it was good.
I'm ready now to be with Thee.

Catherine Smith
Bumpass, VA

[Hometown] Bumpass, VA; [DOB] July 7, 1953; [Ed] high school; [Occ] family administration, housewife; [Hobbies] nature, quilting, photography; [GA] living with miracles

I have always been a romantic with the deepest of my desires centered on God's amazing creations. Through Him I have experienced beauty of sky, earth, and sea. Though my ambitions of being closely involved in the saving of these creations have not been made possible, I still fight for it through my words. Someday perhaps, somehow, my many writings in prose and poetry will inspire others to see His creation's grandeur as well. My children and grandkids are to be the recipients of my words.

Secret Stars

Secret stars
fall to me
be the sparkle
in my eyes
be the light
in my heart
that guides
my way

Sweet sparkle
set my heart afloat
floating to the
heavens above
secret stars
fall to me
set my heart
afloat

Falling stars
floating to the
heavens
send my love
to the secret
stars in my
eyes

Edana Reilly
Chantilly, VA

[Hometown] *Scotts Valley, CA;* [DOB] *June 28, 1980;* [Ed] *high school;* [Occ] *stay-at-home mom;* [Hobbies] *reading and writing;* [GA] *my children*

I have been writing poetry for as long as I can remember. Whenever I have been in a difficult spot not knowing which way to turn, I could always turn to my writing. In November 2000, my brother Ryan died. From that point on, these walls were built around me and my words stopped flowing. In the past two years, especially after the birth of my third child, the walls seemed to crumble down. I could see clearly again. I could write. All my love to my babies, Kaya, Kai, and Katerina! Thank you for showing Mommy the light.

Farmer

As I look out across
the deck
at the field of dirt my
husband left
In four weeks' time green
corn will grow
an occasional deer pulls
a tassel or two
Rabbits eat the leaves
woodchucks will too
Soon the corn will be too
tall for much harm to be done
ears will form, we pray
for rain to put kernels
on those ears
Fall, winter then spring
start the cycle again
Years come and go
They all end the same
They all start with farmers
back in the game

Jackie Geldersma
Sidney, MI

[Hometown] *Sidney, MI;* [DOB] *July 18, 1946;* [Ed] *high school graduate;* [Occ] *homemaker, farmer;* [Hobbies] *gardening, crafts, fishing;* [GA] *my seven kids*

Sidney is a small town—most everyone knows us. I've been married to my farmer husband for nearly fifty years. I love country life. Wouldn't consider living in a town. There are so many things to see here, I'll never run out of things to write about. I'm a great-grandma fourteen times, and I love it.

The Vows

The vows that we spoke are the vows that we broke
We stood before God where you took my hand
then came the exchange of a gold band

I wore a white gown
beads of pearl on my veil
hair pulled back tucked in a crown

You looked so handsome
in your black designer tuxedo
Looking back we were both incognito

You kissed your new bride not expecting a bumpy ride
I grabbed your hand as we rushed down the aisle
Our family and friends await single file

Then came the party, got introduced, had our first dance
and cut and fed each other cake. You looked deeply
into my eyes I never thought you'd tell me lies

It was after the honeymoon things went awry
You were such a cool tough guy
I really didn't mean to make you cry

Looking back at the past it all happened so fast
The fairy tale dream gone in a flash

L. Forthun
Levittown, NY

[Hometown] Levittown, NY; [DOB] June 6; [Ed] executive secretarial diploma; [Occ] medical receptionist, secretary; [Hobbies] acting, concerts, photography; [GA] pursuing acting

I consider myself to be independent, and I am a private person. I had to learn to take care of myself at a very early age; for that I am grateful. Although I'm comfortable being on my own, I looked forward to falling in love, marrying and sharing my life. As you can tell by my poem, it was an attempt that failed. However, that hasn't made me bitter or stopped me from enjoying life or believing in love. Alone does not equal lonely. There are many paths to take—some are meant to be traveled alone.

A Soundless Rumble

The day lies heavy
As do the clouds
Not a smile to meet
Not a voice to greet
Not a sigh to hear
Not a sound to hush

Silent voids ride the wind
Heavy hearted I ache within
Haunted and foreboding
My soul trembles

Alone I stand, I watch, I feel
Waves rise strong and high
Hushed in anticipation
They tremble and rumble
Lightning flash; Clouds crack!
Heavy air squeezes my lungs
Nature's power rules all moments

Susan Ann Horton
Oswego, NY

[Hometown] Oswego, NY; [DOB] January 13, 1958; [Occ] lead job coach; [Hobbies] gardening, cooking, writing, singing; [GA] raising seven children—all productive and employed

The poem is based on a visit with my daughter on Seneca Lake. The sky was brilliant blue and the lake shore, quiet and peaceful. Not fifteen minutes passed and the colors of the sky deepened. Within minutes clouds were billowing! Crack! Lightning! A fantastic light show! Waves riding the wind, crashing on rocks and shore—an afternoon to never forget.

Our Children

Our children of today are
our world of tomorrow.
That is why we must
make sure our children are
shown a lot of love and
respect.

Our children are our
responsibility. We must all try to
be the best parents, because
only we can make things
better for everyone.

Our children are such a
blessing. I thank God for my
children. They have given me
so much strength and love and
a big reason for wanting to be
a good person.

I want to help others feel
like I do.
I will do all I can for
children all over the world.
Our children are our future.

Nora Linde
Lompoc, CA

My name is Nora Linde. I was born in Santa Maria, CA and raised in Lompoc, CA. I am seventy-six years old and am a hairdresser. I've been in the business for forty-three years. I love my work. I have three sons whom I am very proud of. I have three grandchildren and four great-grandchildren. I love them all dearly. I love to write poetry. I hope to keep on writing poetry for a long time. I want to inspire love in everyone!

Sweet Dreams

From the fading mist and shadow
the morning stakes its claim.
Though thy presence from me be stolen
the beauty of thy image remains.
In eastern sky night's vail is torn
radiant beams kiss the day.
Moon's glow from my eyes is hidden
yet the warmth of thy embrace is stayed.
Perched in nature's pulpit
winged musicians play their song.
But for thy melodious laughter
my snared heart does long.
Though I stroll in garden's path
surrounded by the lover's rose.
Joy and solace have abandoned me
till I lay under consolation's sweet repose.
At last the sun is beckoned down
in twilight's serenade through crickets' violin.
With a smile my weary soul drifts away
for in my dreams I shall hold thee again.

Larry Hill Jr.
Shiloh, OH

Christmas Wish

My special Christmas gift to you
A wish to be granted this
night for you. A Christmas
ornament will hang on your
tree, or in a window for friends
to see.
Christmas is a special time,
where family and friends all
combine. Through the years we
have been together, when something
happens and our loved ones are
gone forever. We hold on to our
memories as all we have, we ask
our God to hold our hand.
As we look to the heavens this
snowy eve night, when a star
appears so very bright. A message is
sent from the heavens above,
Merry Christmas to you, my one and
only love.

Patricia Sicurelli-Carapezza
Seaford, NY

[Hometown] Seaford, NY; [DOB] July 17, 1937; [Ed] high school; [Occ] retired banker; [Hobbies] *photography, cooking, puzzles, writing, Scrabble; [GA] raising my two beautiful children*

My name is Patti. I live here on Long Island, born and raised here. I have two beautiful children from my first marriage and two smart grandsons. I remarried a wonderful guy who has ten grandchildren and eight great- grandkids, which we enjoy. We have good times together and are happy when holidays come around. We live in a senior citizen complex, and we are all around the same age—so fortunate to be here. We have been married almost ten years and hope to have many more. It's never too late for a second love. Friends we have lost inspired my poem.

Finding Our Voices

I said the words
I cried the tears
I wanted it to stop
He would not hear us

Mo screamed with pain
Mo cried for hours
Mo was born into this
He would not hear us

Tom said he had tummy aches
Tom said he had headaches
Tom was born into this
He would not hear us

He had no words
He had no tears
Had so much anger
He would not hear us

We said the words
We reached out for help
We wanted him to stop
They could not hear us

We tried our best
I trust God's call
Finding our voices
One day everyone will hear us

Cora Monce
Pleasant Hill, CA

A Winter Afternoon's Walk

As I tramped around the woods on the hill gathering Christmas greens,
I stopped and looked around.
A familiar sight to me, but new each time I saw it.
Looking down over peaked roofs of slate, I watched evening approach.
Grey and salmon colors streaked the sullen December sky,
Covering the dreary landscape of this New England town.
Grey cold stones protruding from the dirty snow
In the cemetery on the hill
Stared down at the town below as if to say,
How lonely we are here in such an empty place.
No Memorial Day flowers to brighten the earth today.
An evening star starts to glow.
The faint moon shimmers dimly in the sky.
Lights appear here and there in windows.
Car headlights reflect in the wet streets below.
When every streak of pink leaves the sky another day will be over.
As I shiver with cold, I can see my breath in the air.
A cheerful warm house awaits me.
A cozy kitchen.
A warm and loving family.
Hugs and kisses from my children.
A soft yellow cat to rub my ankles.
Oh it will be so good to get home.

Mary Hallock Cooper
Leominster, MA

[Hometown] Leominster, MA; [DOB] July 15, 1936; [Ed] Leominster High School graduate, Winthrop Community Hospital School of Nursing graduate; [Occ] nurse; [Hobbies] painting, writing, cooking, reading; [GA] bringing joy to others with my poetry

Having no formal writing education, I didn't write until thirty years ago. Having a long drive to work, these thoughts and ideas struck me like lightning coming from nowhere. I carried a pencil and paper at all times so I wouldn't forget what came to mind. Once I wrote on the bathroom mirror in lipstick. Sitting at my grandma's knee in the kitchen, by the oil stove, I was exposed to learning poetry. I write and paint looking for tranquility. I was a nurse for fifty years. I experience great joy when my words bring meaning to others.

The Ring

It was noticed by the wife
that her husband had lost his wedding ring.
So much grief this will bring.
On his finger is a shadow
of what used to be
now no one can see
that they were ever wed.
For the wife was greatly misled.
She's a wondering what has gone on with this man
because the ring was missing from his hand.
She has lost all her trust.
Right or wrong he has to do something,
this is a must.
Things can't be the same
'cause he changed the game.
Hopefully the ring hasn't been sold.
Their love now is on hold.
He made a solemn pledge
that a miracle will shorten the wedge.
When the ring is found,
two hearts once more will be bound.

Wilma Lee Shifflett
Mt. Crawford, VA

[Hometown] Mt. Solon, VA; [DOB] January 24, 1952; [Ed] high school grad; [Occ] cashier; [Hobbies] art, poems, long drives, gardening; [GA] having my poems published

I have enjoyed poetry since sixth grade in school. I have been reading and writing since then. In my spare time, I spend it with family and friends. Love to mail cards and keep in touch with them that way. I live in the country and still work part time. My ideals come from events in my life, or from taking drives around to places. My poem was inspired by an event in my life. I'm happy to share my poems with others. I live the simple life, love the outdoors and seeing the changing of the seasons.

To Lettie

When I bought you and Rosie in 1909
I felt lucky to have found you.
There are pets, lots of pets, but
You two are the best yet.
I remember when I threw a ball,
You ran, and didn't let it fall.
When I sat down to rest or read,
You jumped in my lap and took the lead.
In August I took a trip, but—
I realized too late that the food was
Too hard for you to chew and eat.
So my dear kitty you had to retreat
To "kitty heaven."
"Rosie and I will miss you"
With love,
Maria and Rosie

Maria E. Herbert
Lead, SD

[Hometown] Lead, SD; [Ed] attended college in Grand Rapids, MI; [Occ] retired teacher; [Hobbies] reading, being with friends, caring for my three cats; [GA] gift of writing poetry

My mom died when I was two, so I never knew her. My dad asked his mother to come help him care for us. There were four of us. My eldest sister was Aurora, my next sister was Claudina. Then there was my brother Pat, and I was the youngest. My grandmother was a perfect mother to us. I bet she is up in Heaven looking and praying for us. Now there are only Sr. Aurora (she is a nun) and I living—all the rest have died. On August 4, I went to Michigan. On that day, my sister, Sr. Aurora, celebrated seventy-five years of being a nun. I am so proud of her. May she have more years, and God bless her.

The Mirror

I look in the mirror.
What should I see?
An image with presence of God and a likening of thee
Showing a love so intense and free—
A soul soaring and flying higher trying to get closer to be nearer to thee,
A reaching hand extended all around to help in times of need,
A spirit of hope and for a future you have planned for me,
A calmness that overtakes me just as Jesus reached out to the sea,
A willingness to forgive others as you forgave me,
An open embrace to accept the Holy Spirit that works in my life to give me victory,
A peace and understanding that one day I will look and see you looking back at me.
My friends, I invite you to come!
Look into the mirror with me.

Bobbie J. Howard
Brooklet, GA

[Hometown] Brooklet, GA; [Ed] BS in business administration; [Occ] retired fashion and shoe store manager; [Hobbies] reading, sewing, flower arrangements; [GA] accepting Jesus as Lord and Savior

As I closed my eyes, I saw the Bible with pages flipping back and forth. Bible verses came rushing toward me. I opened my eyes and wrote the poem. With tears running down my face, I was overcome with the presence of the Lord. At that moment I felt and knew in my heart the greatest achievement in my life was accepting Jesus as my Savior. Two days later I received word my niece, Angela Diane Jenkins Smith, had died suddenly at age forty-four. This poem is dedicated in memory of Angie whose greatest desire was to help others. Angie is sadly missed and will forever be in our hearts.

The Escape

Running down the seemingly endless stairs,
She doesn't stop to think why,
All she knows is nobody cares.
Her reason for starting doesn't equal the reason she continues.
So why stop now?
She'll continue like others have too.
Why should she stay and be mocked,
Why should she stay and suffer?
So she flees from this world that is closed off and locked.
She runs until she see the end.
She reaches for the door,
A dearly loved friend.
She opens the door slowly to conceal
The excitement she now feels,
And she enters into a place of hers, her fantasy, her unreal.

Alana M. Cavanaugh
Panama City Beach, FL

I Had to Try

My love left me today, I never asked her to stay.
She couldn't understand why, what I had to try
Meant saying goodbye.

I guess I'll let her go, it seems to me she should know.
Just because I'm not there, doesn't mean I don't care
Love is something to share.

It's going to take me a while, to forget my old lifestyle.
But I'm happy to say that I've found a way
To better each day.

Living alone is alright, it's just that sometimes at night,
When you're lying in bed, many thoughts fill your head,
Many things that you've said.

When the time is right, I'll bring her home that night.
There's so much to be done before I can have fun
With the love that I've won.

Taylor Ford
Foxboro, MA

[Hometown] Foxborough, MA; [DOB] August 24, 1946; [Ed] BS in archaeology; [Occ] retired;
[Hobbies] music, photography, martial arts

Change

The air crisp on a sunny picture perfect day

Autumn was in the air
Leaves in full bloom
Yellow Red.

The cool air coming off the polluted water
brown down by the bay

A little breeze in the air can't you picture it
as you dream in your bed?

Suddenly reality hits you in the face,

Dreaming now of spring instead
because everything comes to life.

Sadly winter is around the corner
and everything must die.

Soon you will be gone without a trace.

Roaming around by yourself
single no I'm not no one's wife.

The seasons must change now
the question is *why*

Kimberly Listro
Middletown, CT

[Hometown] Meriden, CT; [DOB] June 4, 1972; [Ed] some college; [Hobbies] singing

What inspired me to write this poem, forgive the pun, is that you have to stop and smell the roses. Look around you and let the poem paint in your mind your own picture. Everyone needs someone. Won't you take my hand and explore the beautiful world? If I touch at least one person, that makes me smile. Thank you for reading and publishing this.

All My Little Girls

All my little girls
    move their pretty heads
    as they embrace the sun
Infants poke their heads up
    precociously
    all reaching for the blue sky
All my little girls   some
    heart shaped like valentines
    some tall and willowy
Are precious to me
    growing slowly   refreshed
    with cool water
They delight me   because
    I love them   all my
    Lovely little girls
So quiet   reposing in rows
    some cascading down
    leaves touching gently
They exude strength and beauty
    I impart comfort and care
    they enrich my life and I theirs

Eleanor Shannon Lee Blakeny
New York, NY

This "bevy of little girls" in my living room—these fresh green plants—I have cared for for many years. They are comprised of Sansevieria or Snake Plant, Dracaena or Corn Plant, and Epi— aureum or Pothos—also called Devil's Ivy. I am very much like my mother, who loved all plants. She enjoyed living in Arizona, where I was born, as the desert was her favorite habitat. Had she lived, she would have loved my poetry and paintings. She was the best of mothers.

On This Valentine's Day I Remember

How beautiful the smile of your ruby red lips
when we kiss how my heart flips,

The sparkle of your hazel eyes
say with that gleam, I'm your guy,

The shine of your beautiful auburn hair
when it blows, bounces, and waves in the air,

The smell of your perfume
when it fills the air and our love blooms,

The snuggle of your soft embrace
when you hold me makes my heart race,

The seductiveness of your charms
when you fall into my arms,

Sharon, you make my heart flutter as your love sings
because you are the wind beneath my wings.

Bobby E. Hopper
Linden, AL

[Hometown] Jemison, AL; [DOB] December 13, 1952; [Ed] BA, University of Montevallo; Mdiv, New Orleans Baptist Theological Seminary; Dmin, Beeson School of Divinity, Samson University; [Occ] director of missions; [Hobbies] woodwork, restoration of old cars, trucks and furniture; [GA] first family member to finish high school and earn doctorate

Thank You, Rooster Teeth

Some people say they are pointless,
Just idiots with cameras.
But they are so much more.
Thanks to them I met my best friend.
They make me smile
When I'm sad.
They make me laugh
When I'm about to cry.
They taught me anything is possible,
To follow my dreams,
To fight for what is right,
To use my imagination.
They showed me a world
I didn't know could exist.
For that, I truly am grateful.
Thank you,
Rooster Teeth.

Audiana Mosbrucker
Blackfoot, ID

*[Hometown] Blackfoot, ID; [DOB] July 31, 1997; [Ed] Blackfoot High School, class of 2015; [Hobbies]
video games*

*I am a Rooster Teeth fan until the end. My love for the brilliant men and women of Rooster Teeth have
inspired me so much in my everyday life that I want to show them exactly how much they mean to me.*

Ground Zero

As they came tumbling down
People screamed and people fell.
Smoke and dust mingled with the deaths of many.
Heroes died trying to save the others
Trapped high above.
They lived to die searching,
Crashing twisted steel hiding their deaths.
They were buried in the rubble at Ground Zero.

William Koji
Canterbury, CT

[Hometown] Canterbury, CT; [DOB] August 18, 1927; [Ed] Citrus College, Woodbury College, Los Angeles, CA; [Occ] retired engineer; [Hobbies] painting, watercolor; [GA] living this long

Regarding "Ground Zero": I have never seen, in all my eighty-seven years, killings as vast as those of the World Trade Center. Our enemies complain of our methods of killing. Shut-up!

Looking Back Over the Years Gone By

Now that I have reached the age of ninety-four,
Looking back on those years
Gone like the wind
Leaves like years
All gone like the wind of an eye
My baby years—my childhood years
My school-day years—my marriage years
My motherhood years,
Yet, something never changes—
Winter snow, and snowman scenes,
Sunset, sunrise, and stars so bright,
Or a dark, dark night.
The tree that makes shade in summer,
The trees that bear fruit for all mankind,
The oceans—the fish—the whales.
The rich sod that grows our food
"Oh, How Great Thou Art"
I love to wake up with the morning light
and see God's birds in flight.
I love everything God makes,
and I do smell the roses in June
with their one and only perfume.

My God! How Great Thou Art!

Mary R. Leason
Federal Way, WA

Where Bonnie View Road and Mash Hill Meet

Where Bonnie View Road and Mash Hill meet,
    a landmark can be seen.
The large white boulder placed with care in
    reverent memory.

Old Benny was a presence on the hill each morn,
    was keeper of this land.
Parked his truck out in the field to feed wild turkeys
    from his hand.

A bond between this man and beast was forged,
    over time became well known.
Flocks would gather round his truck, where tufts of grass
    did blow.
Strutted displays, tail feather plumage, danced at break of dawn

Till one day in passing, his truck would be seen no more;
    what barren field and solitary measure, sacred store.
Bring peace as Benny's spirit soars.

Ellen-Ann Christian
Charlton, MA

[Hometown] Charlton, MA; [DOB] August 21; [Ed] nutrition food services; [Occ] nutrition center coordinator; [Hobbies] gardening, sewing, painting, photography; [GA] happily married fifty-four years with five sons

I have worked as a nutrition supervisor many years in my local area for the elderly, providing meals, services, education and socialization in congregate settings; also for Meals on Wheels. The rewards have been many helping elders, working with volunteers on a personal level. Over the years, I've been inspired to write, paint landscapes and other works, purely for the joy of it, and to record what it was. My poem is about a local farmer's history; many small farms are disappearing from rural New England.

The Fields

Horses rear against wild expanses
As rough-hewn herds frolic free among the heartland
These are vistas, visions of perfection
purity and calm, beauty epitomized in simplicity

Leaves pining for the gentle breeze
as a calming sway lifts even the heaviest bird to soar
The sun alighting tall grass as it grows
Like a wild fire, burning with amber incandescence
        A field of blistering beauty
        And a sea of serenity

The wind whispers with its gentle caress
Smiling amid the tall stalks
wishing to ride the waves of good tidings
Amid the amber incandescence
        Like a faithful steed
        Always heeding his master's call

Wooded aromas entice entry
into this world of solitary bliss
Glimpsed freely and longingly
Until it too disappears into the sunset, to rise again.

Eric Bonholtzer
Pasadena, CA

[Hometown] Arcadia, CA; [DOB] April 24, 1981; [Ed] BA from USC, MA from California State Polytechnic University, Pomona; JD from Southwestern Law School; [Occ] writer, trial attorney; [Hobbies] reading, traveling, kickboxing, jiu-jitsu, weightlifting; [GA] becoming a published writer

Writing is one of the greatest creative outlets. To be able to create something from a blank page, a wide-open canvas waiting only for your imagination and your creation, is nothing short of magical.

A Heavenly Party

They're having a party in Heaven
And I'm so ready to go
To be with my friends and loved ones
That I used to know!
We'll walk through the pearly gates
As we enter into Heaven
And Jesus will be there holding
The awards we'll be given
The saints will be singing
The great songs of old
As we dance around on the
Beautiful streets of gold!
Oh what a party
That will be
Singing and dancing
The saints and me!
We'll be standing in line
Waiting to shake Jesus's hand
It will be much more than
We see on this land
I'm waiting here on Earth for
God to call me home
And on this land I'll
Nevermore roam.

Deloris Janik
Greenfield, IN

[Hometown] Greenfield, IN; [DOB] March 27, 1935; [Ed] two years of high school; [Occ] retired after thirty-two years of packing Hostess donuts; [Hobbies] puzzles and word search; [GA] raising two wonderful children

I have written more than thirty songs and poems. My first poem I actually wrote for a song in 1963 called "What a Wonderful World"—my problem, I can't write music. I can sing them, but I can't write them. Even now at seventy-nine, I get a thought in my head and I put it in writing!

My Precious Brother

Since you left to be with the Lord, it's been several long years,
You are so missed, our hearts still ache, and we can't hide the tears.

I remember our daily conversations with your wisdom and wit.
How I long for the days when you had your health and were so fit.

You are with the Lord now, in peace, and in a far better place,
Now there's no sadness or pain, you are in God's infinite grace.

We will never forget you, you'll always be in our hearts,
Our memories will have to suffice for now, until the day we will never part.

Marshelle Carberry
Fresno, CA

[Hometown] Fresno, CA; [DOB] September 21, 1944; [Ed] college degree; [Occ] housewife; [Hobbies] decorating, piano, writing poetry; [GA] International Poetry Hall of Fame 1999

I am a housewife, mother, and grandmother with a desire to help others through my writing of poetry. It all started with writing my own greeting cards for the people I love. Then I evolved into poems of life experiences, songs and honoring persons I truly love and care about. This poem was inspired by the loss of my only, dear brother in a tragic way. I hope it will encourage others who have had a significant loss of a loved one. I was elected into the International Poetry Hall of Fame in 1999.

Daybreak

The daybreak so astounding
And the rain a shimmering sight
Exquisiteness resounding
My awareness does incite
I feel the world's divinity
A sensation so like grace
The commonplace affinity
Perceptions I embrace

But I bear the deprivation
And true sentiment I do seek
So here's my declaration
Though all may think it weak
Removed from you I languish
And my pain within profound
All beauty I felt it vanish
When our lives became unbound

Chris Lundwall
Staten Island, NY

[Hometown] Staten Island, NY; [DOB] June 28, 1967; [Ed] some college; [Occ] IT manager; [Hobbies] gym, yoga, computer gaming, motorcycles; [GA] my son

This poem is about my childhood friend, Linda Margherita, with whom I was reunited in 2013. I find her equally beautiful on the inside as well as the outside.

End of War

We hate and want to
Kill each other,
In our hearts, we don't love
Our brothers,
Let's not seek to destroy
One another.
Wars and violence stalk
The world; no peace is found,
Destruction of life abounds; blood
Soaks the ground,
We must learn to live together
Or mankind will no longer be
Around!

Robert A. Calhoun
Philadelphia, PA

[Hometown] Philadelphia, PA; [DOB] March 5, 1949; [Ed] high school, community college; [Occ] retired; [Hobbies] reading, music, concerts, art exhibits, fishing, swimming; [GA] being a published poet

I love to express my deepest feelings through the medium of poetry. My imagination allows me to see the world as it really is and gives me a firm grasp of reality. By writing I can come to terms with my own inner feelings; put to rest inner turmoil and restlessness. My poem about the futility of war; man's inclination to hate people different from himself, makes it clear that universal peace is only possible when we learn to live together!

Things of the Heart

There are many things that I would say
But somehow the time always slips away.
And the things then are lost and put back on the shelf
And my words are said only to me and myself.

There are many things that I would do
If only I had the time that's true.
Things that would bring a peace to my soul
And make it a quiet place, youthful and whole.

There are many things that I would try
But somehow the time always passes me by.
It never stays long enough to fulfill
All the yearnings of the heart that won't let me be still.

There are many things that mean a great deal to me
Things that I would share only with thee.
And tell you in words that are soft and so wise
That would bring a small tear to your soulful eyes.

But the thing that remains most dear to my heart
Is knowing you love me
Even though we are far apart.

Margaret Hauber
Grandview, MO

[Hometown] Grandview, MO; [DOB] November 16, 1946; [Ed] BA and MA in vocal performance; [Occ] family historian; [Hobbies] photography, needle arts; [GA] a book of poetry published in 2010.

I have always loved to read and sing, but got the poetry bug about twenty years ago. I found I could express myself better writing verse. I love to play with words, rewrite songs, take parts of old poems and turn them around to make new ones. I enjoy learning about new forms of poetry and utilizing them to say what I want to say.

I Wish I Could Call You in Heaven

I wish I could call you in Heaven on the telephone
And say you are the most wonderful woman I have known
You made me feel like I was a king on a throne
Because of all the love for me you have shown

I wish I could send to you in Heaven an email
From the laptop I bought on sale
You were always a twelve on a one-to-ten scale
And you made me the world's luckiest male

I wish I could see you in Heaven on Skype today
To let you know how much I miss you since you went away
When I go to bed tonight, I am going to pray
That we will be together again someday

Chester Williams
Jewett City, CT

[Hometown] Jewett City, CT; [DOB] September 11, 1935; [Ed] tenth grade; [Occ] retired trailer driver; [Hobbies] sports and gambling; [GA] marrying the best woman

Silenced

Wish we could speak, just speak how we feel.
Fear resonates inside us, our fears, so real.
Branded by time, for time tends to steal.
In silence we reside, our feelings we conceal.
Our voice lies frozen, lost somewhere in the tundra.
A love remaining secret, cannot tell them "I love ya."
Beauty lies within our head, photographic camera.
Our silence pushes us away, forever to suffer.
See your faces when we close our eyes, imagining.
When we are near you, cannot stop from clenching.
Alone we dream about you, but fear, the damaging.
Silenced our throats; cannot see where we are landing.
A glamorous butterfly you are, your beautiful wings.
Alone, we strum our guitars, to you we secretly sing.
We know what we see, but we are still grieving.
Our silence halts all we do, cannot stop from fleeing.
Beauty resides in you, beauty more than skin deep.
Silent tears we shed, love that can never be, we weep.
Inside you a glow resides, trueness, in you we see.
Envision a pure spirit; we sit beneath an old oak tree.
Will we find our words or live silenced forevermore.
Downtrodden, abused, crimson tears fall upon floor.
Living different lifestyles; drowning just offshore.
Inner pain, living death each day, lives in our core.
Scared to speak, scared to love, the silence we store.

Ron L. Vernon
Plattsmouth, NE

[Hometown] Plattsmouth, NE; [DOB] September 27, 1968; [Ed] high school graduate and some college; [Occ] writer; [Hobbies] walks, caring for wild animals, collecting movies; [GA] support person for self-harmers young and old

I spent a great many years hiding the facts about my life of abuse at the hands of many, until I finally found a way to speak, not just for myself in writing, but others as well. There lays a secretive society living within the darkness, and sometimes it leads to suicidal ideations and self-harm. Most people do not understand us and tend to shun us out, which makes us draw deeper into ourselves. You may not see the warning signs; it is my hope that society will research the reality of self-harm, learning the dos and don'ts.

Temple of Heaven and Wall of China

I walked on the land of China
To the place called Temple of Heaven
I walked on the houses of Kings and Queens of China
Forth I heard the cry of people
To seek justice and dignity of human beings
It's a place that brings many contradictions to the world
Either the society does not see the bright side of mankind
Or the society is being subject to communist action
But there is the need to release people
Forth they find the truth light from the Son of God
The man who loves mankind, Jesus Christ
In hope for the society to change the face of the earth
Then I walked on the path of Wall of China
Humble upon my life as it is the blood of many people
That impacts people's lives in many ways
The quiet society of China Wall
The wall of isolation from the world beyond the horizon

Vi Nguyen
Portland, OR

[Hometown] Portland, OR; [DOB] April 4, 1980; [Ed] BS in physics from Portland State University; [Occ] life insurance agent; [Hobbies] writing song lyrics, poems, journaling

I visited the Temple of Heaven and Wall of China on April 27, 2007.

On the Mountaintop

On the mountaintop
Where I feel the gift of freedom
That means so much to me,
I feel the gentle, cooling breeze,
Brushing against my face.
I hear the sound of a faraway elk
Calling to its mate.
I think of those who came before me
Who paid the price for freedom.
So I can sit on a mountaintop
And enjoy what's been paid for me!

Roger Jackson
Rocklin, CA

[Hometown] Rocklin, CA; [DOB] April 13, 1956; [Ed] sixth grade; [Occ] disabled construction laborer; [Hobbies] Native American art, jewelry, poetry; [GA] being a mentor to youth

"On the Mountaintop" reminds me of my mother's husband, Elton, who paid the ultimate price for freedom during the Battle of the Bulge in WWII. You cannot put into words how much they loved one another and their country! Mom tells me stories about him from time to time, and even yet, after these many years, sometimes at night I hear her call his name. I hope that this nation will never forget those brave and noble men and women and the ultimate price they paid—to let me be who I am with the freedom I have!

It's Him, My Soul

And God said, stay and hold My hand,
I've chosen the plot, I'm in command!
I'm "we" displayed, with song and prayer,
The soul, that's called for Jesus's care.

This mind of mine was His to tame,
It fought with time and oozed with stain.
His cost began to show in me,
As whole took hold and chose to free.

Attacks of want, lay hold of way,
And stayed the thoughts, of rudes display.
A whisper sought to prove to mind
That move of Christ would soul define.

I've named His own, my close Amen,
He chose my life to twist and bend.
I feel His strong renew in me,
Be still my heart! What love I see!

The best of faith takes hold of share,
To use the name of Lord with care.
Believe He's walked with you today
Else you'd had never found your way.

O, soul, how glad are you and me
That Jesus urged us two to see?
The joyous want of truth be fed,
In song rejoice, we're freed from dead!

Faye A. Deller
Wrightsville, PA

Death's Romance

From the cradle to the grave
We are always trying to save
Another day, another hour
Oh how precious is our stay.

Knowing we cannot change
What God has set in motion
His love is deeper than the oceans
But His word is still the same.

One more year, dear Father
That is our constant prayer.
Let me see tomorrow
I bow my head in sorrow.

Let me see my grandchildren,
I'll be extra good.
I made each one a blanket
Also a coat with a little hood.

I know the great hereafter
Is better with Your plan,
But I'd like to see tomorrow.
Remember I am just human.

Sally B. Ray
Palestine, TX

[Hometown] Palestine, TX; [DOB] October 1937; [Ed] high school and some college;
[Occ] retired; [Hobbies] writing; [GA] salvation

My vision is poor, but my heart is young.

Hair Daze

Why do I do it?
What is wrong with me?
Every day the same old thing—
My hair, my hair.
Why am I so obsessed?

Half an hour, forty-five minutes,
one hour, sometimes more.
It's got to be perfect or
I don't go out the door.

Hair spray, hair spray.
I buy it by the gallon.
Can't let the wind blow a single strand.
The stiffer the hair the better.

Why can't I be like others
and just be happy from the start?
Could a wig be the answer?
Would it be too hot?
Would it stop my ridiculous compulsion?

I know just what you're thinking.
"Why don't you shave it off?" you say.
But then choosing hats to replace it
would waste my time in the same old way.

Anita Tornow
West Milford, NJ

[Hometown] West Milford, NJ; [DOB] March 16, 1943; [Ed] BS in elementary education; [Occ] bank teller; [Hobbies] bowling, Mah Jong, poetry; [GA] having seven poems published

Ever since I was a young girl, I've had negative feelings about the way I look. I seem to feel that if my hair looks wonderful, it will make up for all my other flaws. I've become obsessed with it hoping it will achieve the impossible. No one seems to understand why I do this. I'm hoping my poem will reach out to others who may also share some obsession they hope will boost their self-esteem, and to let them know they're not alone.

Duty Call

When the men went off to war
Women did their many chores
One thing that I can mention
They worked on the railroad engines
Engines that were so very dirty, grimy
Wore their coveralls so timely
Wouldn't do it any other way
No one else to take their place
Some of them ran the cranes
Worked long hours and didn't complain
Others worked in the railroad towers
Keeping track of trains by the hours
One woman that I knew
Wanted to go there and work too
Something her husband didn't want her to do
He happened to look up at work one day
There she was sweeping dirt from box cars anyway
My uncle worked as engineer on Baltimore Ohio Line
He talked to a lady in the tower all the time
He had never met her or saw her face
At our family gathering they arrived at the same place
And he had a chance to match the voice to the face

Elizabeth Thompson
Blandburg, PA

[Hometown] Blandburg, PA; [Ed] no college; [Occ] housewife, proud mother; [Hobbies] collect Indians, SW material, butterflies, refinish furniture, enjoy walking ride trail wooded area, write poetry; [GA] raised handicapped son, he earned two college degrees with many honors and does so many things to help others

The reason I wrote this poem: My aunt was foreman for the PRR. When I was very young, she took me to work with her one day. That's how I know how hard they worked. I have a picture of them on engines and they earned every penny.

People Just Like Us

On the other side of the world
There is a sky not serene and calm like ours
But sonorous and loud
Confused by drones and bombs.

On the far side of the earth
There are people seeking happiness at home
But they live on rubbles of their house.
They take their child to a school
With no window or wall.
They celebrate the birthday of one child
On the grave of another one.

Never mind freedom of speech
No one can hear the suffering of human beings.
They are people just like us, with hopes and dreams
Desiring tranquility and peace
But traumatized by violence and fear
They live a tumultuous life
Human suffering is the price.
They need compassion not drones or bombs.

Mitra Pourmehr
San Rafael, CA

[Hometown] Tehran, Iran; [DOB] April 10, 1951; [Ed] BS in geology; [Occ] teacher; [Hobbies] swimming, reading, writing; [GA] raising two educated children

My bilingual elementary school was the first window to the cosmopolitan world. I received my diploma from an American high school and continued in the American College of Switzerland. I received a BS from Pahlavi University in geology. I married my soul mate in 1974 and have two children. My daughter has her MS from the University of Minnesota, and my son has his PhD from Stanford. I entered the USA in 1996. I have written many stories and poems, some of which are published. I write for my heart inspired from my life. I was in Iran during the revolution and war with Iraq.

Announcement

Life is like an ocean of spirit
With tides and currents
And waterspouts
That ebb and flow and explode
Upon a sandy shore.
We rode in upon such a wave,
My generation of "Boom,"
Just after the end of a heinous war.
We were determined to end all wars
Not only against nations
But also wars against people
Who were oppressed
Because of the colors of their skin
Or because of their gender
Or who they chose to love
Or what aspect of God they worshiped.
And then our tide went out.
It's back again, many-hued,
Marching down streets and into souls,
Rearranging the sands of time,
Beautiful to watch.

Diane Crawford
Selden, NY

[Hometown] *Orient Point, NY; [DOB] February 22, 1946; [Ed] high school; [Hobbies] reading, writing, cooking; [GA] having my books published*

I am recently retired and I love it! I have discovered aspects of myself that I never knew about now that I am living for myself. I am also rediscovering parts of myself that I had to ignore for all of the time I was busy in the world raising a family, working my nine-to-five job and so on. The fighter for freedom is one such part of me.

To See

Heavenly Father, for all the beauty that I see,
Please do not take my sight from me.

I see the blue of the sky above
Given to us by Your tender love.

I see Your flowers with a hundred colored hues
Brought to us by Thy heavenly cues.

I see the children and look with delight
As each one carries Your given light.

Heavenly Father, I come alone
And bow before Thy heavenly throne.

I bring the gifts You bestowed on me.
Heavenly Father, take not my sight from me.

Elsie M. Szoo
Galloway, NJ

[Hometown] Galloway, NJ: [DOB] July 9, 1931; [Ed] high school and some college; [Hobbies] many; [GA] loving life

I was born on a farm in Kipling, Saskatchewan, Canada on July 9, 1931. My parents immigrated to the United States with their four children. At the age of eight, I contracted terrible ear infections, missing a year of schooling. Our family physician met a doctor skilled in a new form of therapy since antibiotics were not available at that time. I received radium treatment. In my adult years, I have had three poly operations, wear hearing aids, and have had cataract operations, glaucoma, and macular degeneration. My abilities in hobbies like sewing, sketching, and painting have diminished greatly, but I continue to create dioramas and working in clay.

You Wore Your Blues

Trading in the strand of desire for the rope of discipline,
Reveille summons us again. Eagle, glove and anchor shine—
preserving, protecting and defending the firing line.

North, south, east and west—our goal in life is to be the best.
More we sweat in peace, less we bleed overseas
and more at ease the pain will be.

John Paul Jones cried: "We've only begun to fight!"
Navy blue fights by air, land and sea,
serving all lines of truth wherever it may lead.

Then we took the warrior's calling card— drilled in field fire,
smoke and steel: For out of blood and guts we grew,
sure, we marched to John Philip Sousa, too.

Advancing abundantly the ideas and ideals of our democracy;
we choose liberty to exalt the beauty of God, nature and art.
In action with fidelity, courage and bravery—
we'll never lose the fight if the cause be freedom,
though it wounds the heart.

All hands held in awe, we recall what America has done
for each of us; we ask what we can do for America in return.
Energy, faith and devotion to your own self be true:
The few strut we to the beat; a cut above a berth anew,
legend has it sir, you wore devotion to your blues.

Jeffrey Cameron
Green Bay, WI

[Hometown] Maywood, IL; [DOB] October 28, 1954; [Ed] BS in social work; [Occ] retired; [Hobbies] go out dancing, listening to music, golf; [GA] graduation from college and honorable discharge from USMC

I have a disability that I've struggled to overcome. I advocate for the disabled. This poem is for those who put their lives in harm's way in the Marine Corps and other services. In social work, I've followed the work of Helen Keller.

My Funeral

Here I am, alone and cold,
    In my box of steel and gold,
A red satin pillow under my head,
    Oh my! This time I think I'm really dead.

I see you pass by me,
    Some stay longer than others,
Some touch my hand,
    Some say, "I'll soon see my mother."

Plants and flowers,
    Notes, saying how sorry.
I hear whispers, I was a bad girl,
    Stayed out late and liked to party.

If I had one more say,
    I'd say, "two-faced people better pray."
They're now standing in front of me, at my gate
    I get to direct them down.
The devil doesn't like to wait!

Too late for them, they didn't pray
    I got the last laugh, as they say
I went to Heaven, they went to Hell
    I'm so dead and I can never tell!
The End!

Terrie Amen
Sterling, CO

[Hometown] *Sterling, CO;* [DOB] *November 5, 1956;* [Ed] *high school graduate;* [Occ] *homemaker, poet;* [Hobbies] *collect art, writing, concerts, jewelry, antiques, Avalanche hockey;* [GA] *my son who led to my granddaughters (Alayna and Claire Amen)*

Sterling, CO is a pretty small town about two hours from Denver. If you wanted entertainment you always had to go to Denver to Red Rocks amphitheater where they have great concerts. At the Pepsi Center, I got to see the Denver Avalanche Hockey Team take the Stanley Cup years ago. I saw John Elway win a Super Bowl and Eric Clapton, Prince, Boston, Keith Urban and many others rock the Rockies. I love Colorado. Skiing, hiking, night life, eating out, flea markets, are Colorado. Everyone should take a vacation and come to Colorado. I love writing. Enjoy my poem. I know it's a little dark. What I see, what I would see, as I lay in state. Want to know what I see? No-No-No.

Summer Going

Soon we must stay out of the pool
That's because the summer is getting cool
Shortly some people will go back to school
Then I think myself a somewhat fool
There are always rules
Some we follow some we don't
Why should we care
Just so we share
Make everything fair
Then it will be fall
Leaves will turn color
Come tumbling down
Most of them to the ground
Then can't be found
But we will have fun
Everyone will want something
Couldn't be a big old thing
Nothing to toss or fling
So nothing is wrong
Summer is never gone too long
Soon it will be winter
But have no fear
Then Christmas time will be here
A time to thank God
That we are all here

Cellesta Loomis Junker
Shelby, OH

[Hometown] Shelby, OH; [DOB] January 18, 1941; [Ed] high school, graduate school, art; [Hobbies] crafts, fishing, art, camping; [GA] helping others

I like to do everything. Some things Mom said I could never do, but I did! I'm happy I did follow all of her rules. Then I did some things better. People liked me more. She couldn't get along with people. I had my own ways. When I was in my late sixties, I was put in a rest home. Some things nurses and helpers say you should never do, but I did, and they didn't like that, 'cause they were trying to slow me down and stop me. I had fun watching them do things. They sure did a lot of talking on others. Some people had their lights on. They wanted help, but the nurses and helpers didn't care. Then I started writing poems.

The Meaning of Love

The meaning of love is
deeply within two hearts
that beat as one which
comforts the heart, which I
hold so closely to my heart,
soul as one.
I cannot bear the grief once
again to lose my love, for his
passion is so deeply inside me
that the long dwelling wrath
would tear my world apart
that I would feel emptiness that
no soul should ever encounter
in a lifetime...
The grief of losing your one love,
one life, one soul, carries such
a bitter taste that you
walk this world all alone!

Dianna L. Bulisky
East Lansdowne, PA

[Hometown] East Lansdowne, PA; [DOB] December 5, 1967; [Ed] specialized associate's degree—paralegal; [Occ] homemaker; [Hobbies] writing poetry, sports, traveling; [GA] going to law school and graduating

I enjoy writing poetry, for it expresses my inner-self and deepest emotions. I wrote this to my boyfriend who has had to deal with my PTSD and our on-and-off breakups, which scare me that I don't want to lose a good man over my PTSD. That he doesn't understand, nor do I, and that's why I write it to this day in poetry. Maybe I'll have that love every woman fantasizes over with my wonderful boyfriend for many, many more years to come.

 Eber & Wein Publishing

Hope's Journey

Where art thou oh beloved heart
Now slept away by tattered tears
Too sweet its memories of treasured scenes
And flowing life in rivers of thought

The fabric of intertwined moments
Haunt its days and dreams at night
Those precious times now washed away
Clouded and distanced as the sky

The soul fights to continue its existence
Struggling on a tightrope to balance with resolve
A new reign of hope to emerge and begin anew

Wisps of life in old photo albums
A tangible of life's collections are reviewed
As years diminish a fading mind and purpose

Yet, the essence of hope rears and hovers precariously
On the ledge of sadness and joy
The balance of one struggle over the other

'Tis a fight to the finish that cannot be won
Until light and hope step in on its journey still ahead
And you can again jump that precipice
To fill life's book to its end

Phyllis M. Anselona
Coral Springs, FL

[Hometown] Coral Springs, FL; [DOB] October 6, 1941; [Ed] high school and college; [Occ] secretary, artist, singer, writer; [Hobbies] tennis, reading; [GA] The Concert Company

There are no words to describe the loss of a loved one. I experienced this in my own life and have expressed this in my poem, "Hope's Journey." If it touches your heart, I have achieved its purpose in the promise of hope, a new future and a new beginning.

Empathetic Abilities

Life is full of surprises and pays to appreciate life's simple things.
God blessed me with an empathetic gift, meant to help others
with joys to bring
With spiritual gifts comes power.
But never will I be for power, only the joys and other
emotions to others I will shower.
From others I feel pain as well as joys.
As I reach out my hand and heart to help; never with this
gift will I toy.
Sometimes it's unnerving to feel other's pain.
But that goes away when I bring the person sunshine and take
away their rain.
All the pieces fell together of why I am how I am.
I live to give with open arms, this is who I am.
Opening my heart to others comes naturally to me
As I bring out their unknown emotions to set them free.

Joylene Rios
Sacramento, CA

[Hometown] Sacramento, CA; [DOB] March 7, 1983; [Ed] college student pursuing my bachelor's in human/family and child services; [Occ] in-home care; [Hobbies] beads and writing; [GA] when I published my book of poetry

I was diagnosed with epilepsy at age nine. Epilepsy has taught me to appreciate life in every way, never taking life for granted. Epilepsy is my blessing in disguise. I published my book entitled The Joys and Disappointments of My Life So Far *with great pride—my life's work, my diary put into poetry form. Next to be published will be my children's book entitled,* Tales from the Stars. *I couldn't care less about fame, never pushing my inspiration or writing just to write. I write because I need to write.*

Who Are You?

As I went walking in a woodland track,
I felt two eyes staring at my back.

Turning slowly around, I asked
Who are you?
Those two eyes just answered
Whooo.

I asked you first, you know.
Answer me or I will go.
Those two eyes just answered
Goooo.

I started to leave that woodland track
With those two eyes still staring at my back,

As if to say, *Don't you know*
Who you are, my good man?
I certainly know whooo I am.

Marjorie C. Tate
Harrisburg, IL

[Hometown] Harrisburg, IL; [DOB] April 25, 1932; [Ed] business college, creative writing; [Occ] retired minister, bookkeeper; [Hobbies] crafts, gardening, traveling; [GA] visited thirty-eight of the states, visiting museums, churches, and old graveyards

I love the outdoor activities. I like to write about the creatures of God and what they would say or think about people—squirrels chattering, butterfly lives, the earth worm—to name a few. "Who Are You?" about the owl is a favorite at the nursing homes I visit. I go to a small country church outside of Rudement, IL (Social Bretheren denomination) where everyone is made to feel welcome, just as God intended.

Upon Seeing the Sea

For Norman

I who have loved you
Did not know
The pain your absence would bring
Nor could I have guessed the searing blow
Of seeing you again.
The carrion gulls laugh and reel mockingly
As drunken sailors in sodden dress whites.
There is salt enough in my unending tears;
Who needs the sea who proves no friend to me.

Oh, treacherous void!
I could not fathom your tyranny,
Your desperation to make all things an empty shell.
Luring my love with sparkling sprays
Of countless gleaming jewels
Undulating and tugging at her heart
You overpowered and held her to you;
Her secrets known, her prayers quenched
Though many waters could not quench my love for her.

And so, my loves have come to this
Silent, broken treasures cast about my feet,
Ruined in the wake of one who waits,
Crouched and still disarming.
But I....I will love the Sea No More,
Forever.

Joan Kathleen Swartz Clellan
Galloway, OH

[Hometown] Wapakoneta, OH; [DOB] March 14, 1952; [Ed] BS in education, Juris Doctorate; [Occ] attorney at law, artist, arbitrator; [Hobbies] painting, song writing, creating fashions, jewelry; [GA] being born again and spirit-filled

Reared on a farm in north-western Ohio, I was surrounded by books of poetry and prose. Mother always had several books by her living-room chair and even more on her night table. Dad quoted at length great poems and carried a copy of his favorite until his death at age ninety-five. The younger of two girls, I began creating poetry before I entered school and learned to write. My poem was inspired by the drowning of Nora Flowers caught in a riptide while her husband, Norman, frantically attempted to save her.

Hope

The earth trembled, the trees shook, windows shattered.
The trembling became rumbling, buildings folded,
Collapsing as if they were made of cardboard.
Roadways opened up as if by a giant can opener.
Big waves rushed violently to shore,
Crushing everything in its path.
The earthquake took no mercy.
People running, screaming frantically,
Bleeding, searching for their loved ones.
Nothing was left, schools, hospital, all in ruins.
Stunned and in a state of shock
The man walked aimlessly through the rubble.
As he reached a pile of concrete
Where once a school stood
He saw a hand reaching upward.
Panic stricken, he started digging.
As he moved the rubble aside, piece by piece
A face emerged, it was a girl.
As he gently brushed the dirt from her face
A smile appeared on her face, her hand grasped his—
Out of tragedy came Hope.

Sandra Llewellyn
Greenfield Center, NY

[Hometown] Newark, NY; [DOB] July 29, 1958; [Ed] high school graduate, some college, diplomas in fiction, non-fiction and children's writing; [Occ] home health aide; [Hobbies] writing, photography, reading, music, crafts, nature walks; [GA] Editor's Choice Award—outstanding achievement in poetry by Poetry. com and International Library of Poetry

I started writing poetry when I was in my teens. I would carry a blank journal everywhere I went and write down my ideas. This inspired me to start writing about my life experiences and how I saw the world around me. My poem "Hope" was inspired by the 2004 tsunami—ocean earthquake disaster. It affected so many people around the world. These were my thoughts on the devastation it created.

The Big Game

Dedicated to Jerry and Brianna, my grandchildren
and the kids across the street

An old mop handle
their baseball bat
the street became their field
on that Saturday afternoon
They were filled with so much
zeal
and the boy who was up to bat
squirmed
before the throw
the pitcher threw that tennis ball
and he struck a mighty
blow
I stood in my doorway
caught up in their mood
squeals and squeaks of laughter
that Saturday afternoon
You would have thought
by all their shouts
that it was a major game
but instead
a bunch of little kids
playing baseball
just before it rained

Charlotte Neukam
Hanford, CA

[Hometown] Cedar Lake, IN; [DOB] March 1, 1945; [Ed] high school; [Occ] retired, Bank of America; [Hobbies] dancing, painting, reading; [GA] this writing; I am so grateful

I am now sixty-nine years old and I currently live in a small town in the San Joaquin Valley in Hanford, CA. I have not written anything in recent years. I stumbled on this writing group by accident. I was lonely and this filled some time. I knew no one here. Poetry seemed to come naturally to me. This poem is inspired by a baseball game played in the street, and went just as it reads. All the children are under the age of eleven. Jerry and Brianna are my grandchildren, and several kids (boys and girls all from the same family) live across the street.

Heavenly Treasures

Every day is a gift from God,
His love is everywhere
And when we give Him thanks and praise,
our burdens we can gladly bear

His love is there for everyone,
It's not for just a few
For those who live in faith and trust,
His words will all come true

So, do not waste another day in seeking
earthly things
Seek those that are of Heaven and receive
the gifts His love can bring

And when you get to Heaven,
you'll find the treasures you have stored
It's then that you will taste and see
The Goodness of the Lord!

Frances Vickers
Malverne, NY

[Hometown] Malverne, NY; [DOB] September 7, 1945; [Ed] high school graduate; [Occ] retired library clerk; [GA] climbing Mt. Podbdro, Medjugorje, Yugoslavia

My greatest accomplishment was making a pilgrimage to Medjugorje, Yugoslavia in April 1987, where the Virgin Mary appeared to six visionaries on June 24, 1981. Today, all but three of the visionaries have daily apparitions of the Blessed Mother who conveys messages of conversion, faith, prayer, fasting, penance and peace to lead us back to her son, Jesus Christ. I didn't realize I had the gift of poetry until February 25, 1999. I truly believe it was a gift from God and I think you will too when you read my poem, "Heavenly Treasures," written on September 3, 2001. I also believe that my love for God and the inspiration of the Holy Spirit led me to write these words. As the Blessed Mother once said: "If you have received a gift from God, you must be grateful and not credit it to yourself. Say, rather, that it is God's."

My Mom Rode a Dinosaur to School

When my mom was a little girl like me, she also went to school.
She said there was no bus to ride and she did not own a mule.

It was too far for her to walk, so a dinosaur she did ride.

But when she got there, she could not bring him in.
So he had to stay outside.

When it rained she did not get wet.
His tail held her umbrella as he did stride.

When it snowed he did not slip,
And she felt very safe outside.

Coming home was so much fun.
With friends she would race.

She tells me that she always won,
But that certain smile is on her face.

When my mom was a little girl, it was so very long ago.
But I will not tell her that there were no dinosaurs.
Even though that is what I know.

Suki R. Kaplan
Manchester, CT

[Hometown] New York City; [DOB] March 2, 1952; [Ed] master's degree in performing arts; [Occ] para educator; [Hobbies] writing; [GA] raising two amazing children

When my children were experiencing their first years of school in Connecticut, I would prompt them to be ready and not miss the school bus. They asked if I ever missed the bus. I explained that I grew up in NYC, where there were no school buses. They insisted that I tell the truth. I explained that my mom let me ride my dinosaur to school. They accepted this at first. But one day, my son came to me and said, "Mom, I know you're old, but there were no dinosaurs when you went to school," which inspired this poem.

Green Bay, Black Ocean: Two Lives

A warm sun danced across the water,
But you were all a-shiver, lips blue,
Evilly I splashed water on you.

Now the years have rolled swiftly by,
And the colors of our paths have grown,
But so very, very differently.
My color was pink, three tiny girls,
But yours was single, wild, airy, free.

Richard, you were lost,
Drifting, still searching
For peace in your soul.
You ran to Texas, Mexico, who knows where.

But your mind soared
Above all the rest;
Genius can be cruel.

I am so sorry that the black depth
Of your darkness I could not see.
On a frigid November night
The black Atlantic claimed you.

Many saw you dive into the sea;
Nary a one thought, even the police,
You were worth a trip to see what was.

Laura E. Turpin
Millville, NJ

*[Hometown] Toms River, NJ; [DOB] September 10, 1948; [Ed] one year of college; [Occ] banquet server;
[Hobbies] gardening, writing, painting, crocheting; [GA] three lovely daughters*

*Never have I wasted time searching for my place in this world; long ago I decided to carve it out with my
actions, words and various creations. God put me here for a reason, and I may not know why, yet I sense my
purpose through observing my surroundings, and do what I can, in my own way, to better myself and those
closest to me. All the tools have been given to us by our maker, we just need to learn how to use them. Poetry
can be one of those tools.*

The Outcasts

We live in exile, in isolation, together both Amber and me. It's people we want to avoid, our faces we don't want them to see. Though our presence most people tend to shun and abhor, I love my Amber dearly, now, and forever more. We don't know why we're the victims of such an unfortunate turn of fate, why we have to be targets of ridicule, prejudice, or even hate. If people have such feelings, such attitudes towards people like us, that's unfortunate, that's their problem and we don't care. We're content to live our lives happily, as long as we're left alone, and people stay out of our hair. I love my Amber very much, and unto her I shall cleave. I'll never abuse, mistreat her or even leave. We have a powerful bond between us no one can shatter or break. Our feelings, our love for each other is all that's at stake. We have an eternal relationship that will always endure and last, even if we have to spend our lives as unwanted outcasts.

Alan Knight
Champaign, IL

[Hometown] Champaign, IL; [DOB] July 30, 1958; [Ed] high school diploma; [Occ] hospital cafeteria worker; [Hobbies] watching videos, trains, taking walks; [GA] having donated nineteen gallons of blood in my life

God may have created us all equal, but each of us is a separate individual. We are all unique and special in some way. We need to stop judging each other by appearance, religion, social background, etc., and accept each other as we are, not as we would like for them to be. It would be a better world, by far, if we overcame our natural prejudice and bigotry and accepted one another as unique separate individuals, talented and special in our own way.

Patrolling a Legacy

Meandering through philosophical oracles in pretense of
judgmental hypocrisy, consuming numerous droughts of
celestial seasonings in mandarin orchard, pondering the
universe...stumbling upon the puzzle of science and
philosophy strolling hand in hand along a path of
ancient wizardry...What will range the corridors of
the mind? What will snuggle in the coffers of the soul?
Driven to perusing the historical documentation and
pronouncements of copious literature, what river of
knowledge will flow into the future? What will the
vaults of ancient wisdom preserve and offer up to our
infrangible laws and perspicacious searchings?
Seductive wit and wisdom, wobbling on the edge of
immortality, excites my intellect. Indulging, I
experience surrealistic verse exciting the heart,
crafty rogues of dark passions haunting the mind.
A surreptitious glance at uninhibited free expression
tempts the mood. Next, horror, like a junkyard canine,
bites at the spirit...Enraptured by the usufruct of
wealth and treasure in a wonderland of didactic
offerings, feeding on fruits plucked from great trees
of anthology, plodding along the paths scholars and
dreamers trod, I'm grateful to be trudging.

Glenn D. Brennan
Council Bluffs, IA

[Hometown] Council Bluffs, IA; [DOB] March 15, 1944; [Ed] bachelor of arts; [Occ] retired teacher; [Hobbies] writing poetry, swimming, teaching; [GA] helping a homeless man secure employment

I have approached the literary field seriously only since I retired from daily employment at age sixty-seven years, eight months. I enjoy teaching Bible, attending church regularly with my wife and reading and studying poetry. I got into Frost, Milton, Keats, Tennyson, Longfellow, Wadsworth and more. Patrolling a legacy was inspired by my love and appreciation of good literature. Patrol: the action of traversing a district or beat. I thought it fit perfectly into what I am doing in the field of literature. I spent several hours writing this piece.

Untitled

I am a book of secrets
Most pages filled with lies
There is no soul inside me
For I have no eyes

Of the innocence you see
The light begins to fade
Slowly it consumes
They should be afraid

For darkness shines through light
Little left to save
There is no use in running
Everyone's a slave

Desiree Hinton
Mentor, OH

[Hometown] Mentor, OH; [DOB] March 30, 1994; [Ed] high school diploma; [Occ] sales; [Hobbies] writing, video games, photography, outside

This poem is about all the dirty secrets, or secrets in general that we hide away inside ourselves— all the lies spoken or received.

Autumn

Autumn is one of my favorite seasons of the year.
I love the way it makes me feel the cool breeze
and watching the falling of the yellow and brown leaves.
Early in the morning, as you step on to the floor,
It makes you want to tuck back in and sleep some more.
It's a good feeling when you can just stay in bed
Because you can just peep out from under the cover.
Feel the coolness and then pull the cover back over your head.
But when you do get up, the kitchen is the place to be.
Will it be coffee, cappuccino, chocolate or hot tea?
Either one of these hot drinks will make you feel good
Before you leave your house, regardless of where you have to be.
If it's a lazy day for you curling up on the couch with a good book,
regardless if it is a hardback, paper or your Nook.
Because if you're like me you will fall asleep anyway,
but who cares if you take a long nap—
remember it's your lazy day.

Emma L. Hawthorne
Brownwood, TX

[Hometown] Waco, TX; [DOB] February 10, 1956; [Ed] Jefferson Moore High, US Career Institute, certified billing specialist; [Occ] medical claims and billing specialist; [Hobbies] writing poems, drawing, sewing; [GA] being a mother and my career

I was born and raised in Waco, TX. I am the middle child of three sisters and three brothers. I became interested in writing and reading poems in junior high. I also love to draw in my spare time. I made my home in Brownwood, TX. I am a mother of two beautiful young ladies, Domonique and Linette, of whom I am very proud. This will be my third poem published. My goal is to someday write a children's book and that will be among one of my greatest achievements.

Farewell to a Friendship

Many moons seemingly have slowly passed
Reminiscent of a friendship that never was
Secrets and laughter shared never to last
Deceitful your selfish heart, even at pause
Overcome me, with warm angry sacred tears
Resting weakly on knowing southern walls
Over ill-defined and artificial happier years
Hushed in betrayal wrapped in deafened ears
Yet, the impartial air allows a deep-taken breath
That sustains universal things we all have met
How sadly now I mourn your ways to the death
Of that part of you I will need to try to forget
Moments tainted in truths, dipped to betray
Ashamed a bit, I do claim such dislike for you
Shrouded in a private funeral, no words to say
Even in your postured mind, I see it through
Dare I cement your ways in lessons learned?
Draped in goodbye before your shadow turned
Luckily, I stay ready to embrace pieces of good
In spite of dark crooked turns so boldly stood
For I will always hold smiles and joy in my heart
Every day giving thanks to music in God's art
In every corner awaiting, where I mind a turn
Sojourning, surely in life, I too again will learn
How to take great comfort in God's embrace
Through precious tones of life I readily face.

Ella T. Hall
Yonkers, NY

[Hometown] Yonkers, NY

Life Encumbrance Are Memories

Life is but a walking shadow, a treasure of
Family, friends and miles of acquaintances still standing
But yet for those who have passed are mussing shadows
Decorating the corridors of one's mind
Nothing more than wall paper to tantalize the cerebellum
From time to time allows us to immortalize their images
I do so cast the loving memories that fill my life
From whence the beginning that hones loneliness with compassion
Defines loss with direction and doubt with purpose
All these things and much more that comprise my existence
That which fuels my exuberance and fills my vessel of life
Can it be that life teaming with such love be compromised in loneliness
To meander among the shadows of memories not in shroud of darkness
But thought to invigorate the effervescent of healing and celebration
Bless these spirits that decorated my life and I too as planned will follow
These courses of events and thus in time you also shall celebrate my existence.

Theodore P. Colterelli
Middletown, NJ

I was named after my dad, who was named after a president of the United States, Theodore Roosevelt. I have always felt proud to live within the confines of such a glorified "Rough Rider" and for my grandfather's inspirational namesake. Time allots me the intelligence not to take for granted my heritage and be made to appreciate our ancestry that is exhumed in the spirit of good will in all endeavors.

Paige "Sunshine" Hensley

Here we are again
at the long end of the cross roads
begging for the fight to end.
I'm crying and pleading
for you not to leave.
Don't you dare run away.
Don't you dare say
that you're on your way
to growing up today
to putting my child at bay.
We can't separate
not this way
not in different states…
Please don't go away.
Just one more day, please stay…
I don't know how to let go.
How do I move forward
when the past is all I know?
You are my daughter, my friend.
I don't want this to end.
Life is but a blink in time
and I don't want to say goodbye.
Let's just sleep on it,
and only say good-night.
I love you sunshine, for life…

Christina Potts
Leicester, NC

[Hometown] Leicester, NC; [DOB] January 1, 1977; [Ed] high school graduate; [Occ] appraiser's assistant; [Hobbies] writing, painting, and music; [GA] being a published poet, mother and wife

All my life I was told I can't do many things, that I'll never become anyone worthwhile, but here I am, a mother to five and married to the most amazing man. My family means I have accomplished more than most. With their support, I've been published over seventy-five times, and above that I have received the best prize ever: Paige, Sarah, Zackery, Katelynne, and Brooke, and Kenny.

Do We *Really* Know Anyone?

Do you really think you know your friend?
Your own mate, do you comprehend?
Have you walked a ways in *their* shoes?
Have you ever felt *their* lowest blues?

Have you tossed and turned in *their* bed?
Have you ever crawled into *their* head?
Have you known when smiles were hiding tears?
Have you thought them strong, though they had fears?

Sure, you've heard a million stories
Of their pain and of their glories,
Witnessed some of *their* achievements,
Listened to *their* sad bereavements.

No matter how very close we are,
We all are oh, so very far.
Our *own* road in life, is walked alone.
No one sees where our mind doth roam.

Our purposes and goals are single,
Do any *two* minds really mingle?
We will win or fail at our own scheme,
But only *God* knows *our true dream!*

Lavaughn Ogren
Torrance, CA

Brothers and Sisters

A troubled teenage boy
I abandoned you.
For that I'm sorry.
I wasn't there for you.
I didn't protect you.
So you grew up without me.
But we are family.
We belong to each other.
It isn't about eggs and sperm
Or DNA and blood types;
No, being brothers and sisters
Is about hugs and kisses.
It's about caring and loving.
I didn't realize then
The life lessons I'd learn from you.
Oh, how your heart-set changed me.
Your love rescued me.
Your love changed my life.
I didn't realize it then; I do now.
Thank you for sharing your life.
I'm so proud of you.
You're so special to me.
I love you.
I have always loved you.
I will always love you,
My brothers and sisters!

Bill M. Watt
Fayetteville, NC

Dedicated with love to Steve, my brother! Bill Watt 3/24/2015

[Hometown] *Fayetteville, NC;* [DOB] *December 20, 1950;* [Ed] *PhD;* [Occ] *college professor;* [Hobbies] *racquetball, chess, GO, PS3;* [GA] *married Katherine Young*

One of God's many blessings was my placement in foster care when I turned fourteen; however, the difficulty for me as the eldest child in a single-parent home was that I was separated from my brothers and sisters for several years while I attended high school. I did gain two foster brothers and two foster sisters whose love I cherish to this day, but it was hard being separated by hundreds of miles from my blood-siblings. Fortunately, after graduation I was able to reunite with them. Over the years they have blessed my life beyond measure with their love.

251

Life's Seasons

Spring is like all things new
flowers bloom kissed by the morning dew
grass is all green warmed by the sunlight
children play and the world seems so right

Summer is a time for growing
with warm sunshine and gentle winds blowing
the days are all fair sunny and bright
at the end of the day a starlit night

Fall is a time when things start to fade
flowers no longer bloom and the earth turns brown
leaves on the trees fall gently to the ground
and nature's harvest no longer abounds

Winter is often seen as a time of gloom
when all the beauty has come and gone
I look up at the sky on a crisp clear night
and there is a star shining so bright
letting us know there is beauty in all things
even in the night

Betty J. Russell
Cleveland, TN

[Hometown] Cleveland, TN; [DOB] November 6, 1951; [Ed] high school; [Occ] Peyton's Southeastern, Krogers; [Hobbies] reading, writing, fishing, swimming; [GA] my family and writing poetry

I have lived in the same town my whole life, of all the places I have seen while on vacations, I have never seen anywhere else I would want to live. My husband of forty-six years inspired me to write this poem. He believes in me and encourages me in anything I choose to do. My son, grandchildren, two dogs and one granddog keep my life full and busy.

Four More Heroes Gone: Dedicated to the Benghazi Victims

Four more heroes gone on September 11, 2012
It was incredible when late afternoon they asked for help.
The terror attack and it was no phony scandal as indicated;
now we all know the truth, the real truth was never anticipated.

What happened with this administration and this great nation?
The heroes that survived the terror attack defended you with passion.
I heard about your bravery in defending the humble.
I was praying that you got out of trouble.

You sure didn't mind helping others.
Courage was in your heart to find your brothers.
The present administration couldn't comprehend your determination.
The entire world knew your bravery and so did our nation.

Your departure from Earth has given us sad goodbyes.
Many Americans are still waiting for justice and please no lies.
The hands of God and his angels exposed the truth.
The present administration are lacking with uncouth.

The US troops waiting in Europe and at Benghazi wanted to participate in your rescue.
But the top guy and his administration forbid your brothers from going near you.
Rest now our brothers, rest our true heroes that the world knew.
They will always be remembered as great Samaritans.
Our four heroes defended many people with helping hands.

They are the ones that carefully noticed that they needed to be benevolent.
When you were denied help for the administration that was malevolent.
Equivocally there's no doubt for God, that he knows your heart.
Thank you, guys! We hope that in the near future we will meet in paradise

Diana R. Gonzalez
Passaic, NJ

[Hometown] Passaic, NJ (born in New York, NY); [DOB] April 1960

My parents migrated from Puerto Rico and returned to their origin year later. I dedicate this poem in memory of our four great heroes. Their motto was, "Have an inquisitive mind, demonstrate to be ambidextrous by defending their beliefs and trusting that a better world is possible." Learn to do right! Seek justice, encourage the oppressed. Defend the cause of the fatherless, plead the case of the widow. Isaiah 1:17

Upon a Pole

When flags are made to gently fly against the breeze,
The way is ours for peace to afford its price

Each tiny thread was sewn together to show what love
For neighbor may represent, and when the charge of
Bayonet and gun have statements of their own, the
Flags are standing proud upon the poles

Untouched by mankind though worn thin by wind and
Rain, we claim our victories on land and sea

All wars must always change our ways since searchings
For power have proven that man and God have earned
Their justice in the sod!

Gerold D. Mathewson
Sioux City, IA

[Hometown] Sioux City, IA; [DOB] November 16, 1935; [Ed] BS in architecture; [Occ] artist, poet, designer (residential); [Hobbies] free-expression, impressionist art; [GA] residential designer for niece Jean's family

My poem is an original free-verse work initially written when I found inspiration from a friend who attended a flag-pole at a residential area known in this neighborhood as Cook Park Housing. Throughout Gerald's later years of writing poetry and original art framed by the author, his major inspiration has been beauty in architecture and nature as well as a creativity recognized by his son, Jay. Our younger generation also has inspiration derived from the flag of our nation's heritage.

The Queen Has Gone to Be with the King

To my grandchildren

In the great getting up morning, who shall be able to stand?
We all will have to stand before the King
We do have earthly kings and queens
God knows who they are, by all means, insects, bugs
There are ants, bees and others
So be careful how you treat your sister or brother
It may be a king or a queen
He calls all of us home when our days are done on Earth
He had a special call to make the other day
He chose among His very best
He said you have fought a good battle, you have kept the faith
I have a crown waiting for you
Come on up and join the throne of grace, you have had a good life
So much love and care
Loved ones don't weep anymore for her
For her, rejoice and be glad
Because all the days of her life, she loved and prayed for you
It gave her so much joy
While waiting for her call to glory
To meet the King and tell her story

Clover L. Winston
Pine Bluff, AR

[Hometown] Pine Bluff, AR; [DOB] August 19, 1925; [Ed] ninth grade; [Occ] mother and nurse; [Hobbies] gardening, fishing; [GA] mother and grandmother

I have always loved to write and draw. When I was growing up, I drew almost any kind of bird or dog. When I would see a doll in a store window, I would keep it in my mind, then I would go home and draw it from memory. Now I am eighty-nine years of age and I still love to fish, tend my flowers and garden. My husband passed away when I was thirty-five years old. I gave birth to twelve children. I have ten living. God keeps on blessing me and I praise Him every day.

Lil' Bro

Precious little ragdoll kitty,
big blue eyes, cream coat so pretty,
think you're such a big tough guy
until your brothers make you cry.

Blaze and Smokey, patience waning,
growl and hiss at Rory Mac,
their re-direction sadly failing
when he bites their tails and jumps their backs.

This little cat 'cat-astrophe' is a pushy, pesky, kitty dude,
who tears at warp speed through the house,
hiding his brother's red stuffed mouse
then scarfs their favorite wet cat food!

The day is ending, eyelids heavy, it's now time for sleepybye.
Kitty Sandman hums a kitty ditty
while his brothers sigh a lullaby
and bow their heads and cross their paws
to thank their Father Cat on high.

Meow meow mew,
in faith we plead our prayer to you.
Please let us all sleep through the night, and that means Rory, too!
Please get him through this stage all right,
Then we'll start the day, patience renewed. Amew!

Maureen Opal
Fountain Hills, AZ

I've been an avid reader since childhood and sporadic poetry writer the past twenty years. I have even been a finalist twice in the National Library of Poetry contests and a semi-finalist in the last Eber & Wein contest. I retiring two and a half years ago after a forty-eight-year career as an RN. I enjoy flower gardening (28 rose bushes) and am a voracious reader (favorite authors: Shakespeare, and poets Shelly, Keats, Brownings, Robert Frost, Maya Angelou, Emily Dickinson, E. E. Cummings and Satirist Ogden Nash). I also enjoy mystery writers Michael Connelly, James Patterson, Lisa Gardner, Mary Higgins Clark, and many others. My last published poem, "Soul Mate," was about Smokey Joe. This entry is about him, Blaze and, primarily, Rory Mac. Singing alto with two different choirs is also a passion, and spending time with three grown children and five grandchildren.

Wintry Days

We ask how shall we know when winter is really here
When will we know it is time for cold weather we fear

We do know somehow wintry cold days surely belong
Suddenly days grow shorter and nights just linger along

Since wind blows in and becomes rather tiring and bold
Just know that it is time when weather turns very cold

Whenever snow piles up and there is a need for a plow
Then we know for sure that it is really winter somehow

We heed the rules of winter and wear our heavy coats
Usually we enjoy our morning meals of cereal and oats

Crops have long ago been planted and well harvested
Enjoy through the long cold winter since we invested

"Trick or Treat" the children always look forward to this
Showing off their costumes seeking candies and bliss

What about Thanksgiving when most families do gather
Eating turkey or foods that they somehow would rather

Do not forget holidays of Christmas and the New Year
These are the ones most of us hold sacred and dear

We ask how shall we know when winter is really here
When will we know it's time for cold weather we fear

Dorothy E. Kissman
Austin, TX

[Hometown] Quanah, TX; [DOB] June 30, 1931; [Ed] high school; [Occ] retired secretary, typist; [Hobbies] collect depression glass; [GA] being a wife and mother

Most of my life I wrote poems, but in the eleventh grade my brother was killed in an accident. Later we were asked to write a poem as a class assignment and I wrote about death. A teacher rejected my poem and said I was too young to have deep thoughts about death. I gave up writing but later started writing again. Family and friends say my poems are good. I joined the International Library of Poetry and participated in conventions in Las Vegas. A few of my poems got standing ovations. Writing poems brings enjoyment.

My Living Will

We are prodded more and more to draft up a
    living will
Directions for when life is teetering on the brink—
    and in the hands of a doctor's skill
So mysteriously and suddenly, we may begin to croak—
    gasping for our final breath
Our incoherent muttering straining to convey
    what's been beating within our breast
A feeding tube or other device could perchance
    connect to jump-start our body alive
Merely postponing however, that ultimate final exam
    by Who's breath we all survive
So dear caring loved ones, I long to have you
    gather around me singing old Calvary hymns
With your billowing tears bidding farewell
    to my faltering body and limbs
Sending up sweet prayers to heaven while I soar
    upward towards those pearly gates above
Freed from the most well-meaning medical invention
    to enjoy forever my precious Savior's love

William H. Shuttleworth
Jacksonville, FL

[Hometown] Philadelphia, PA; [DOB] May 6, 1937; [Ed] Philadelphia College of Bible; FCCJ night course; [Occ] retired furniture restorer and lay preacher; [Hobbies] photography, acrylic painting, travel; [GA] hopefully, a life pleasing to God

Despite wordy privacy protection notices from doctors' offices, insurance companies, banks, etc, modern technology can easily retrieve personal information on any of us. Forms we must fill out require so much sensitive information that it becomes mind-boggling at times. Describing our personal strategy concerning our own end-of-life plans is about as tough as it gets. Therefore, being a poet, I decided to express my innermost thoughts and feelings on this unavoidable subject, poetically. I just couldn't stomach filling out some excessively detailed form concerning my departure from this world. As a result, I have provided "My Living Will" for anyone curious enough to read it.

Rumors

They said I'd hear a blaring, thunderous roar,
That I'd see lightning streaks crash through the floor.
They said there would be music so sweet to my ear
That surely angelic harps must be playing near.

They told me my heart would pound, stop, sing, and soar.
My knees would be wobbling like never before.
What do people learn to say such silly things for?
They talk about the birds and bells forevermore.

Lies! Lies! Lies! Because how it happened to me
Has never been described correctly previously.
Now I can tell you firsthand not to believe all you hear.
Just nod your head at what's said and smile whimsically.

There was no music, fuss, or muss, no angelic trill.
It wasn't long and lasting, like the reading of a will.
It happened uneventfully, his lips just brushed my cheek.
He did not hold me tightly until my knees were weak.

Silly! Silly! Silly! That bunch of zany stuff,
People talk about it like they can never say enough.
Where do loony rumors start? There was no shattering thrill.
I did notice, however, that the earth stood perfectly still.

Sharon D. Proehl
Henderson, NV

[Hometown] Newark, NJ; [DOB] October 26, 1927; [Ed] doctorate in Theology; [Occ] retired; [Hobbies] writing, gardening, music; [GA] integrating females into Essex County vocational system, only black female in the entire school

By Nosetradamos

Noses can come in all shapes
and sizes,
Some are gross and give unpleasant
surprises.
Many are bulbous and others quite
scanty,
But there's only one Jimmy 'Schnozzola'
Durante!
Cyrano's nose could put an anteater
to shame,
He's in the Guinness Book and the
'Probiscus Hall of Fame.'
You should cover them when you
sneeze or cough.
(Although there's no danger of a nose
blowing off!)
When you cry, tears run down and
over your lip,
If your nose is sympathetic, it
also will drip! Sniff!

Norm Smith
Columbus, OH

[Hometown] Washington D.C. and San Francisco, CA; [DOB] August 30, 1921; [Ed] San Francisco City College; [Occ] retail manager; [Hobbies] poetry and military round tables; [GA] eligible to wear seven WWII medals

I was invited to attend San Jose College for track and journalism. WWII ended that dream for four years. For military service I wound up as Message Center Chief on West Field Tinian Island during the A-Bomb raids on Hiroshima and Nagasaki. I was awarded the Meritorius Unit Citation and WWII Victory Medal. I continue to speak at high schools on WWII experiences. I've been married fifty-eight years to the same wonderful gal! I met Olivia DeHaviland, Tyrone Power and many of the famous folks, i.e., Ronald Reagan, Max Baer and John Glenn, to list only a few!

A Blessing from God

Lord, I saw You last night,
Your hair was made, such a mess.
Your face and Your body, beaten and bruised.
And yet, You had nothing to confess.

With Your head hung down,
Pilot questioned You
Then washed his hands
Of this matter, he said, "I am through."

Then I saw You dragging the cross
Through the cobblestone streets,
Passing by people, shouting,
And some that watched and weeped.

Then finally, at Calvary,
As You gave up the ghost.
I saw Your head slump down,
This hurt me the most.

Then, I closed my Bible,
And in a dream, my mind did sway,
And, one more time, I saw You, my Lord.
And we were flying away.

And I was singing a song,
Giving all praise unto Thee.
And there at my side was my wife,
Mom, Dad, and the whole family.

Lawrence Melvin
Greenup, KY

[Hometown] Wurtland, KY; [DOB] January 2, 1949; [Ed] GED; [Occ] retired; [Hobbies] hunting, riding, working; [GA] receiving God's grace

I am a Vietnam War Veteran and now retired from the CSX Railway. My wife, Ruth, and I have four children and eight grandchildren. We have been married for forty-five years. I am sixty-five years old and I am of Baptist faith. My writings of poetry, to me are as a gift from God. They are the best way for me to witness of my Lord and Savior, and to let others know of Him and of His plan of salvation. May God richly bless you with His love. "Live now, to live forever."

Paradox

Autumn with its shorter days
affirms its vulnerability…
Allowing for the touch of death.

Leaves shout their vivid colors;
boldly they cry out…
Cold winds are on their way!

Leaves beckon. I pause, reflect—
looking, thinking, wondering…
Do fallen leaves sense defeat?

Leaves are grand masters
at fully letting go…
Falling, twirling, spinning, gliding.

Nearly dead, yet dancing still
stabbed by icy frost…
Shimmering in the morning sun.

Continuing to walk my path—
trees are secretly smiling…
Winter death assures new life…spring!

Barbara W. Grygier
Medina, OH

[Hometown] Medina, OH; [DOB] July 30, 1948; [Ed] BS in elementary education; [Occ] retired teacher, grades four to six; [Hobbies] photography, drawing, painting, needle arts; [GA] I am an "overcomer"

After a rewarding thirty-three-year career teaching children to become the best "thinkers" and "doers" they could become, I am actively retired. Ever since fifth grade, when I won first place in a composition contest, I have longed to have time to practice the arts that I so love. Many of my poems are inspired by photographs I have taken. Equally important to me is my volunteerism. I am a hospice volunteer in addition to my church ministries. Many people I have encountered have deeply touched me. They have also inspired my writing and art.

Addiction

Addiction is a frightening and lonely place where paranoia runs wild. Fear of being found out, watching and waiting for something. Always wanting; for that addiction's strong hold calling!

Addiction is being out of control, always looking for a way out. Panic lies just beneath the surface as you scan the room looking for any evidence that might have been left behind. Paranoia is playing with your mind again.

Addiction makes the decisions on where and what you do. After all what if you're found out? Maybe the shakes or nausea and vomiting will hit, what then? The weight loss gets too much attention. No, friends are no longer welcome in this world of addiction; it's too dangerous!

Addiction means you're no longer there for yourself. You can't make the right decisions or be trusted as the addiction is powerful and all consuming. You want help but fear and uncertainty grabs hold making you think, "What if?"

Addiction is a disease. It's being at dis-ease with you! Like other diseases, it won't go away without treatment. You hope someone loves you enough to help before it's too late and you're dead, but do they? Why look the other way, make comments or even support the habit?

Addiction belongs to everyone! Are you frightened and lonely desperately wanting help? Are you watching someone sink in despair and loneliness? Are you the addiction, anchor, or the life raft?

Addiction, what is it to you?

Debra Knapp
Ocala, FL

[Hometown] Ocala, FL; [DOB] August 29, 1962; [Ed] RN; [Occ] critical care RN; [Hobbies] hiking, kayaking, writing; [GA] happily married

I am a critical care registered nurse and I worked with another nurse who had a drug problem. After knowing another nurse who almost died from drugs when no one even tried to intervene, I did try to help this girl. After two interventions, she remained drug free. I then wrote this poem thinking about her.

A Journey by Faith

Two souls from separate states online
A writer and past baker with time on their hands find
That they have more in common than age can define

A social network was the place they met
521 miles was the trip that was set
To greet each other and sit and talk
To meet each other and maybe walk
In the township of Wingate, North Carolina
Where people are social and weather is finer

Your destination is reached you extend a hand
To a short and stocky fan
Who doesn't wait for the car to stop and park
Before the door opens and a little dog barks
Arms wrap around your neck
And hugs and kisses are exchanged in a sec

It takes faith to journey to an unknown place
But to be a friend you need to meet face to face
You give your book as a gift before you leave
There is no telling and you believe
That you will see your friend again
You hope and pray this friendship never ends

Linda Hendrick
Jonestown, PA

[Hometown] Jonestown, PA; [DOB] May 2, 1949; [Ed] Thompson Education Direct, pharmacy tech; [Occ] housewife, writer; [Hobbies] knitting, crocheting, reading; [GA] my poetry book Inspiration from the Heart

I am a mother, grandmother and presently going to school for drafting with CAD. I am handicapped with Parkinson's but love to travel. I write my poetry on what life has handed me and where I have traveled. I've been married for thirty years to a great man. We live where history was made near Gettysburg, where some of my poetry was written experiencing the Gettysburg ghosts. I am sixty-five years young and trying to prove that life goes on even when there are trials. I forgot to mention, I am also a minister.

Decades of Life

When a toddler is under the age of ten and unfamiliar,
then the toddler is a friendly acquaintance.

When a teenager becomes of age it is aggravating,
then a teenager has a temper it is annoyance.

When the age of twenty is achieved they become conquering,
then the age of maturity has been invincible.

When the age of thirty has arrived not conquered,
then this age ego has a touch of conscience.

When the age of forty most conquering has alibis,
then the conquering attitude has most adjustments.

When the age of fifty has arrived there are life moments,
then numbered moments have passed by.

When sixty has become the savory pleasantness,
then this age has achieved moments to remember.

When the ripe old age of seventy approaches,
then the cemetery is necessary of late life.

When the soul sings songs to the solitude,
then cloud research results in rain.

Ronald L. Libengood
Colorado Springs, CO

[Hometown] Erie, PA; [DOB] December 31, 1940; [Ed] high school; business management semester; English semester; [Occ] disabled veteran; [Hobbies] enjoy life to the max [GA] re-manufactured 1935 Auburn

I became disabled around the year 1972 while employed in the USAF due to an electrical current in a storm. The effects involved my mind and also my physical body—especially my back, which needed surgery. I've been married thirty years, and I do own a home, car, truck, and motorcycle.

My Angel

When I was six years old
I had a story that needs to be told.

I had pneumonia and wasn't expected to live.
An angel appeared in the early morning hours with a special gift to give.

She knelt by my bed and held my hand.
She had no wings—dressed in light green—
with a halo that made a gold band.

She smiled and prayed for me, then left my side.
To this day, in angels I abide.

My dad believed the story I told—
He said, *You will always remember her visit*
even though you were only six years old.

To this day, I collect angels. I have around 140!
Gifts from my children, grandchildren, friends, and various countries.
I love them all!

Patricia A. French
Longmont, CO

[Hometown] Longmont, CO; [DOB] March 16, 1932; [Ed] high school, early childhood education classes;
[Hobbies] watercolor painting, writing poetry; [GA] owner/teacher—Wonder World Preschool

I was born and raised in the small town of Mead, CO, one of eighteen children. I love writing poetry for holidays and special occasions. My poem is a true story. To this day, I can still see her! I am thankful my dad didn't say, "Oh, you must have been dreaming!"

My Love for Twirling

When I was a little girl, oh how I loved to twirl.
Standing high on my tippy-toes,
with my arms out to the world.
Around and around I'd twirl,
Twirling, twirling, twirling until I fell.

When I was a young woman,
it was still there. That love I have
for twirling, always close and near.
My friends would laugh and kid me,
"It's Disco, not twirling!"
But for me it will always be,
twirling, twirling, twirling.

Now I'm an old woman, sitting in my chair.
But boy, I still have my memories
of twirling everywhere.
Twirling here, twirling there,
twirling, twirling, twirling,
until.

Connie R. Knight
Yakima, WA

*[Hometown] Yakima, WA; [DOB] May 26, 1951; [Ed] trade school, cosmetology; [Occ] retired; [Hobbies]
reading and music; [GA] having my poems published*

*My inspiration for this poem came about while I was daydreaming about my early childhood. Growing up in
a large farm in the northwest corner of Missouri, there was lots of room to roam and play. Twirling was one
of the first things you learned. And it's so true, I do have a love for twirling; how about you?*

Soul's Song

It is a wondrous sight!

Thousands of minute hot-air balloons
Ignited, steadily ascend on musical currents

Different shapes on some: oval, cubic, round
And the colors vary too, constantly changing

There is a candescence about them
And they modulate as they rise
As though responding

To a higher impulse

Lura L. Genz
Broomfield, CO

[Hometown] Broomfield, CO; [DOB] February 24, 1931; [Ed] Mary Washington College and George Washington University; [Occ] retired; [Hobbies] writing, reading, movies, gathering with family and friends; [GA] finding my life's mission

A seeker of spiritual truth for many years, my poetry reflects, in some small way, my interest in bringing truth, wisdom, beauty, and spiritual freedom into my everyday life.

3:29 a.m.

You have been teaching me how to hold my breath
but I have forgotten how to exhale.
You said that if I held my breath,
my thoughts would organize themselves

I always take everything too seriously.
There are two tanks within my ribcage
that are full of rusted filters
and my hands do not remember
which level will resuscitate them.
Panicked thoughts gasp for air like tired horses
I wave severed arms to get their attention.
I need more tattoos so that when I dream of bodies,
I know if they are mine.

Last night I watched my hands try to unlock my jaw.
They scurried like mechanical spiders
but the muscles compressed like padlocks
and I stare at the ceiling every night
waiting to stand in the path of every recollection
but all I hear are wheels on pavement
and the echoes of other people's words
shutting the valves sitting below my sternum.
I am small and made of nothing
All the multitudes I have,
they slip through the cracks in the whites of my eyes.

Claire McDonald
Oakland, CA

[Hometown] Oakland, CA; [DOB] January 20, 1992; [Ed] BA in American literature; [Occ] fundraiser for non-profit organizations; [Hobbies] writing, reading, printmaking; [GA] completing two months of archival research on John Steinbeck

Morning Song

Often in the early morn
I'd walk the meadow near the corn
Down the hillside where below
A crystal spring fed stream would flow,
And squatting there I'd fill each tin
To fetch the morning water in.
On such a morn one early May
With buckets full I turned away
To start my trek back up the hill
When pierced the air a songbird's trill.
A song so sweet I'd never heard,
'Twas truly some enchanted bird.
I softly sat my burden down
And careful not to make a sound
I searched around until I came
Upon the songster—damp and lame!
"'Twas surely not the Maker's might
That caused you such a painful plight!"
As I in sorrow sadly sighed
He cocked his head in certain pride
As if to say, "Is something wrong,
Do you not like my morning song?"

Dave Rempe
Westerville, OH

[Hometown] Westerville, OH; [DOB] July 24, 1935; [Ed] two-year university in English literature; [Occ] retired; [Hobbies] writing free verse, rhyme, limericks; [GA] motivational training system

"Morning Song" is based on an actual experience. My great-aunt lived alone in a cabin in the Serbian farming in Southeastern Ohio. Each spring I would go down to help her prepare for summer. Without running water, it was one of my chores to bring it in each morning from the small field stream. The particular morning of "Morning Song" provided me with a life lesson that has served me very well these many years.

The Hurricane of 1938

It didn't have a name
No one knew it was coming
But up the coast it came
And people started running.

It hit with a fury never seen before
It rattled at our windows and pounded on our door
Big surprise to a New England Town
A hurricane had tracked us down!

And the rains came, and the winds raged
And the whole house was shaking
The lights went out, the wires were down
No chance for evacuating

We huddled close in the darkened room
Lit only by lightening flashes
Frightened by the roaring sounds
And sudden, thundering crashes

Hours went b—and the storm surged on
All we could do was pray
Trees were falling all around
Hoping none would come our way

I was a mere child of ten
My mom had died, my dad had gone
I was really afraid my world would end
As I hid in the corner, quite forlorn

My grandma came and held me tight
And dried my lonely tears
She told me it would be all right
And calmed my wildest fears

At last the nightmare ended
And we were safe and sound
But oh, the damage it rendered
When we went out and looked around

Many years have gone by
Since that perilous day
But I still remember when
My grandma made the storm go away—
when I was a child of ten

Dorothy P. Martin
Edgewater, MD

[Hometown] Edgewater, MD; [DOB] January 25, 1928; [Ed] New England School of Art; [Occ] had many, now retired; [Hobbies] art, astrology, writing; [GA] my ten children

I was born in Boston and lived there nineteen years. When I moved to D.C. to work for the government. I was always interested in poetry and writing. When I was living in New Carroltown, there was a hurricane one day, which brought back all the memories of the hurricane that terrified me as a child. I just had to write about it. They say it did more damage than the San Francisco earthquake of 1906.

Power of Love

What is the power of love?
It's a feeling within and strength from above.
It's always having you by my side,
My partner in life, along for the ride.

Together we make an unbelievable pair.
Our lives together, so much to share.
Sometimes too serious, not always fun,
Life gets that way, we're always on the run.

Taken for granted over time so much,
I almost lost you, just fell out of touch.
You and I equal the power of two,
Simply said, I love and need you.

I get it now, it's not just about me.
It's about tomorrow, together we will see.
I can change over time, if given the chance.
Always and forever, to our last dance.

Ed Kielkucki
Bethel, CT

[Hometown] Yonkers, NY; [DOB] February 17, 1952; [Ed] BBA in marketing, Iona College; [Occ] senior sales manager; [Hobbies] poetry, New York Yankees, collecting; [GA] my family

There is nothing more important than family. It has been my source of strength throughout the years. I enjoy writing poetry, but I know it comes to you when it wants to, on its own schedule. It would be nice to be able to just sit down and write something, but that's not how it works. I need to be inspired by something or someone to get the words to paper. Only then will a poem get created. This particular poem was written for my wife, Joyce. Through the ups and downs of marriage, we have been married for almost thirty-seven years.

Looking Forward

My dear friend is looking forward
To the freedom of a butterfly and bird.
In her next life, after this one
The hitch in her get along will be gone.
The cane she can use for decoration
And that's the end of that frustration.

My special friend is looking forward
To every sound that used to be heard
Birds singing, the wind sighing, a speaking voice
To hear them all would be her choice.

Upon the re-opening of her eyes
The bright colors a great surprise.
She now is blind, but then she will see
After many years, what a blessing to be
Able to paint, to read and to write
Light and cheery, not always night.

How does she know this will all occur?
That's up to her loving Lord and her.
Her Bible says no more suffering or pain
So no hearing aids or glasses or cane.
She knows she can depend on His word,
Most of her life that's what she's lived and heard.

C. Elaine Ricketts
Cañon Caon City, CO

[Hometown] *Cañon City, CO;* [DOB] *December 8, 1937;* [Ed] *high school graduate;* [Occ] *bookkeeper, title clerk;* [Hobbies] *reading, writing, crocheting, picture post cards;* [GA] *sharing love, friendship and good times with the elderly folks and handi-capable adults I have volunteered with.*

A dear friend says I can take any idea and make a poem out of it. Well, not by a long ways, but I have played with words and rhymed them since grade school. This poem was inspired by a very dear friend who is blind, at the assisted living facility where we both reside.

Profile of a Dead Neighborhood

Pastries
Pushcarts
South Brooklyn
Italian immigrants
Congested tenements
Hard working dock workers
Human and multifarious odors
People living on stoops on hot nights
Infamous neighbors who were never seen
Tough kids taken by the ear when late for supper
Clashes of culture, generations, language, dialects
The ruthless separation of the chaff from the wheat
The often repeated tragedy of the American nightmare
The often times repeated triumph of the American dream.

We never really transcend our beginnings

Joseph Tuccillo
Brooklyn, NY

[Hometown] Brooklyn, NY; [DOB] November 3, 1936; [Ed] bachelor of sciences

Antiquity's Breeze

Above wild sea
on high beach bluffs
goldenrods twirl
with moving shine
as lyre's gold
that Aeolus strums
away in sorrow
to grieving shrieks
from Sapho's heart,
before her leap
to waves below,
cold roll deep
at Sanguines' keep

Christopher L. Dinas
Huntington, NY

[Hometown] *South Farmingdale, NY; [DOB] June 17, 1956; [Ed] college graduate, fine arts; [Occ] custodian/warehouse picker; [Hobbies] painting, designing; [GA] self-realization*

As a longtime progressive activist, using my God-given artistic abilities to create 'art banners' for progressive causes to enlighten (with beauty!) messages from antiwar, no nuclear power and war, destruction of old growth forests to homelessness and health care for all! Those were on TV during massive rallies for three decades before the Patriot Act branded US terrorists—so now I paint with passion my visions of nature as reflecting our lives filled with mystery in wonder.

Mad Alice

Alice, Alice, where have you gone?
Trapped in the memories of your fiery past.
Wonderland holds no solace for you.
Listen to my advice and you'll survive
the horrors of being eaten alive.
The Hatter feeds tea to his dead companions,
while an evil train races down the tracks.
You cannot stop it, Alice, let it go.
For soon you will certainly know
the blackness that grows
inside this hole,
which seeks to drown you
in the blood of your lost soul.
                    —Cheshire

Holly Johnson
Columbus, OH

[Hometown] Ashland, OH; [DOB] July 20, 1989; [Ed] BA in English; [Occ] librarian; [Hobbies] reading, Xbox, music, photographer; [GA] yet to occur!

I don't know where it began, but I have an obsession with Alice in Wonderland. After playing the video game, "Alice: Madness Returns" by American McGee, I was so inspired I had to write about it. I hope I captured Alice's persona, plus a twist of my own.

When I'm Gone

Life will be different for you
When I'm gone.
Life will be simpler for you
When I'm gone.

No more worries on how I feel
When I'm gone.
No concerns if I need help
When I'm gone.

No more discomfort for you
When you're in my home—only memories
When I'm gone.
All will be at your disposal
When I'm gone.

Yes, life should be
Much simpler for you
When I'm gone,
But always know I loved you
When I'm gone.

Selma Gutierrez
Raton, NM

[Hometown] Raton, NM; [DOB] April 21, 1936; [Ed] high school graduate; [Occ] retired; [Hobbies] reading, writing poetry, volunteering; [GA] county jobs I have held and my family

The Crab's Funeral

Tiny footprints lead the way
through drifting sand mounds
and seaweed strands.

Lit by the rays of the setting sun,
a heart, crudely drawn
by a child's hand,

in the center, an arrangement
of red-orange baby crabs
left behind by the receding tide,
now dry and lifeless,

lovingly gathered
and given a proper burial.

Joan Hunt
Lebanon, OR

While I did some writing in high school, I wasn't really inspired to write on a regular basis until my husband and I moved to the banks of the North Umpqua River in 1961, where we began a non-stop adventure. This led me to be a writer and photographer. My parents were to follow us in a short time to remodel the restaurant, tavern, and cabin overlooking the lovely river. What seemed like paradise at first soon became a nightmare, when we experienced a once-in-fifty-year flood. I lost my first baby, and my beautiful dog got run over and killed on the busy mountain highway. I began to write first of the beauty of living in such a lovely setting, then of the trails, and pioneering on the Oregon coast range where we lived in a tent until we built an a-frame cabin, and several log houses. We raised chickens, goats and bees. Our living was made logging, cutting, selling firewood, and doing helicopter Christmas-tree harvest. I got a job working for a local paper, writing a weekly column of local happenings, feature pieces on people of interest in the community. This also inspired me to write for magazines. I have had pieces published in Oregon Coast, *the northwest edition of* Farm and Ranch, Looking Back, *and* Good Old Days, *just to name a few. Although, my first love remains, writing short pieces on wild-life and nature in free verse poetry. We live in a rural ranch and farm area where our daily encounters with wild life and the beautiful surrounding country gives me much food for thought and paper.*

Escaping Reality

Escaping reality...The bad I don't want to see...
I want to live in a fantasy...No hate no enemies.
Where people have love to share
And people's lives are spared.
No wars, no fights,
And people know how to care.

This isn't the way it was intended to be
We came into this world blind you see.
To learn as we go and learn from what we didn't know.
To let our spirits shine and make our own world divine.

Escaping reality...The bad I don't want to see...
We can live in a fantasy...Why can't us people see...
We still have people who love and share
But people's lives aren't being spared.
We have wars and fights but
We the people have forgotten our rights.
Escaping reality that's where I'd rather be!

Joan Williams Krueger
Bastrop, TX

[Hometown] Bastrop, TX; [DOB] April 23, 1984; [Occ] CEO Krueger Monuments Works; [Hobbies] singing, writing, hunting, fishing

I am a very proud mother and have a wonderful husband. My poem was inspired by finding a way to look at positive in the times we are in.

Moving On from Free

Clouded mind hazy thoughts
Gut-wrenching pain inside of me
You woke up one day, said
"I'm moving on, moving on from free"
Crippling fear struggling to be
Suspended silence in the nighttime air
In the morning light you said
"You gotta go, 'cause I'm moving on
Moving on from free"
You were my rock, you were my friend
You brought me strength until the end
With tears in your eyes and a lump in your throat you said
"I love you so much, I love you so
That's why I…
I'm moving on, moving on from free"

David Polebitski
Merrill, WI

[Hometown] Merrill, WI; [DOB] May 17, 1976; [Ed] BS in comparative religious studies; [Hobbies] outdoors, writing, reading; [GA] eagle scout, college graduate

To me inspiration comes from life experiences. All experiences give us an opportunity to grow, learn and change. Some are fun and uplifting while others are painful. All are inspiring and life changing. When I sit down to write, I try to not have anything planned out. I like it to be spontaneous. If I had to, I would characterize my style of writing as no style or stream of consciousness. Writing like that makes it seem like a snapshot of where I am mentally, creatively—so I generally do not rework what I write.

Loneliness

Who says that
I am alone loneliness?
Can't you see
The present of God
When you look at me?
Loneliness loneliness
Can't you see
The Lord is here to see?

Gilberto Melendez
Philadelphia, PA

[Hometown] Philadelphia, PA; [DOB] August 10, 1932; [Ed] tenth grade; [Occ] security; [Hobbies] writing; [GA] to help people

I am always thinking about life and I love to help people to live in good action because good action makes the world move around to better life.

A Precious Gift

Children are a precious gift from God.
They are given to us just for a short time.
We are given the honor and pleasure of being their caretaker and protector.
Like a gardener tending to his garden, they provide what is needed in order for their plants to grow and flourish into a bountiful harvest.
Our children are the same, with tender loving care along with a mixture of worries, heartaches and pain, we watch them grow into these wonderful beings of personalities.
But how they grow up so fast and we soon forget that they are a gift on loan for just a short time.
No one can measure the span of time from birth until death. Death has a contract with each living being and that contract must be honored.
How can we forget that they are only a gift that must be returned back to the sender one day, stamped with received and cherished, but then carefully returned with love and stained from years of loving heartfelt tears that were shed.
They are a precious gift form God.
A gift so precious and so meaningful that the mere sound of their laughter and the joy of their presence blinds the eyes and hearts racing. Although, in the back of our mind, we know that it may only be for a brief moment in time, when they will have to return to the giver who sent them. What a wonder it is—the cycle of life.
No one can imagine the pain or the heartache of giving a child up whether in life or in death. When we remember the moments, the smiles, and the laughter and, yes, even the pain and heartaches our loss is not too hard to bear. Because within our heart, every beat it beats brings a moment of comfort and of peace and love for that precious gift from God—our child no matter how brief or how long their life may have been. At least we got to share that moment in time when nothing else mattered except the love between a child and their parent.
A child is an awesome and precious gift from God.

Willie F. Dunn
Silver Spring, MD

[Hometown] Kinston, NC; [DOB] September 8, 1961; [Ed] Kinston High School; [Occ] executive assistant; [Hobbies] writing, cooking, running marathons; [GA] retiring from the US Navy

It seems like I have always had this gift for writing poems and poetry as long as I can remember. I used to write poems for my high school classmates for different occasions. One of my teachers—the late Oran Perry—told me one day during English class I should become a teacher since I love to write so much. But as fate would have it, I joined the military but continued to write off and on everywhere I was stationed. My poem was inspired by my niece "Missi"—Janelle C. Grant—who succumbed to MS in September 2014. She was given six months when she was diagnosed in 2011. But she asked her family not to give up on her. She fought a courageous battle for three years. This poem is in memory of Missi, a beautiful, thirty-six-year-young lady (August 23, 1978–September 17, 2014).

Transitions

The world has always been in constant transition.
Our lives are in transition from the time we are conceived.
Some come to us unbidden, quicker than a stroke of lightning,
while some only appear very slowly, gradually and sneak up on
us like a spirit in the night.
A few transitions are carefully planned; some can leave us
dumbfounded and momentarily paralyzed; but make no mistake,
as sure as the wind blows for better or worse, they will come
and we must try to be ready.
The final transition will take us through the Veil, into Eternity.

Marilyn S. Vatter
Oskaloosa, IA

[Hometown] Oskaloosa, IA; [DOB] June 8, 1937; [Ed] BA in languages, post-graduate study; [Occ] retired language teacher; [Hobbies] travel, reading; [GA] working with high school students

I taught French, German, and English for forty-one years in California and Iowa. I spent a lot of time running student tours to France, Germany, Austria, and Switzerland. I traveled widely both in the United States and Europe. I have been very active in my church and the community. I was married for fifty-one years and have been widowed for two. I have one daughter who is married and has two college-age children. She and her husband are professors of theater in South Dakota. I have always enjoyed writing and have written a few children's stories, which have never been published. I am still involved in travel and planning certain tours for adults.

Power for Peace

"Because I exist, man lives," said the sun.
"True," said the wind, "but you know I'm the one,
Who can creep under doors; make myself known;
Gather seeds of peace; see they are sown.

I'll whisper so softly in an infant's ear,
And rage or howl—so all will hear.
I'll implant this message to incubate;
Your warmth will nurture and germinate.

'Twill take a thousand years—or maybe never,
For this growth in man—for some are clever;
They reject or stifle, but for self, any plan,
That will improve society, or benefit man.

What care they for all of humanity?
Instead of wisdom, they reap insanity,
Their weapons more lethal—themselves less strong,
Will not join others who try to right wrong."

"Ah, yes, we'll do all we can," said the sun,
"To change human nature—one by one,
But if evil persists in spite of our might,
I'll extinguish myself, and kiss them goodnight!"

Gladys P. Bowman
Redmond, WA

*[Hometown] Redmond, WA; [DOB] April 1, 1923; [Ed] high school graduate; [Occ] normal
routine of age ninety-one and a half*

I Write What Is Real

The things that I write are simple but real.
I write not to bore you but to give you a thrill.
Some poets write like doctors, giving scripts to the ill.
You can't understand a thing that you're reading,
Just swallow the pill
And make sure the bottle comes with a seal.
Some poetry you must assemble in order to build,
Trying to figure out where to screw on the wheel.
If you like to feel poetry, just read mine and chill.
For all that I do is write what is real.

Saundra Brown
Brooklyn, NY

[Hometown] Brooklyn, NY; [DOB] September 30, 1952; [Ed] college, business administration; [Occ] shop owner; [Hobbies] sky diving; [GA] writing poetry to touch a soul

Through the Years

I once was a puddle, then a small stream.
Through the years, I became a brook.
As I grew older, I became a river, with twists and jagged turns.
Some thinning and others with splendid fluidity.
One day I will meet the ocean,
With all of my transgressions and good deeds.
And we will become one.

Elizabeth A. Garcia
Edinburg, TX

[Hometown] Edinburg, TX; [Ed] BSW; [Occ] caregiver, life coach; [GA] every day is a great achievement

Legacy

To all humanity, I leave this world, Earth,
All my sorrows along with my tears
The unrest and insecurities that grip my very being;
Loneliness, that hovers over me as a shadow in twilight
Inferiority, like a dripping faucet pours through me
Torment, like an enemy hunting me night and day.
My very fibers cry out to be released
My soul to be freed from life's nightmares
I have become so weary and tired of being on life's stage
No more do I wish to be confronted with another play act.
Oh, ugly, cruel, torturous world
Release me from this purgatory
I haven't any more need of you.
Let the shovel dig up dirt and my miserable body laid to rest
Embraced by the coffin
Hugged by the bowels of the earth, let the clods of soil drop
Down to cover me well.
I have stepped down from the stage of life, the curtain for me shall
not be raised again,
Goodbye, planet Earth.

Antoinette (Nettie) Goodlow
Union City, NJ

[Hometown] Union City, NJ; [DOB] January 24, 1921; [Ed] some high school; [Occ] homemaker, secretary; [Hobbies] writing poetry, cooking, sewing, crocheting, knitting; [GA] my family

I come from a close-knit Italian family. My mother and father and a very loving aunt helped shape my life. Even so, my dreams of experiencing all that life offers led me to writing, especially poetry. I had three children of whom the oldest, my son Jim, was also a great writer.

Winter Garden

Vibrations of light...
bring brushstrokes of color
Crescendos of orangebursts and eggplant purples
feather the dusky twilight sky
Treasuries of sugar-spun snow
frost the landscapes into iced perfection
Majestic trees dressed in white linen
stretch forth their limbs unto the heavenlies
Pine boughs heavily encrusted with prisms of frozen tundra
bow in reverence
A winter white snow owl perches stoically
watching with great expectancy
A winter garden with lessons to teach
Vibrations of air...
bring supernatural manifestations
Faint sounds of music and voices and singing become audible
to those who have ears to hear and eyes to see
Wafts of sweet roses and exotic fragrances
surround the secret things
Three o'clock in the morning
Dark creatures of the night scatter
and bid adieu
Glistening in Divine Glory we enter into the sweet rest
Then suddenly...
God walks amongst us

Vicki Gonchoroff
Macomb, MI

[Hometown] Macomb, MI; [DOB] June 18; [Ed] securities and insurance license; [Occ] financial representative, retired; [Hobbies] reading, writing, travel; [GA] son Rob; grandsons Kyle, Jordan, Charles

My ten-year passport expired happily. I visited Italy, Brazil, and Israel (2014). Visiting Israel was one of life's greatest adventures. I feel truly blessed. I was baptized (Tevilah) in the Jordan River. I toured the Holy Land and walked where Jesus (Yeshua) walked. I even rode a camel! Needless to say, I stand with, support, and pray for Israel. Le-hayyim

The Fear

Conquering Heaven
not one tear
Conquering earth
he falls to the fear

The fear that devours,
the fear that dissolves,
the fear that is ours,
the fear that revolves.

It revolves like the cylinder
on a loaded gun,
the gun that shoots the bullets
right through the soul,
the gun with the powder
pitch black, like coal.

The powder like the dirt
that clings to the earth,
the powder like the clouds,
the clouds in all their girth

Tell me now, how the clouds in the sky
The clouds that hold heaven, the clouds that can't die
gave way, way to a child, who fell to the earth
who lost himself, to his own self-worth?

Cassie Farris
Caneyville, KY

[Hometown] Canneyville, KY; [DOB] May 12, 1998; [Hobbies] writing, playing music

Ernest Hemingway said, "There is nothing to writing, all you do is sit down at a typewriter and bleed." I may not have a typewriter, but I do have a love for books and that screeching noise that a pencil makes as you dump your thoughts out on a blank canvas. I think what inspires me is the way some words seem to fit so well together, and some are like polar opposites on a magnet. I love manipulating words.

I'm Not Old

My number in years keeps getting bigger, but I'm still
sixteen no matter the number, grandkids name change
from time to time, be nice if they would make up their
mind, But I'm not old.
   I've three new friends Arthritis, Bursitis, Tendinitis,
With regular dates with Doctor D.O. and M.D.
up and down the hall I go, To spend time with
        Ben Gay and Icy Hot.
I go out more than I used to, this joint or another.
My hearing is not too swell, and eyes are fuzzy, hands
shaky as well, sixteen candles, a light and wish as well.
Fingers and back bent to straighten I dare not
As I may flop.
        Off to the sock hop.
To stand up I must get to rocking to get a start
The number of tries you need not know.
While walking my direction is not too certain as my
legs gotten a mind of their own. Driving is a lot of fun
for I may not recall the road or what I'm doing?
Was that a red light that you went through?
        Oh, you are not the one driving
But as I read this, did I write it or did another send it to me?
        I'm not old
     Later years one's luster shines
     Cast off the bow line and set sail

Tim Reiners
Mt. Grove, MO

[Hometown] Mt. Grove, MO; [DOB] June 15, 1952; [Ed] high school; [Occ] Air Force, carpenter, truck driver; [Hobbies] fishing, hunting, music, reading; [GA] neighborhood-watch certified

Spending considerable time along a creek or river as elders explain, on a dreary day, their age, capacities are many. Come wake of morn to see what may be down the way. Insecure as it be afforded, I too experience more ere you go desire all the same quiet life or fame rather than age, carefree and young at heart, I'll stay. Later years luster shines. Cast off the bow line and set sail.

Untitled

I've peeked in the windows of Heaven
Say, what's going on over there?
Are those my darling sisters?
And my mother with silvery hair?
Ah, yes, there's my dad and all my brothers
Calling, come on Ruthie, we've been waiting
So the family can be complete
We will worship our Savior together
And humbly fall at His feet.

We shall dwell in the realms of glory
Where no sorrow or pain will prevail
And the beauty of Heaven will thrill our hearts
As we dance down that golden trail
Our Lord, Savior, Redeemer, will hold us
Close to His compassionate breast
And we will whisper, "I love you"
As we enjoy our eternal rest.

Ruth Thorud
Eden Prairie, MN

[Hometown] Minneapolis, MN; [DOB] June 12, 1917; [Ed] high school; [Occ] homemaker, salad chef; [Hobbies] reading, gardening, poetry; [GA] two wonderful sons

The Great Depression denied me further education than high school as I had to go to work. I never intended to show my poetry to anyone and kept it hidden in a drawer for eighty-five years. I wrote for solace to my soul. On my ninety-fifth birthday, I reasoned my two sons might enjoy them, so I had them typed up. A niece entered a poem that you published, "Dawn's Dream," and I was quite delighted to realize my poems were of interest. My eldest son, Gary, has been a fundraiser for various charities such as "Care Walk for Mankind," etc., and has traveled all over the world. He is retired now and lives in Pine Bluff, NC. My youngest son, Bruce, has been in the retail world and at present is manager of Boscov's Department store in Lancaster, PA. They both are compassionate human beings who love the Lord. They are my greatest achievement.

Why Shampoo?

Are you aware that I have no hair?
So what use do I have for shampoo when I get
anywhere?
I am clean-shaven and have no beard
(To use shampoo is kind of weird.)
To be honest and true
What need do I have for shampoo?

Marvin D. Goldfarb
Sunnyside, NY

[Hometown] Sunnyside, NY; [DOB] January 20, 1939; [Ed] year of college; [Occ] retired; [Hobbies] poetry, chess; [GA] being in Who's Who in International Poetry

Marvin Goldfarb has been writing since the age of twelve and has written over 4,000 poems. He has performed all over NYC and has established his reputation at such venues as The NY Poetry Forum Army-Navy Airman Club, Cadman Plaza, (The Poets of the Round Table), the YW/MHA of Forest Hills and the Kew Gardens Community Center (KGCC). There he hosts "Show us your talent" at the KGCC bi-monthly show. Mr. Goldfarb has had four poems published by Eber & Wein Publishing. Those included: "Who Is This Admirer?," "My Cat Says," "Marvin the Millionaire," and "Reverse Skydiving." A fifth poem published by Great Poets Across America, Washington, DC is called "Moses Gets the Ten Commandments" and won an award. Mr. Goldfarb has written over six hundred challenge winners on starlitecafe.com and allpoetry.com and is currently a judge of the allpoetry.com contests. His first book, self-published in 1999 by Menasha Press, orchestrated by Marvin Goldfarb was entitled, Out of the Words of Birds, Forest Hills, NY and was a sell out. It has pictures of birds and about twenty-five poems. In addition, Marvin has initiated performances at the City Coffee Shop in Jackson Heights, Queens, where he will introduce an upcoming publication of a children's book called Zoo Dreams involving works of his own book and seven other poets. Most recently, he was published in Who's Who in International Poetry for the poem, "The Psychiatrist and the Proctologist."

My Little Rose

You are a blessing from above,
The one who created you
With love and care.

Oh, my little Rose,
You light up my heart
With so much joy;
You are gorgeous,
As the horizon in the sky.

Your blue eyes sparkle
Like the stars in the sky,
Deep, so deep ocean blue.

Even though you have just been born
Oh, my granddaughter,
My little Rose, how
You fill my heart with

So much love; you are
So precious, so precious to me
In every way.
I thank the Lord for you, my little Rose.

Jane Roberts
Citrus Heights, CA

To my beautiful granddaughter, whose short life brightened all our lives, May 6, 2014–July 5, 2014.

The Fond Memories in Grandpa's Garage

Such were the great times Grandpa and we shared,
In his garage on a hot summer day,
Grandpa smokes cigar; Jim and I—root beers,
Sitting in lawn chairs—love the shady elms,
And some cars and trucks pass by down the road,
Summer Vacation, in our elation,
Grandpa loves to fish, we pass the candy dish,
Sharing our stories—school and work glories,
The birds fly above, camping we dream of,
We spy tools, pipe, board, sack, can, wheel barrow,
Buckets, nails, saws, cord, wire, rotor tiller,
Hose, rope, license plates, pitchfork, hay in loft,
Lawn mower, shovel, rake, camper and His truck.
Brother and I love Grandpa very much.

William D. Irwin
Princeton, IL

[Hometown] Princeton, IL; [DOB] June 23, 1956; [Ed] completed two years of college at I.V.C.C.; [Occ] work in a local restaurant; [Hobbies] hiking, picnicking, camping, fishing and writing; [GA] being a locally known poet and author of eleven books

Possessing a God-given gift of a creative imagination, I am very rich with all of my life experiences (people, places and things), which I learned from and can gratefully write about. So, therefore, besides honoring God and my family, I am also thankfully inspired by my friends at school, the US Navy, my places of employment, in churches and spiritual/religious groups, and everyone else I met and associated with all during my life.

A Childhood

On those dark and gloomy days there's sunshine in
    the memories that we hold.
Our childhoods are there forever and their
    images are so bold.
When we're sad and feeling oh so lonely
    we can always go back and smile.
It's a safe place to go whenever we choose
    if for just a little while.
Childhoods should be joy and laughter
    but sometimes they are sad.
When we sit and think about them
    you see they really weren't that bad.
In good times or in bad times there's always a
    lesson to be learned.
Our parents did the best they could at
    each and every turn.
With bedtime stories and homemade donuts
    before we went to bed
We were always kissed and tucked in tight
    and sleep tight was always said
The lessons that they taught me are instilled
    in me today.
I just want to tell them thank you in each and
    every way.
Keep what you learned inside you and
    never ever stray
When you just keep being who you are
    the tomorrows will be okay

Peggy Lanese
Chagrin Falls, OH

[Hometown] Bedford, OH; [DOB] July 2, 1955; [Ed] Bedford High School; [Occ] business owner; [Hobbies] cooking, writing; [GA] my two children

I was born on July 2, 1955 in Bedford, OH. I have lived here my entire life. Some achievements I have made are my two daughters, which have led to my four grandchildren who are my greatest joy. I started my own business in 1997, and it is still going strong. I want to keep putting my thoughts and memories into my poetry for as long as I am able to and can't wait to see what tomorrow brings.

Homeward Bound

Saying *goodbye* to a bustling day,
Springing about in my favorite way.
Where gongs don't sound, nor breaks jam,
Nor whistles blow, nor doors slam.
Feeling a connection of nature so dear,
A shelter and direction driving me near.

The cooing of a sweet turtle dove,
Soft whispering or a puzzling hum above.
Selective sounds can be so wild and high,
Starting on the earth, then flying to the sky.

A colorful turkey or a playful katydid,
The brown chipmunk skittering in the hedge hid.
Shimmering sights can be so light and bright,
Starting in the dawn, then winging to the night.

Saying *hello* to the green acres I love the most,
Where horses, cows and sheep I daily host.
From the hills, valleys and fields all about,
The bounty is beckoning without a doubt.

Sometimes it appears as I fictitiously opine,
The next century must be entirely mine.
So I may claim a functional financial field,
With the city's sounds and sights, as a
Tremendously popular, productive yield.

Janet M. Receski
Indiana, PA

[Hometown] *Indiana, PA;* [DOB] *December 25, 1941;* [Ed] *BS in education, MA in education;* [Occ] *elementary teacher;* [Hobbies] *gardening, cross stitching, hiking, traveling*

I have worked as a primary education teacher for many years. Poetry has been something that really caught my attention. I particularly enjoy nursery rhymes and the play on words. Raised with eleven siblings, there was plenty of fun in our household. Every day was full of many surprises. There is still much more yet to come.

A Remnant

Each of us is just a remnant
In this world of vast design,
For our shape, our size,
And our color too
All form a pattern of splendid hue;
For when God made this world
And put us where we are
He gave us many talents,
Although few, if any, may be a star.
Since I only am just a remnant
Of this Universe so great,
Or even just a part thereof,
May God grant to me a giving heart
That I might make a difference.

Berniece M. Boyett
Rogers, AR

[Hometown] Mulberry Grove, IL; [DOB] May 28, 1932; [Ed] two years college; [Occ] retired secretary; [Hobbies] crochet, writing; [GA] country music song publication

Growing up a country girl on a farm in southern Illinois, I was the youngest of four. I attended a country school and enjoyed poetry from early childhood. I recall sitting at my mother's knee as she read poems to me from a very large volume of poetry that had belonged to her father. Although I never heard my grandfather read from the book it was cherished by our family and writing a poem seems to be, to me, an appropriate way to express one's thoughts.

Dangerous Dan McGrew

Dangerous Dan McGrew,
drove into town in a black Daewoo.
He walked into the only bar in town,
pulled out some money and threw it down.
The barmaid came over and said what'll it be,
he said 3 fingers of red eye and then we'll see.
She got down the bottle and poured him a shot,
he said I'm here for a man name of Harley Potts.
He threw back the red eye then turned around,
this man name of Potts ever come to town?
The bar went silent no one dared say a word,
the man with the Daewoo was about to be heard.
I'm here for Potts so somebody better start talkin',
He's wanted in Texas for killin' a man and stalkin'.
I'll take him back to Texas, he'll get a speedy trial,
then we'll hang him from the oak tree out on the trail.
My name is McGrew and I'm here to tell you son,
if you're in Texas and you fight or use your gun,
I'm McGrew, and I'll stick like glue,
So don't screw up because I'm watchin' you.

Elmer Doerr
Trempealeau, WI

[Hometown] Winona, MN; [DOB] May 12, 1941; [Ed] high school grad

My wife and I have been married for fifty-five years. We raised four children. We have nine grandchildren, four step-grandchildren and eight great-grandchildren. I worked as a Foreman in a Tool and Die Shop for thirty-nine years. I am a woodcarver. My work has been published in a woodcarving magazine. My poems all rhyme, the subject matter varies from humorous to emotional to intense. I am retired and now have time for hobbies and such.

Seasons: Come and Go

Summer, winter, spring and fall,
A favorite season for us all.
Summer trips to the beach,
To relax and tan, within our reach.
A snowy scene comes so fast,
It's great to watch, but doesn't last.
One day it's spring and no more snow,
The flowers bloom and trees glow.
But don't get used to warm days,
Fall colors create a maze.
Four seasons that never bring a tear,
Always changing, for a great year.

Helen L. Bryla
Edison, NJ

[Hometown] Perth Amboy, NJ; [DOB] December 8, 1933; [Ed] high school; [Occ] lab and library; [Hobbies] reading and sewing; [GA] wife and mother

I was born in Perth Amboy, NJ and am eighty years old. I am the youngest of four siblings and had a great mom and dad. I enjoyed school from kindergarten to my senior year of high school. I worked in a lab for eight years, then married and had my first child. My second son came two years later, and they both grew up to be fine men. I am now retired and enjoy living in New Jersey, where there are four seasons and not just one.

Celebrate the Differences

Dedicated to Christian Nichtern
A very special young man we miss every day

God blessed us with babies, animals, birds, flowers,
trees, the sky glowing with stars sparkling,
oceans that never end and mountains that
seem to touch the moon. We pray for mankind
to prosper, teach, learn and give back to those
who need it now or very soon.

Children become adults and have children of their own
around the world, hoping they stay healthy, yet
different in their own special way.

One day as I walked through an evergreen forest
with its fresh, distinctive smell, I noticed a
sapling just a few feet away. Not a maple, oak,
cedar or pine, it caught my attention as the
trees began to sway. Never moving a branch
or dropping a leaf as if to say, "Look at me,
I'm different and I like it this way."

I never stopped thinking about that tree
hoping nature would show its grandeur in a
glorious way. God makes us all different and
unique as if to say, "It takes only one brave
enough to believe I deserve to celebrate
each day."

Renette JoAn Colwell
Lake Almanor, CA

[Hometown] Carrington, ND; [DOB] May 26, 1951; [Ed] business and legal administration; [Occ] retired paralegal; [Hobbies] gardening, antiques, classic cars, travel, rock & roll; [GA] publication of my first poem

I am proud to have been born, raised and educated in North Dakota. I presently live in northern California on beautiful Lake Almanor with my husband, John E. Colwell. My inspiration for my poem, "Celebrate the Differences," came from my best friend's son who was gay, who loved life and was sadly taken from us at a young age. I have been inspired to write poetry by the interesting people I have been privileged to meet in my travels around the world and my community. Thanks to Eber & Wein, I am able to pursue my passion for poetry.

Rain

Rain
Come
Wash me away
Melt into me until only my soul can stay
Crystallized drops cling to earth and petal and vine
These tiny beads of tears that hold rainbows inside
Wash me away, rain
Until I have nothing left but light inside

Heather Hauser
Safety Harbor, FL

[Hometown] Safety Harbor, FL; [DOB] November 22, 1987; [Ed] BS in early childhood education from USF; [Occ] first grade teacher; [Hobbies] yoga, biking, writing; [GA] my beautiful daughter

Children and writing are two of my greatest passions. Although I make a living educating children, writing stories and poetry has been a part of my life since an early age. My poetry is inspired by nature and the ever-changing beauty of the earth.

Wake Up, America

Wake up, America
Before it's too late,
'Cause the Muslims are causing us trouble
And our future is at stake.
They don't want to understand America
For all the good things we do,
'Cause they have their own goal in mind
And that's to destroy me and you.
Wake up, America
And lift up your voice,
'Cause if we wait too long
We may not have a choice.
Don't be misled by the liberals
Who will tell you Muslims are good;
That only the radicals are causing trouble,
And that the rest are misunderstood.
The radicals are really the forerunners
And the rest sit quietly and wait;
And if the radicals are successful
Then they will join in for the take.
Wake up, America
If you want to save our state.
And when we all wake up together
We'll be the ones that will decide our fate.

Samuel Lombardo
Destin, FL

[Hometown] Caraffa, Calabria, Southern Italy; [DOB] July 12, 1919; [Ed] two years college; [Occ] retired army; [Hobbies] golf, making wine, writing, gardening; [GA] first American to cross the Rhine River in WWII Flag at Museum, Ft. Benning, GA

I was born in Caraffa, Calabria, Southern Italy, on July 12, 1919, and arrived in America (Ellis Island) on October 3, 1929 with my mother and two sisters. I grew up in Altoona, PA through the Great Depression. I joined the Pennsylvania National Guard on November 11, 1939 (Armitice Day). February 17, 1941, the 28th Division federalized and became fully active. I volunteered for Europe during WWII and was rifle platoon leader during the Battle of the Bulge. I fought to the end of WWII then attended Ariey Language School to study Japanese. I served as intelligence officer through the end of active service in Japan, Korea and Vietnam. I had to quit school during the Great Depression to help my family of eight. I learned stone masonry (artistic) under my father's teachings. After retiring, I owned and took care of an avocado grove. I practice gardening, beekeeping, and wine and champagne making. I've done tree and grape crafting and played golf. I have always loved art sculpture, classical music and beautiful things. When inspired by beauty or any strong feeling of patriotism, I write.

Early Morning Prayer (3:45 a.m.)

Even if I walk alone,
Please help me walk.

Even if I stand alone,
Please help me stand.

Even if I live alone,
Please let me live.

Even if I give alone,
Please let me give.

Even if I love alone,
Please let me love.

Even if I pray alone,
Help me reach God above.

Help me walk, to stand,
To live, to give, to love.

I look to you, Jesus,
To give a hand,
To live a life of love.

Lydia M. Money
Saint Helena, CA

[Hometown] Saint Helena, CA; [DOB] November 6, 1942; [Ed] two associate's degrees in photography and humanities; [Occ] family property management of commercial rentals; [Hobbies] photography, writing, art; [GA] keeping a family diary since 1979 and writing a family genealogy

I have been writing poetry since I was fifteen years old and recently compiled an anthology of over fifty-seven years of work, which I am sharing with family and friends. Poetry is the soul of a nation and I try to encourage other writers to share their work too. I have an active prayer ministry for those who are suffering, and prayer is very healing and necessary no matter what faith heritage one is from.

Adventure

Oh Time Traveler,
Time Traveler
Take me away,
So I can see another day.

Let's go to a place,
When the dinosaurs happened to stroll along Earth's face.
Or maybe we could go and see
That one place with the 400-foot trees.

I've heard Shakespeare is great,
But we should hurry up,
So we aren't late.
The seats sell fast,
People pay to stay,
Maybe it'll be a tragedy today.

Oh Time Traveler,
Time Traveler in your simple blue box.
Or maybe you prefer
To use a wrist watch.

Out of all that time,
And all those days…
Could you perhaps pick this one?
Because I'll be waiting for you…
Yesterday.

Barbara Allen
Auburn, AL

[Hometown] Auburn, AL; [DOB] August 4, 2000; [Ed] currently ninth grade; [Hobbies] horseback riding, playing video games, piano; [GA] not enough life experience yet

Common Sense

Walk with me from the rising of the sun
Until it settles in the West.
See the forests waltzing in the wind
As falling acorns are put to rest.
Hear the rolling thunder high above
in answer to the rain dove's frantic plea
to quench the thirst of flowers that we love
and join the streams that flow into the sea.
Be amazed when the moon turns the world to velvet
and splendor meets the sky.
There's no power on Earth can melt it.
Our four seasons on it rely.
Think about the sounds of nature.
Look at beauty all around.
Feel the wind with all its power
as is whirls so many leaves around.
Hold the beauty of creation
Close to your soul and heart.
Mark it well within your memory
before your thoughts depart.

Ruth M. Blessing
York, PA

[Hometown] Red Lion, PA; [DOB] August 24, 1932; [Ed] twelfth grade; [Occ] LPN; [Hobbies] reading, writing, sewing; [GA] great-grandmother of nine

I became interested in poetry when I was twelve, when I forgot words to a song. I made up my own to rhyme with the lyrics, I won a contest with Ray Zaner, who scouted students when I was a junior in high school. My teacher in a one-room school gave me a copy of Longfellow's poems as a gift for effort and I fell in love with his poem, "Day Is Done." I've never forgotten it.

Christmas Colors

As I looked up
In the sky
I bowed my head
As I passed by
The sky was painted
In red and green
Christmas colors
You should have seen
In Heaven so fair
It will be seen
Why God chose the colors
Of red and green
In case you saw it
Oh what a mix
It was the year of our Lord
Two thousand and six
I wonder why
And someday I'll know
Why Christmas colors
Are mixed with snow

Marilyn Love
East Bernstadt, KY

[Hometown] East Bernstadt, KY; [DOB] March 8, 1954; [Ed] twelfth grade; [Occ] retired; [Hobbies] art, music, poetry, decorating; [GA] qualified to be a doctor in US Army

"Christmas Colors" is a true poem. Most of what I write is. I was on my way on Christmas Day 2006 for Christmas dinner with my family. I looked up in the sky and bowed my head in reverence to God. I saw the clouds rolling in red and green. I was breathless, the beauty and knowing the awesome power that our Lord made the majestic scene above me. I had a wonderful day that day. It was like walking on air. No one can ever imagine, no eyes have ever seen, what God has in store for those who love Him. Christmas colors are just a sample to me.

Thoughts, but Nothing to Say

There are so many times that I pick up my pen,
And find that I have nothing to say.
There are so many things that a mind does ken,
But cannot express in any way.

I have seen, it seems, a thousand dreams,
That I would love to tell to you,
But when I reach for the nearest one,
My thoughts all go askew.

There are so many events about which I could write,
Yet they dwindle before my quill,
There are so many events that a mind does sight,
But cannot adhere to my mental will.

I have experienced, it seems, a million things,
That I would love to share with you,
But, alas, these things are not of this world,
And, by me, cannot be filtered through.

There are so many times that I lay down my pen,
Because I have nothing to say,
There are so many things that a mind does ken,
Yet, unable to express in any way.

Howard H. Mackey Jr.
Edgewater, MD

[Hometown] Edgewater, MD; [DOB] May 10, 1926; [Ed] bachelor of architecture; [Occ] retired architect; [Hobbies] writing poetry, fishing, Lladro collecting, (non-firing) gun collecting; [GA] raising a family of achievers

I was born in Washington, DC and married Anna Catharine Thompson, my high school sweetheart. We raised four children, Howard III, Stanford, Karen and Adrienne. I am a WWII veteran, having served in United States, France, Belgium and Germany. I studied architecture at Howard University after Army service. I married while in college and graduated in 1953. After thirty years of marriage and the passing of my wife, I moved to Annapolis, MD. I retired and married Ernestine Mebane who passed after nineteen years. I moved to Edgewater, MD in 2001. My many life experiences were the inspiration for writing this poem.

I Saw a Ghost in My Tub

I saw a ghost in my tub.
My back he started to rub.
He picked up my rag
And tore off the tag.
He didn't have no manners.
He wore no banners.
He picked up my soap.
He won't no pope.
He dropped what he was
doing and went through the wall.
I got up and ran down
the hall!

Joseph Mercer
Garysburg, NC

[Hometown] Garysburg, NC; originally Elizabeth City, NC; [DOB] October 4, 1955; [Ed] eleventh grade; [Occ] minister; [Hobbies] music ministry; [GA] getting saved by grace

I wrote this poem somewhere around September 1, 1982. We lived in a well-documented haunted house back in the mid '70s. It was a big two-story blue house on the corner of a block—the only house, there. Well, one day, my eyes closed sitting in my easy chair, I saw the apparition of an elderly white lady with long hair float into the dining room adjacent to me and then float on across the room to the wall facing me from which she then vanished. My eyes were closed the whole time.

Eulogy for the Last Mountain

A voice called me to the mountains
where, as a youth, I had roamed without care
The sight I beheld brought a silent stare
All but one had disappeared, lying in rubble
Helpless, hopeless victims of the coal and gas bubble
I climbed the last mountain, knowing not what I'd see
Mother mountain screamed, crying out to me
Why do those below refuse life here be still
Force their cold steel, foul poison deep down inside
Don't they care that I feel?
My sisters and I have lived God's dream
Birds flocked to our trees, fish thrived in our streams
Lifeblood pure water, for all here and below
The circle of life, love, a gentle wind blows
Why did man destroy my sisters and me?
Can't you, my son, stop this insanity?
All have a deaf ear, those greedy men, forfeit their
Souls for what I hide within
My sisters gone—I am the last—my tears stained memories
Of harmony past
God's promise of tomorrow was sacred words; I'll perish
Man will follow, falling on his own sword
Leave now—go down, warn all that you can
A bleak, barren world is the future of man
The End

Ronald Michael Pafford
Greeneville, TN

[Hometown] Kingsport, TN; [DOB] August 24, 1952; [Ed] high school, some college, school of life; [Occ] retired educator, environmental causes; [Hobbies] songwriting, singing, guitar, poetry; [GA] talking my wife Susie into marrying me

I am most inspired, and feel closer to God, when I'm in these beautiful Appalachian mountains, where I am so blessed to live. I am Cherokee/Anglo descent; I try to follow the path of good medicine taught by the Cherokee. This poem was inspired by the late Paul Hayden—a great friend—executive director of Middle Nolichucky Watershed. A true champion of woods and water, we really miss him. Also, my late father, Marvin C. Pafford Sr., who taught me at an early age to respect the earth, and all creatures have their place and purpose—Thanks, Dad.

The Storm

The never-ceasing storm wreaks havoc all night long
Lightning lights the sky as thunder plays its song
The ship rocks back and forth, waves wash o'er the deck
Passengers are thrown around, dear God they ask what's next
The Captain shouts, "Stay below, it's not safe to walk around."
The women pray their endless beads, they pray to reach safe ground
A mother clutches her babe and prays for the life of her son
Please dear God spare us this night, his life has just begun
The endless rocking back and forth, eerie sounds of the ship are heard
They bring a haunting silence throughout, no one speaks a word
Heaven smiles as the morning sun breaks through the blackened clouds
The sea is calm once again, cries are heard among the crowd
Hugs are given with shouts of joy as the ship now heads towards land
Some are very weak while others can barely stand
On the horizon land is seen lit up by the morning sun
The horrific night is over, a new day has begun

Cherie Chilvers
San Bernardino, CA

[Hometown] South Haven, MI; [DOB] September 8, 1947; [Ed] high school graduate, Bryman medical assistant; [Occ] retired from thirty-five years as a lab assistant; [Hobbies] writing poetry, traveling, reading books; [GA] giving birth to three amazing children

Hearing on the news about ships in distress, I thought a poem about writing what the people are going through would be important. My husband and I have been on seven cruises. We love to sail and explore other countries.

Numbingly Dumb

Confusion rises but there's nothing to tell,
Mind is silent for everything has passed through hell.
The grass may be brighter but it's all the same,
Settle the conflicts to resolve such pain.
The eyes are the soul and they hold many thoughts,
The conclusion I come to is to not be distraught.

Heather Nickey
Safety Harbor, FL

[Hometown] Safety Harbor, FL; [DOB] January 29, 1986; [Ed] college student; [Occ] supervisor, esthetician, nail specialist; [Hobbies] painting, reading; [GA] publishing a poem

I'd say that I'm a pretty crafty gal—always been an artist, love writing, gathering opinions and voicing ideas that can solve problems. I've traveled some. I would describe myself as unique, talented, and genuine. I'm a jack of all trades, college student, artist, poet, supervisor at one company, and a full nail/esthetician specialist on the side. My poetry is based on life events; it's a way of connecting.

We

Come float with me
In the sky above
And be with me
In the space of the doves

Flying on a cloud
In a sky of blue
In a private place
Far away with you

Knowing you care
And I do too
Makes it all so right
And so very true

Wilma J. Scherrer
Tuscon, AZ

[Hometown] Tucson, AZ; [DOB] August 20, 1921; [Ed] ninth grade; [Occ] raising two children; [Hobbies] contactees and UFOs; [GA] above son and daughter

I became a widow on October 12, 2014 after seventy-five years of marriage. I was born in Bergholz, OH and was rescued three times from water, and was kidnapped two times and escaped. I raised a son and daughter and worked with people all over this planet who have had contact with ETs and UFOs. I love humanity and the things God created. All kinds of pure love makes the world healthy.

A Mother's Chores

She starts the day with prayer,
and tries to make things pleasant
for those she loves.

She mends broken hearts and fixes
numerous things that no one else
dares.

The day is seldom long enough to
accomplish all her plans,
but still she presses on with courage
to all the demands.

With soft words of simple sound,
and an understanding touch,
she continues to take the lead
and do more than her part.

When all are tucked in, she's the last
to retire, and with great care she
prays for strength and guidance for
those that are in her care.

Nona B. Ryder
Lake Charles, LA

[Hometown] Lake Charles, LA; [DOB] April 6, 1934; [Ed] high school and business school; [Occ] retired office manager; [Hobbies] poetry, exercise, gardening; [GA] wife, mother, grandmother

Born April 6, 1934 in Lake Charles, LA, I finished high school then went to business school. After finishing my schooling, I got married and had two wonderful children. I later went to work and retired after twenty-five years. I was active in my church for years. Now that I am eighty years old, I am taking it easy and traveling abroad. I have two wonderful grandchildren. I have been writing for thirty years. I have been married to a wonderful guy for sixty-two years.

The Harmonica-Playing Poet

for James Montgomery

You know...I love the harmonica
it's like carrying a piano in your front pocket...
without the added weight
it's like playing in a band...
with only one player
it's like you swallowed a juke box
and with every breath notes leak out...uncontrollably
It's like a forever happy blues-chasing machine
right in the palm of your hand...
no batteries required
you know...I used to use it as a gimmick
to set me apart
from all the other poets
They may have the clever turn of a phrase
in iambic pentameter
but could they bend or twist a note
like a sweet Louisiana Delta
or an Alabama sharecropper sitting on his front porch
sharing his sorrows of another dry season
I think not...
but sometimes...
it backfires on me
and people ask me about those train-stopping whistles
and wailing half notes
and forget that I have just poured my heart out in a poem

Alan R. Howarth
Braintree, MA

[Hometown] Braintree, MA; [DOB] April 2, 1950; [Ed] BA in history, BS in education, MS in psychology; [Occ] graduate gemologist, wine specialist; [Hobbies] performance poetry, collecting fine wine, cycling; [GA] completing three marathons for my kids

I have been writing since I was in the third grade. For me, writing is a life-sustaining necessity. Sometimes it comes to me in the middle of the night like a radio tower receiving special poetry signals. On other occasions, it comes to me on a plane flying to Tucson, AZ, like this poem. I have played the harmonica as long as I can remember, not seriously, but just for the fun of it. I sometimes use it as part of my performance poetry. Ironically, people sometimes ask me more about my harmonica than the poem I have just read. James Montgomery is my favorite blues harmonica player.

You Do Not _____ Alone

You do not have to cry alone.
For I am always near.
I share your troubles and your pain
and know the things you bear.

You do not have to walk alone.
For I am always there.
I share your passion and your dream.
and know the things you dear.

You do not have to live alone.
For I am always here.
I share your friends and your home.
and know the things your mind does wear.

You do not have to die alone.
For I am always somewhere.
I share your treasures and your love
and know the things you fear.

Debra DeVeney
Ione, CA

[Hometown] Ione, CA; [DOB] March 16, 1965; [Ed] high school graduate; [Occ] delivery of the local newspaper; [Hobbies] bowling, darts, crosswords; [GA] being a mom of three girls

I never went to college. After I graduated high school, I joined the US Army. I spent the majority of my time in service at Ft. Campbell, KY, which is where I met and married my husband of thirty years. I wrote this poem to my husband for our twentieth anniversary.

Epilepsy

There is an ugly beast
That lurks within the mind.
It strikes when you expect it least
And will at any time.

It will grab you and it will hold you fast within its grip,
It takes away your consciousness until you start to slip.
You shudder, shake and roll your eyes until they turn so bland,
The life force in your body won't even let you stand.

The beast is cruel and mean, it has a lot to gain,
So when you fall and hurt yourself, you cannot feel the pain.
It holds to you and lets you go when you begin to fall,
You never feel a single thing when you break through the wall.

Sometimes it seems to play a game and just take a little nip,
You lose your mind and say something, with quite a nasty quip.
The things you say can really hurt the ones that you hold dear,
But you are not aware of it, even when you see the tears.

The beast is always lingering near,
And doesn't really care,
About the life you live in fear,
It laughs at you and mocks you with a horrible blank stare.

James William Rose
Camden, DE

[Hometown] Camden, DE; [DOB] May 3, 1953; [Ed] BA in business management; [Occ] retired US Army; [Hobbies] reading, cooking, fishing, carpentry; [GA] soldier, husband, father

I was in high school the first time I felt that I could really compose poetry! I had prepared a poem for an English assignment and I asked my mom to read it before I turned it in. She read for what seemed the longest time and then looked over the top of the paper and asked where I had copied from. Since then I've written poetry for my wife, short stories for my grandchildren just for the pure joy of putting my fleeting thoughts to ink. This latest poem is inspired by my wife and our battle with epilepsy.

Hands

The hands of a baby are smooth and soft
And thrilling to the touch.
And all who see and hold the child
Enjoy them very much.

The mother's hands are slightly worn
From dishes, many chores
Yet children crave to feel them
For comfort, healing sores.

And Grandma's hands are wrinkled
With blood spots, signs of wear.
But still bring joy and comfort
To their loved ones everywhere.

Great-grandma's hands are withered
And tender to the touch.
And still their children love them
Feel comfort, joy and such.

No matter whether young or old
The loving hands inspire—
Give forth the blessed tenderness
That people all require.

Lloyd S. Foote
Tempe, AZ

[Hometown] Gunnison, UT; [DOB] November 10, 1932; [Ed] law degree; [Occ] retired; [Hobbies] writing and volunteer work; [GA] marrying the right woman

As a Tree

As a tree
    Cut my limbs.
        I'll never grow them back.
As a tree
    Pull on me.
        I'll cry tears of sap.
As a tree
    Sit under me.
        I'll provide the shade.
As a tree
    Eat my fruit.
        I'll love you every day.

Alec Elzinga
Kalamazoo, MI

[Hometown] *Portage, MI;* [DOB] *October 10, 1994;* [Ed] *high school senior;* [Occ] *arts;* [Hobbies] *arts;* [GA] *won teen film festivals*

My name is Alec Elzinga. I just turned twenty years old. Until the ninth grade, I attended a small private school in Kalamazoo, MI. The school believed in developing the whole child and exposed us to many forms of art that allowed us to develop our creative talent. When I was twelve, I started writing, directing, and producing short films using neighbor kids for actors. I won a couple of teen film festivals. I then used those talents to write and produce advertisements for a nonprofit group I am on the board for—Proper. Proper's main mission is to encourage people of all ages to "leave it better than you found it." In high school, I started a couple of t-shirt businesses in which I designed creative logos and had them printed on t-shirts. For the past couple of years, I've been writing and producing rap songs. We just finished our first complete CD with another one almost finished. I've always liked writing; it's an outlet to express my views and thought process. I've submitted this poetry with hopes to have it published to utilize another avenue to share.

School Starts

Small feet dance, skip and hurry
Along pavements or dirt roads
Eager to explore the now
Study the then
Mesmerized in tomorrow
Carrying backpacks of innocence
Held fast with a dot of glue
Or a zipper of hope
Determined to catch rainbows
And puzzle out the stars
While packaging ideas beneath
The microscope of a child's eyes
Small hands and tiny fingers
Shape the future in
Crayons, paint, Popsicle sticks
A rock, a leaf, a doorway
Leading to a theater of stars
As the chrysalis of education
Awaits the birth of its butterflies

Paula Compo-Pratt
Westville, NJ

[Hometown] Westville, NJ; [DOB] December 22, 1950; [Ed] BA and MA in English and certified floral designer; [Occ] teacher of language arts for thirty-nine years, writer of children's books (Boo Boo's Story, Boo Boo in the Land of Mists and Dreams, Boo Boo Meets Tiger Too Tall and Boo Boo and the Valley of Secrets), poet, receiving thirty-seven major awards nationally and internationally in the field of education, becoming a US ambassador, participating in the United Cultural Convention

I Have Seen

Bright blue umbrella,
man in sky blue work pants, shirt
walks through rain, smiling

On the naughty list?
Let's play nice and get off it.
Santa is coming

Small black butterfly
flitting about in bright sun,
disappears at dusk.

Standing in sunshine
with rain falling on my head
I see a rainbow

Cotton-wood seedlings
arrive along with fish flies
soon gone with fresh breeze

Oh my dear brothers
four were born, now four are gone
sadly no others.

Constance Warren
Detroit, MI

[Hometown] Detroit, MI; [DOB] May 3, 1933; [Ed] attended Wayne S. U.; [Occ] licensed practical nurse; [Hobbies] plate and music box collecting, poetry; [GA] learned to fly on the GI bill after spending three years in the USMC

As I survey my yard and neighborhood, I see these things and the Haikus write themselves. I always carry a pen and notebook with me because I never fail to see something noteworthy that I want to share. I appreciate the chance to send my verses in because I live alone so have no one to share with. Many people don't appreciate poetry. I love to read the old masters. I don't understand some of the modern poets I have read.

Untitled

In a hurry, scurry world
In a bustle of today
In a world filled with technology
Whatever happened to peace, quiet and harmony
So hard to find in today's society
Where did the slow-paced life go
Lost in a different era
Go to a park, lake, mountain or beach
Find a place that speaks to your heart
Listen to the sound of the birds sweetly singing
The wind rustling in the trees
Water flowing
Feel the sunshine on your face
And inhale fresh air
Go and find your serenity as often as you can

Veronica Durre
Long Beach, CA

[Hometown] Long Beach, CA; [DOB] May 12, 1963; [Ed] AA degree; [Occ] caregiver, home-based business owner; [Hobbies] photography, being in nature, cooking, art; [GA] finding confidence in myself

I have been writing poetry for many years, but it wasn't until recently that I dared sharing them with anyone but my secret drawer. This past year has been an incredible journey into myself, where I discovered many things, one of which is my confidence. This discovery took me on many adventures, including swimming with dolphins. I am humbled and honored to share my work. I know now it is not only a joy, but also my responsibility to share my gift, so it may inspire people to go on their own journey and share their gifts with the world!

6 Hours

After today
Where will I go?
Is there a place for me?
So different in many ways
That I don't wear shades
And the light in my heart is going down
That sometimes I can act like a clown
Just to make my frown go up instead of down.
I am quite unique.
I do many things that I think I can't.
I believe in many things like in hope and forgiveness,
Which I thought I wouldn't.
Changes may appeal to make up for the mistakes.
I wouldn't say everything will come out okay.
I have dreams that I know that I cannot have.
I care of others that don't really think the same way as me.
I try to understand why things happen the way they do.
I make sure that I can write a few words or two that can help my day or
someone else keep on going through the process of feeling blue.
Oh what oh what am I doing wrong?
I try and try but all I want to do is cry
Because I am tired of the way I feel inside.
Some times I am all right,
but then I do something to make myself feel good.
But then someone says or does something
that makes you just want to jump from the highest mountain in your mind
and then say yes that is the end of that feeling,
And then deal with the next one that wants to come through.

Sendia Gomez Gonzalez
Brooklyn, NY

My name is Sendia. Is there a person that feels the same way I do? Let your words be heard because when the time comes, then you will not be anymore and the worries and the feelings will go with you, and the memory will go too.

The Red Rose

Climbing red roses
Upon a splintered wooden fence
A honey bee floats
From rose to rose

There she sits in the green grass
In her hand a rose she holds
A diary lays open upon her lap
Revealing the secrets of her past
Of her younger days she daydreams
Of the life she lived of youth and beauty

A prick from the thorn of the rose
Brings her back to where she is now
Lightly she kisses her wounded finger
And places the red rose in her diary

She now arises
And walks in to her life
Of today

Deborah A. Fogel
Nazareth, PA

I was born in a family of seven, including my parents, I was the middle child and was very quiet and shy. We lived in the country in a farmhouse surrounded by fields and woods, scattered with small towns here and there. I grew to love poetry when in fourth grade we had to read a Robert Frost poem. Since then I have come to use poetry as hobby and outlet for my emotions and as an inner sense of who I am as a person. Poetry for me helps me perceive a sense of calm and a truer outlook on a better way to see life in a different light.

Ah Love, How Heavenly

Love's special time brings happy faces as lovers create
shared romantic places. Songs are held with personal
meanings, etched in memory for romantic recall. Happy
hearts burst forth with love's new reflection, bonds form
through long-lasting connections, like minds mesh
together blending compatible perceptions, as nature's
beauty is enhanced in visual repose. One's sparkling
eyes reflect love's truth serene, and through another's
gazing eyes that same treasure's also seen. Lovely moments
we can't do without, that dissolve all chance of fear
and doubt. Dreams burst forth of floral gardens, where
we whisper sweet sonnets, and kiss with ardor, brushed
like the wind sweeping through the soul, filling our
hearts with further dreams untold. Sensual touches where
soft currents flow, giving the body a blushed radiant
glow. Warm connections at the touch of another,
meshing as one under warm, cozy covers. Hearts basking
in feelings so sublime, believing those senses will
last for all time. How beautiful life gleams when love
murmurs its sound through heart's quietest hours when
love stirs all around. Enamored by many when on that
fateful day eyes lock with another standing not far
away, the face of our future, as the heart skips a beat,
with the feeling this person will make life complete.
How blessed we are when love comes to call, those magical
moments desired by us all. Ah love, how heavenly.

Carol E. Gange
Baltimore, MD

[Hometown] Halethorpe, MD; [DOB] July 17; [Ed] high school and business accounting night school; [Occ] retired office manager for thirty years; [Hobbies] creative writing, painting (watercolor/ink), singing; [GA] surviving Stage 4 cancer (five years in May 2015)

I love to write about love. It's the most beautiful feeling a person can have, and it varies in so many ways. It takes you to the highest height of happiness, but, if lost, it can hurt to the depth of the soul. It's just so powerful, but an emotion we wouldn't want to live without. I just feel that if you have a good, kind heart your life will be better for it. It pulls in the positive constructive nature of life and you'll always find love waiting there. Surviving cancer afforded me the opportunity to publish my poems.

Roses

Red soft petal rose
with her sharp thorn touch bloom in the air
filled with sweet perfume smell
exude in her high graceful stand
in her green flourish display
so captivating to the scene
bring vivid memory to the sight
with great passion love
Yellow soft petal rose
with her sharp thorn touch bloom in the air
with her radiant smile
showcase in her bright and vibrant
distinct color of display to the world
with a sense of hope and revive
Pink soft petal rose
with her sharp thorn touch bloom in the air
embrace you with its warmth feeling play
cast its own beauty splendor
to her secret admirer
with a sense of peace to mankind
White soft petal rose
with her sharp thorn touch bloom in the air
imprint you with
her pure innocent image
with a sense of honesty care
So, which is thou favorite pick?
Each flower carries in a unique way
Like a woman portray
Only to see her inner beauty side to form a mind

Hanh N. Chau
San Jose, CA

[Hometown] San Jose, CA; [DOB] March 4, 1973; [Ed] master's degree; [Occ] radiology aide; [Hobbies] writing, public speaking, ballroom dancing; [GA] earned my MBA

I enjoy writing because it provides me with the opportunity to share and express my feelings with other people. I'm grateful to be gifted with a talent to write. I started writing when I was in high school.

Taking a Chance

Reading is like kneading
The brain of a writer
To capture the essence
Of thoughts wonderfully wider.

Words on a page
Carefully crafted for impact,
Readily reassembled
By another, soon sidetracked.

That's the chance
The writers take;
What of their work
Will readers make?

Mary Millemann
Harriman,, TN

I earned a BA in elementary education at Ohio Wesleyan University in Delaware, OH. I am an avid reader of many genres. Reading and writing poetry are both every enjoyable to me. Though I realize rhyming isn't mandatory, I prefer that style in writing poetry. I taught elementary education for some years, have two grown offspring, and have enjoyed tutoring as a volunteer in public schools. Thank you for this opportunity to share one of my poems.

Time Once Was

Time once was
when Mama could sit out on the front
porch watching her children playing
up and down the street.

Time once was
enjoyment without fear, fun places
to go, things to see, things to do
and friendly voices saying, hello,
how are you?

Time once was
a friendly face, a lending hand from
the next-door neighbor,
the happy sound of the ice cream
wagon coming down the well-kept
streets.

Time once was
saying good night, leaving the windows
open, the door somewhat crack so you
could feel a little relief from the
summer night's heat.

Time once was
all of this and so much more, but I
still hope and pray that the time
once was will return and live again
someday.

Barbara A. Kelley
Detroit, MI

[Hometown] Birmingham, AL; [DOB] March 10, 1944; [Ed] medical secretary and administrative medical assistant degree; [Occ] homemaker, babysitting, grandmother; [Hobbies] writing poetry, crafts/puzzles; [GA] family and new accomplishments

I appreciate the beauty of Mother Nature along with God's creations. It gives me such joy and inspiration each morning as I rise and look out my window to begin expressing the thoughts of my mind. From my children and my sisters and brothers at my church, Antioch Missionary Baptist Church, from them support comes to me through love and encouragement, pushing me to sharing words of my soul and touching the hearts of many. I thank God for giving me this gift to share with others. I love life and all that it has to offer.

Breeze

freshman tone
from breath
of hills
rolling in their light

blinks in blue
like morning star
finding I
in my eye

and lands in
oat seed breeze
of green wind
in shadow black boughs

urging moon's edge
from end
to no end
with poet's piano

drifting in
polyphonic lift
painting autumn bright
with my daughter's hello

Michael Smith
Baltimore, MD

[Occ] registered land surveyor

To Those We Meet

Came to
in a positive haze of misty memory.
Slow is the depth of sleep
where dreams seldom remain.
To wake and walk upon the day
is a wonder of what became of night.

There is really never
a casual acquaintance of those we come to meet,
but rather
a taste of time and place
where the mind traps…
a sound, a smell, a face.

In the shallow breath of darkness
there leaves but a lasting drool of life
sliding down a wanting chin
dripping off into a positive haze
of time and place
where dreams seldom remain.

John Schmoyer
Schnecksville, PA

Tattooists Wanted

We are looking for artists in a closed-minded world
to fill the vast empty canvas of skin while seeking openness and meaning.
Everyone is a masterpiece.
You have already decided to be yourself, to quit wearing a mask.
Your walking road signs warn the public to see you as you are,
not as they want you to be. We struggle to find identity.
Neck tattoos are conspicuous inks needing attention.
In your face, flash the world, defined by opposition, honoring the dead,
symbolizing boldness, rebellion, fighting upstream.
Easy to hide flowers and butterfly wings.
Print your own rules on your own body, so you don't forget who you are;
so everyone sees your fierceness, your boundaries, your courage.
I feel confused when looking at my son,
I want to celebrate his peacock feathers, his vitality, his burgeoning self.
Instead I see a confluence of bright colors, a tasty whackadoodle pie, a celebration of his artistic
eye that I am committed to honor.
Tattoos are supernatural smudges reminding us to wake up our souls.
Meditations, written reminders of our essence, our purpose.
Integrating our frayed, fragmented selves. Only conflict leads to respect.
Don't join the culture of the entitled!
The cowboys on the loose, lassoing workers brought to their knees.
The xenophobic and pure, victims of wealth, clubs of anachronistic prejudice,
controllers who, demonizing the poor, stick their nose into everyone else's bedroom.
Fight back, find solidarity. Join the culture of inkblots,
which give only integrity.

W. Roger Carlisle
Birmingham, AL

[Hometown] Tulsa, OK; [DOB] August 6, 1945; [Ed] MD; [Occ] physician; [Hobbies] hiking, nature, writing; [GA] father

I am currently working two days a week as a volunteer physician in a free clinic. I am in several writing groups and enjoy sharing my poems with my friends. I am married with two children. I love writing every day. It keeps me in touch with my real self and keeps me on a spiritual path. Writing is a growth experience and has been a source of great joy. Prizes and fame are not on my list of goals. I also work as a wilderness ranger and am a trustee with the nature conservancy. I love to travel and also paint landscapes.

Captions of a Moment

Through the muck and through the mire
I will astain higher,
Of my goals inspire;
You led me ever so nearer
That everything is so much clearer.

We never have the need to borrow
With gain of sight of the morrow.
As the ocean beats upon the shore,
We don't need to be torrid and torn
Until we are worn.

For a time we were in a dark abyss
With no lost moments to miss.
Of the ever passing terrain.
To see the beauty of the rain.

My thoughts are ever surer
To a love that is ever purer.
Sensing the moments of total bliss
That there is nothing amiss.

Ever measured, ever worn
To cherishing moments of a brand new morn.
Seeing things in a whole new way
Total involving a brand new day.

Dorothy Safko
Harrisburg, PA

[Hometown] Harwood, PA; [DOB] March 17, 1943; [Ed] high school, trade school; [Occ] prep cook, pump jockey, nurse's aide; [Hobbies] walking, reading, poetry, crafts, Christian music; [GA] being published

My inspiration came from watching a movie: soldiers were going through vast, high, dirty and infected waters, carrying their weapons above their heads. It was supposed to be a time of renewal, but little did I realize I would fall into the same trap that nearly took my life. Therefore, a death-bed miracle.

Indian Friend

A long time ago,
I met this Indian friend,
She is so wonderful to me.
She helps me with all my problems,
Some are small, and some are big,
But wherever they are,
She is there for me.

And then there are times,
The things she helped me with,
Work out great,
So when I need her, I know where to go,
It is my Indian friend,
And I love her so.

Loretta Aul
Belle Vernon, PA

[Hometown] Belle Vernon, PA; [Ed] high school; [Occ] housewife, retired; [Hobbies] sewing, writing, garden work; [GA] to be a poet

I dreamt of writing poetry for many years until Eber & Wein came along and published my poems. I am grateful for all of their help. I am retired from working at the bank in the office. I love to relax by writing.

Index of Poets